FUNERAL CUSTOMS
THEIR ORIGIN
AND DEVELOPMENT

THE PROTOTYPE OF THE "MOURNING COACH"
(from an old drawing).

FUNERAL CUSTOMS
THEIR ORIGIN AND DEVELOPMENT

BY

BERTRAM S. PUCKLE

Wood Block by John F. Hunter

THE LAST VOYAGE

LONDON
T. WERNER LAURIE LTD.
30 NEW BRIDGE STREET, E.C. 4
1926

**Vincennes University, Junior College
Shake Learning Resources Center
Vincennes, Indiana 47591-9986**

Library of Congress Cataloging-in-Publication Data

Puckle, Bertram S.
  Funeral customs : their origin and development / by Bertram S. Puckle.
      p.   cm.
  Reprint. Originally published: London : T.W. Laurie, 1926.
  ISBN 1-55888-750-4 (lib. bdg. : alk. paper)
  1. Funeral rites and ceremonies.   I. Title.
GT3150.P8   1990
393'.9—dc20   89-63010
                                                              CIP

♾
This book is printed on acid-free paper meeting the ANSI Z39.48 Standard. The infinity symbol that appears above indicates that the paper in this book meets that standard.

PRINTED IN THE UNITED STATES OF AMERICA

FOREWORD

An exhaustive treatise on funeral customs, ancient and modern, has yet to be written.

Leaving to the theologian and philosopher the thankless task of assigning the *mystery* of death its proper place and functions in the scheme of creation, the writer has confined himself to a general survey of those practices which surround the *physical fact of death*, a subject which is as immense as it is fascinating.

Whilst investigation shows that almost all our present usages have their origin in stupid pagan superstitions, they have none the less an interest of their own to record.

It is a wholesome sign that a more enlightened public is slowly releasing death from much of its ugly trappings, for—" Death, beautiful in itself, is only made terrible by groans and convulsions and a discoloured face, and friends weeping and blacks and obsequies." So wrote Bacon three hundred years ago in his " Essay on Death." " But above all, believe me," he concludes, " the sweetest canticle is *Nunc Dimittis*."

Bertram S. Puckle.

Richmond,
    August 30th, 1926.

ACKNOWLEDGMENT

THE Author wishes to express his sincere thanks to many friends who have helped him with this book. In particular, he would mention the following public bodies, firms and individuals who have lent pictures for reproduction: Messrs. J. D. Field & Son (for some particularly interesting material, including the 1824 funeral cost account), Messrs. J. Lyons & Co. Ltd., Messrs. Odhams Press Ltd., the Trustees of the British Museum, the Cremation Society of England, Mr. Emery Walker, Mr. John Tussaud, Mr. W. R. Leech, Mr. W. Edgel, Mr. Francis J. Bigger and Mr. Edward Good.

CONTENTS

CHAP.		PAGE
	FOREWORD	5
I.	THE PROVISIONS OF NATURE	11
II.	DEATH WARNINGS—WHEN DOES DEATH TAKE PLACE?	17
III.	PREPARATION FOR BURIAL, COFFINS, "GRAVE-GOODS," SUTTEE	31
IV.	WAKES, MUTES, WAILERS, SIN-EATING, TOTEMISM, DEATH-TAXES	61
V.	BELLS, MOURNING	82
VI.	FUNERAL FEASTS AND PROCESSIONS	99
VII.	EARLY BURIAL-PLACES	129
VIII.	CHURCHYARDS, CEMETERIES, ORIENTATION AND OTHER BURIAL CUSTOMS	139
IX.	TREES, FLOWERS, BODY-SNATCHING	163
X.	PLAGUE	182
XI.	STATE AND PUBLIC FUNERALS	191
XII.	CREMATION, EMBALMING	209
XIII.	IN MEMORIAM	232
XIV.	MEMORIALS, EPITAPHS, RINGS AND MOURNING CARDS	253
	INDEX	279

LIST OF ILLUSTRATIONS

The Prototype of the Mourning Coach	*Frontispiece*
	To face page
Fretted Memorial Card Mount	30
The Capucine Vaults, Palermo } A 13th Century Stone Coffin }	54
"Honouring" the Dead	96
Method of constructing Funeral Pyre (Grecian) } Wailing Women }	112
The Dismal Trade in Council } Early Form of the Modern Hearse }	128
Loculi in the Roman Catacombs } Vault in the Roman Catacombs }	138
Old London Burial Ground	148
Burke and Hare } Ballad Card }	178
Death Mask } Heart Casket }	194
Invitation to Funeral of Duke of Wellington } Lord Nelson's Funeral Car }	202
Roman Funeral Pyre } Early Horse-drawn Bier }	214
An Egyptian Coffin } Modern Crematorium }	220
Early Undertaker's Sign	230
Images of Dead Children in Japanese Temple } Funeral of the Comte de Paris }	232

10   LIST OF ILLUSTRATIONS

To face page

Memorial Cards - - - - -	244
Epitaph of Robert Preston } Tombstone of Daniel Defoe } - - -	260
Memorial Brass of a Knight } Invitation to a Funeral, 1799 } - - -	264
Mourning Jewellery - - - - -	268
Mourning Jewellery - - - - -	270
Cost Account of Funeral, 1824 - - -	273-5
14th Century Wrought Iron Hearse } Modern Votive Candle Stand or Hearse } - -	277

FUNERAL CUSTOMS

CHAPTER I

THE PROVISIONS OF NATURE

IN the animal kingdom a dead body arouses no feelings of fear or repulsion. In most cases it is looked upon as a generous gift of Nature, of which the fullest advantage is to be taken, or the opportunity lost to competition.

It is difficult to appreciate how vast a number of birds, beasts and insects inhabit the fields and woods, and we may well ask ourselves the question " What becomes of their dead? " In a day's search we may not find among all the teaming wild population a single stiffened body, or one bright eye glazed in death. Here in a clearing we may have chanced upon some blood-stained grass, and a few scattered feathers, which gave evidence of the hawk or carrion crow, but this is very far from accounting for anything like the greater proportion of the short-lived race.

Has Nature, then, her undertaker? Certainly she has. He is appropriately known as the *Necrophorus mortuorum*, or more popularly as the sexton beetle, for he is equipped with spade and all that is necessary for "undertaking."

There is much that the human variety might learn from this humble and industrious insect. Whilst he is dressed in a conventional garb of black, he seeks to enliven matters by means of two broad bands of yellow on his back. He is cheery, and when his duties are over for the day he indulges in a little music, not perhaps entirely a matter of art for art's sake, but like most joyous notes of nature, his immediate object is to attract the attention of the opposite sex.

In praising the *Necrophorus mortuorum*, we must admit that in his work he is not actuated by motives of disinterested philanthropy any more than is the case with the human undertaker.

Nature is indeed far too wise to entrust any important work to the spasmodic efforts of the well-intentioned. If she wants a job done thoroughly, she does not grudge a reasonable wage for services rendered.

If during our lives we are often able to disguise from ourselves that we are but superior animals, the disabilities of birth and death bring the fact unmistakably before us.

The helplessness of a new-born babe is proverbial, but Nature has provided it with the means of making its urgent necessities unmistakably apparent, and she has not been less considerate to the corpse.

We must not be shocked to hear that it is by means of the olfactory organ that the sexton beetle is made aware of the proximity of a new "client." Once having sensed a job, he communicates the good news to his wife, and together they fly off to the house of mourning by the shortest possible route—for competition is keen.

Arrived at the spot, they find the corpse to be that of a recently deceased mouse.

"Having feasted," other helpers having also arrived, the male beetle proceeds to excavate around the body, till by a process of gradual under-

THE PROVISIONS OF NATURE 13

mining it sinks into a considerable hollow, thus prepared for its reception.[1]

The work is finished by piling the earth neatly on the top.

For the purpose of excavation Nature has provided the sexton beetle with club-shaped antennæ, which are supported by strong muscles equal to the work that they are called upon to perform. It should be stated that Mrs. Beetle remains in possession of the body in which her eggs are laid. Surely this is a sanitary and logical conclusion to a commonplace event, in which everybody concerned is paid off and satisfied.

It teaches a lesson that burial is a natural method of disposing of the dead, and it gives more than a hint, that believe what we will of the prospects of a future life, death is only a rather misleading term for a changed, by no means an impaired, activity.

It will be self-evident that in dealing with the larger animals, such as bears, lions, etc., the sexton beetle, however numerous and industrious be his kind, would be sorely taxed if he received a call from a client. We must not, however, under-rate the extraordinary power of the insect world when working together with a common objective.

In the jungle the greater feeds on the lesser, and the jackal and vulture scavenge what remains.

The busy workers living in organized communities deal with their dead on lines more akin to human necessities. Their own dead, or a chance intruder into the ant-hill city, will be treated with system and dispatch, and the body removed long before it has any opportunity to prove offensive or dangerous to the community.

The ants, being carniverous, will quickly devour any beasts or insects which may die near their nests,

[1] Grant Allen, " Nature's Workshop."

14 FUNERAL CUSTOMS

and if anything uneatable remains, a squad of workers will be summoned at once to remove the offence to some more convenient place.

The bee, having no use to make of the body, has but one idea, and that is to expel the corpse, or so deal with it that the carefully regulated atmosphere of the hive shall not suffer from the presence of any poisonous fumes.

The workers of their community who are set apart for scavenging purposes, will soon eject a body by shouldering or pushing it out of the hive. If the intruder be a slug or snail, it may happen that it has climbed into such a position that its bulk will render it impossible for the bees to deal with it in the ordinary manner. In such a case the unhappy adventurer is quickly walled up with wax in the position in which he is found, and the tomb hermetically sealed past all fear of any harm to the city.

At exactly what period superstition affected death and burial, it is of course impossible to say. Perhaps it was taught to man by the sigh of the wind in the trees, or the dramatic terrors of the thunderstorm—however it came about, we know that the possibility of a spirit world was an early consideration.

The valiant hunter, undismayed by fierce encounters with wild beasts and his own kind, learned to crouch and shiver at the shadows, or, having slain his adversary, he fled from the accusing eye and hid from the avenging spirit. Even to-day, amongst savage tribes, it is quite common to find the shadow of a man attacked by the witch-doctor, in the belief that it is the soul.

We may well suppose that in such matters a very long time would elapse before anything concrete enough to be called a religion took possession

THE PROVISIONS OF NATURE 15

of man's mind. Asked by a missionary what were the gods he worshipped, a savage replied: "We know that someone walks amongst the trees at night —but we never mention it."

This is probably the state of mind of the early inhabitants of the earth.

With a belief in good and evil spirits inhabiting material things, we can at once trace this influence in funeral customs, for there is hardly a practice which has not had its origin in the old dread of haunting and revengeful ghosts.

When the next stage is reached—a belief in a general participation in a future life—a whole range of interesting happenings develop.

These are the foundation stones upon which our present day usages are built, varying in accordance with all sorts of minor considerations, such as climatic environment, etc.

Belief in a future state presupposed a material existence after death, with corresponding material necessities. Food must be provided, weapons and clothing, and a supply of charms with which to ward off those evil influences which the soul might expect to encounter on its journey.

Special provision would be made for those of rank—wives and servants for the chief, and a horse and attendant for the warrior and hunter.

This early attitude of mind was based on the supposition that death would surely bring with it that completeness of desire too often unsatisfied during the earthly existence.

That the ultimate state was one of happiness, seems to have been generally taken for granted. Can we say that the symbols used by a past generation as expressions of a state of bliss—such as crowns, harps, streets paved with gold and gates of pearl—have not often enough been accepted literally, and on no higher lever than the "Happy Hunting Ground" of the American Indian?

Amongst these materialistic views we may place the idea of death as an endless sleep or physical rest, too long denied to tired laborious lives.

We shall have evidence enough that a literal acceptance of this figure of physical rest and sleep in the grave represents the real aspirations of a number of people to-day, as in a past generation.

Thus we find a conception of the soul linked in various ways to earthly associations.

Loosed from the body, it was once supposed that the spirit quickly returned to its old surroundings, gifted with many supernatural powers, against which the living were unable to conceal their thoughts.

It is indeed a sad insight into the human conscience to discover what elaborate precautions were considered necessary in order to avoid the persecutions of the revengeful dead.

CHAPTER II

DEATH WARNINGS—WHEN DOES DEATH TAKE PLACE?

IT is perhaps natural that around the three great mysteries—birth, love and death—a crowd of superstitions cling, the children of those unnamed fears which accompany so many of us from the cradle to the grave, and which certainly dominated the lives of less enlightened generations.

That death, the greatest of all mysteries, should be singled out to be embroidered with many fantasies does not surprise us.

Many of the superstitions which we shall note are obviously nothing more than a chain of associated ideas; such as, for instance, the very general belief that it is unlucky to sit down thirteen to a meal, it being held that the first to rise from the table will go to his death.

The origin of this superstition is, of course, the Last Supper, from whence Judas, one of the twelve, left the table and went out into the night to betray his Lord.

"Death warnings" as they are called, have nearly all an obvious origin. A raven or other black feathered bird is seen to alight on the thatch of a cottage where a man is dying. Simply by force of associated ideas the gossiping neighbours agree at once that the bird is an omen of speedy dissolution, which event taking place shortly after, a new warning is added to the ever growing list. There are, however, certain superstitions which cannot be readily accounted for, unless we are prepared to admit the existence of supernatural intervention.

There is, in fact, a considerable amount of testimony in favour of certain hard-dying beliefs, the origin of which it is outside our purpose to consider, such, for instance, as the well-authenticated cases of dreams, in which a warning has been given of the approaching death of friends and relatives, or in some cases of the dreamer himself.

We are familiar with stories of persons so condemned who have thought by special precautions to avert the fate of which they have been warned. It has been said that once the mind of the person has been infected by a belief that death is inevitable on a certain day, the action of the mind upon a frail body may well be responsible for the physical result. This is an explanation which many will prefer to hold.

Amongst such beliefs, perhaps the most familiar is the frequently repeated assertion that a clock has stopped at the very moment that a death took place, with which may be classed our old friend, the falling picture, and the supernatural summons to the bedside of a dying person.

It would be quite impossible to attempt to chronicle anything like a complete list of death warnings, but the following are worth noting:

It is generally believed by sailors and fisherfolk that death is delayed till the ebb of the tide (it will be remembered that Dickens used this superstition in "David Copperfield"). "It being low water, he (Barkis) went out with the tide."

In Scotland a white rose blooming in autumn is accounted as an omen of an early death.

In Devon, if a sick person begs for a draught of cider, it is also a sign of death. This superstition rather suggests that the desire being gratified, the patient might well succumb from the effects of that ungenerous beverage.

The ebbing tide and the unusual appearance of the white rose in autumn may be safely catalogued as associated ideas, and also the very general belief that the fire burning black on one side is a token of a death in the family, or the peculiar formation of wax round a burning candle which suggests a white shroud.

Similar explanations might be reasonably given for the following:

When a dying person "sees something white" or if he "sees something black" a less enviable fate awaits him.

When fruit and flowers appear on the same tree; if you should be so imprudent as to wash clothes on a Good Friday, you are said to "wash someone out of the family."

If you chance to drop a mirror in which you have seen your own reflection, you have killed the reflection, hence you are doomed.

If you shiver it is said by the gossips that "someone is walking over your grave."

If you dream of nursing a baby and the baby cries, you will either die yourself or lose a near relative.

All these superstitions are foolish and harmless enough, but one might be mentioned which has lead to much trouble and has a wide influence even over the minds of people who ought to be better informed —the belief that if a person makes a will it is a sign that they will die shortly after.

The following has a less obvious origin and may well be a survival of the belief in nature spirits.

It is said to be unlucky to save a drowning man, for on being brought back to life it is thought that he will wreak vengeance on his rescuer at the dictation of the water spirits who have thus been baulked of their lawful prey.

We see the nature spirit again in the legend of the " Pool of Brereton " (Cheshire), in which the trunks of trees are said to swim on certain days before the death of the heir of the estate, as also in the legend of Credenhill Court (Herefordshire), where an ancient elm, known as " Prophet Elm," is supposed to shed its branches as a token of the death of the head of the house.[1] The connection between certain trees and funerary customs should be noted, for here we shall find later many traces of the most ancient of all religions—the worship of trees.

" It is certain," says Carew (" Survey of Cornwall "), " that divers ancient families in England are forewarned of their death in the mansion by oaks bearing strange leaves." An example of this is an oak in Lanhadron Park (Cornwall), which bears speckled leaves before a death in the family.

In some country estates the rooks are said to abandon their nests at the approach of death, and do not return until after the funeral, as in humble homes the crickets and the mice retire in like manner from the domestic hearth.

It is perhaps in the nature of things that royal and illustrious families receive special warnings not vouchsafed to meaner men, otherwise it would be difficult to account for a number of instances where a special forerunner of disaster appears to be provided for their exclusive information, one of the best known examples being " The White Lady " of the Hohenzollern. This spook is said to have appeared to Napoleon, and has been frequently seen in Karlsruche and other royal palaces since the middle of the seventeenth century, as the invariable herald of disaster to members of the family.

[1] Reginald B. Span, *Occult Review*.

DEATH WARNINGS

The royal houses of Bavaria and Romanoff are also credited with ghostly visitants; it is, however, worth noting that their generous services are of little value, as we have no instance where the illustrious persons have been able to avoid their fate by virtue of these dramatic "warnings."

At the marriage ceremony of the Crown Princess Louisa of Saxony, "three archdukes who were standing close to me became so impatient that in order to find another way out of the chapel they jumped over my train. My brother-in-law, the Archduke Otto, noticed this, and said in rather perturbed tones, 'Do you know the Hapsburg superstition, that anyone who jumps over a bride's train dies in the same year?' 'Well, it's November now, so they will have to be quick about it,' I said, trying to pass it off lightly, for I saw that Otto was really upset at the occurrence, for many uncanny things happened to us Hapsburgs."[1]

If it was a coincidence it was truly a remarkable one, that in a fortnight's time the Archdukes Sigismund and Ernest died, only to be followed at the end of December by the third archduke, Karl Ludwig.

The same Princess relates having seen in November, 1902, the phantom black cat which is said to appear on the altar of the royal chapel in the Zinzendorf Strasse, Dresden, to presage disaster.

The Banshee or "woman of the fairies" of Irish legend has always a very select clientele, and can only be induced to wail or "keen" as it is called, for the very best families.

In Wales this spook is known as the witch of Rhibyn, whose lamentations are not to be confused with the Cyhyraeth or "groaning spirit."

[1] Ex-Crown Princess of Saxony, "My Own Story."

Before we examine the rites and customs of burial, in their natural sequence, there is one aspect of the subject which deserves some special consideration, and that is the very debatable point as to *exactly* when death may be said to have taken place.

The thought of the possibility of being buried alive is a very real and haunting terror to a large number of sensitive people, as we may be assured if we study the curious clauses in wills which frequently appear in the Press.

Two recent examples of this may be quoted.

A lady dying at Hever, in Kent, left substantial sums of money for charitable purposes, and directed " that my body shall be stabbed to the heart to make sure that life is extinct." And the following from the will of a wealthy man who recently died at Herne Bay: "At my death a medical man shall make such experiments as may be necessary to make sure that life is extinct, and until the burial my remains are to be watched over by two nuns." Such requests have always been quite common, and show how deep is the fear of being buried alive.

In the year 1896 the Association for the Prevention of Premature Burial was founded to safeguard its members against premature burial by arrangement with medical experts in various localities, who would scientifically certify death in accordance with certain tests laid down by the Association. A further object of the society was the scientific investigation of trance.

Writing in support of this movement, the matter was well summed up by Sir W. J. Collins, M.D., F.R.C.S. (ex-Chairman L.C.C.) who said: "It is morbid sentiment that precludes the adequate consideration of the subject in this country, while it is only too easy to dismiss it with ill-directed jest."

Suppose that a person has "passed away," he no longer breathes, the action of the heart has ceased and the doctor has pronounced life to be extinct. Perhaps some test has been applied, such as breathing on glass—a very popular expedient—and there appears to be nothing left to be done but to make arrangements for the burial. It would be somewhat startling to the average person to learn on the authority of Dr. Brouardel, the eminent French specialist (Director of the Morgue, Paris) who made a life study of the subject, that this is "a grave popular error," "for many persons *who no longer breathe* have been recalled to life by means of care and skill." He says further, "the moment of death cannot therefore be assumed to be identical with cessation of respiration."

As regards the beating of the heart, he recalls a case where a man was executed at Troyes, whose heart beat for an hour after decapitation, the body being accompanied from the scaffold by two doctors who verified this fact.

Dr. Brouardel gives several instances of *apparent* death, and quotes the following case, in which he himself was present, from verbatim copy of notes taken the same evening.

" Ploingneau,
October 1st, 1867. Midnight.

" I exhumed at eight p.m. Philomèle Jonetre, aged twenty-four, buried at five p.m. in a grave six feet deep. Several persons heard her tap distinctly against the lid of the coffin. These blows appeared to me to have left visible marks, but I did not hear them myself."

He then goes on to describe the absence of all the ordinary signs of death, "rigor mortis" and the like. "Ammonia and other restoratives were applied." He then continues: "She was not dead, but like a candle, the flames of which had been extinguished, though the wick continues to glow. *No definite sounds of the heart*, but the eyelids moved in my presence. The body was kept unburied till the following day. This," he adds, "is an authentic case of burial during life."[1]

From many sources, more or less reliable, similar instances of premature burial might be quoted.

In the churchyard of Rye, Sussex, there was a tombstone, now defaced by age, depicting the figure of a woman sitting upright in her coffin, of whom the following curious story is related. She was subject to attacks of syncope, and was supposed on one occasion to be dead. Wrapped in a shroud, her body was placed in a coffin in the old Flushing Inn which is still standing. Thus she lay till the morning of the day appointed for her burial. The oven was being heated for the baking of the funeral repast when she awoke, climbed out of her coffin and walked downstairs, where she was found by the horrified cook, standing before the kitchen fire, complaining that she "felt the cold." She lived for some years after this extraordinary experience. It would seem that there is a period of suspended animation which may occur from various causes, and which is very likely to be mistaken for death.

Evelyn the diarist gives the following quaint account of a resurrection.

"Supped at Sir William Petty's, famous for having brought back to life a poor wench who had been hanged for felony, her body having been begged as the custom is, for the anatomy lectures;

[1] Dr. Brouardel, "Death and Sudden Death."

DEATH WARNINGS

he had her 'put to lie with a *warm woman*'[1] (surely some credit is due to the warm woman), and with spirits and other means restored her to life."

A full account of this exploit was published at the time in a pamphlet entitled, "News from the Dead, or a true and exact relation of the miraculous deliverance of Anne Greene, who having been executed December 14th, 1650, afterwards revived and by the care of a certain physician, is now perfectly recovered."

It is well known that the Indian fakir and his kind, under the influence of control, allow themselves to be buried for three weeks or longer; at the end of which period the flickering flame of life returns.

When does death take place? Anyone who has assisted at the restoration to life of a body recovered from the water, who has seen the miracle of returning animation to an apparently lifeless body, as a result of scientific treatment, lasting perhaps an hour or even longer, will hesitate for ever after to judge the matter on a basis of appearances, for it is between the time when the ordinary symptoms of death are apparent, and the actual setting in of putrefaction, that science may find a means to revive life.

It is rather by a combination of recognized signs than by dependence upon any particular "test" that life may safely be pronounced to be extinct, and it is only a qualified person, after careful examination, who has any right to give such a verdict.

In both the animal and vegetable kingdom examples are not wanting to show the wonderful provision of nature to protect the life of her children in extraordinary circumstances. The common

[1] Evelyn's Diary.

pond trout frozen in snow will remain apparently lifeless for days, but will revive at once if placed in water again. Despite the far-fetched stories of toads who are often said to remain embedded in trees, or built up in walls for years, and to come to life again on their release, there can be no doubt that such creatures are able to suspend animation for lengthy periods, in unfavourable conditions.

Before leaving this subject, there is another side of the question of which even less is known, and that is—granted that man has a soul—when does the soul leave his body? It has been the general practice in all ages to reserve the corpse for a certain period before burial. The actual time has depended somewhat on local conditions, climate and the like, and the custom is further influenced by the natural desire of affection which dictates that the body should be kept from dissolution as long as it is possible, but woven into these practices is the dim consciousness that the soul may not have finally severed the link which has bound it for so long to the body. Various customs, which we shall presently consider, show how deeply this thought has a hold on our minds. At the present time, when men of science are no longer ashamed to be associated with a belief in a spiritual existence after death, it is interesting to follow the results of their investigations, to confirm by demonstration what we have hitherto accepted, perhaps with a flickering faith.

We gather that the modern spiritualist holds that the soul dominates the physical life, and only when it leaves the body can death take place and decomposition set in. So far he would seem to agree with the general practice of all ages, that the body should not be buried till these signs are unmistakably present, but he takes us a step farther, for he

DEATH WARNINGS

professes to have proof that the soul is attached to the body by an elastic cord of unlimited tension to the various vital parts of the body, and we are told that for a period lasting for days, or weeks, in the case of an active man meeting with a sudden death, the soul is not severed from the body, even if burial has taken place in the meantime.[1]

How far we are prepared to credit such evidence must be a matter of personal consideration—to scoff is wholly irrational, for we shall find that many of the observances we cherish to-day have their origin in the grossest superstition of which any intelligent person might well be ashamed.

Various experiments have been tried with a view to overcoming the possibility of premature burial. What we know as mortuary chambers were established in Germany. They were built for the purpose of providing a resting place to which bodies could be removed immediately after death had presumably taken place, in order that they might be systematically under observation till putrefaction had definitely set in. Every possible precaution was taken to this end. A bell-rope was placed in the hand of the corpse, so that, should any return of consciousness take place, it would be immediately notified. As an additional precaution an official was in constant attendance, whose duty it was to inspect the bodies in his charge from time to time.

It will be some consolation to those who suffer from a horror of being buried alive to learn that no instance has been recorded of bodies placed in these mortuary chambers having "come to life."

These institutions are not to be confused with the Mortuary or Morgue.

Amongst the very many evils existing in con-

---

[1] J. Hewat McKenzie, "Spirit Intercourse—Its Theory and Practice."

nection with our methods of disposing of the dead may be cited not only a general lack of proper mortuary accommodation throughout the country, but particularly the attitude both of the officials and the public towards this most necessary institution. The thought that the bodies of friends and relations should be taken to a mortuary suggests to the average mind an indignity, a social degradation. The mortuary is regarded as especially provided by the State for the bodies of unfortunate outcasts picked up from the gutter, or dragged from the river, or at the best, as a place where the suicide or a person meeting with some dreadful accident is impounded till a jury can be called together for an inquest. We associate it mentally with the prison and the workhouse. Yet, when we are called upon as citizens to sit on coroners' juries, we see nothing incongruous in the fact that a public-house is considered a fitting place to take the corpse for the purpose of an inquest. This attitude is entirely wrong and a relic of Bumbledom. When we consider the vast floating population of London alone, housed for the most part in hotels, flats, boarding-houses or in lodgings, it must be seen that from a moral, hygienic or economic standpoint, proper and decent accommodation should be provided by the State in every district, to which bodies should be *compulsorily* removed immediately after death has been certified. It should, moreover, be a punishable offence to keep a body in any house, unless a special permit be obtained from the medical officer of the district, showing that he was personally satisfied that suitable accommodation had been provided for the purpose. The following story is not beautiful, but it not only has the advantage of being true, it is also typical of what goes on around us in our overcrowded cities.

DEATH WARNINGS

Dr. Brouardel quotes an instance from his own experience, where a man, living with his family in one room, died of *smallpox*. Here, on reaching the house, he found the family entertaining their friends who had come to "watch the body." He says: "There were bottles everywhere, even on the abdomen of the deceased. This," he adds, "is by no means an isolated case."[1]

One can picture the insanitary conditions of such a "chamber of horrors," crowded with persons whose ideas of personal cleanliness at any time were not very urgent. The blinds would probably be drawn, the window shut, and the family with the usual complement of small children and babies, would eat and sleep in the poisoned atmosphere. So overlaid are all our primary customs by empty sentiment and clown-patches of tradition, that this crying abuse, which is relatively as bad for the vast population of small villa residences as for those who inhabit the "slums," can only be effectively attacked by the example of those whose doings are aped by lesser minds.

Do we not find an opportunity here for the undertaker to justify himself? Could he not provide suitable mortuary accommodation to meet the needs of those who still have a "feeling" about public mortuaries. Certainly in some cases he has risen to the occasion and has provided (for a substantial consideration) a temporary resting-place for his "clients." The writer had a recent opportunity of inspecting the premises of one of these super-undertakers. He was shown with pride a "chapel" where the rich might "lie in state." Needless to say, it was resplendent with every conceivable vulgarity dear to the Dismal Trader's heart, where imitation stained glass and bastard Gothic decora-

[1] Dr. Brouardel, "Death and Sudden Death."

tion gave an air of theatrical sanctity; in place of what was required, a simple well-ventilated chamber, furnished only with the necessary provision for bearing the coffin, it was tricked out to resemble a place of worship, plus all his beastly trappings of death. When will it occur to the Trader that his province is to supply a box and a decent vehicle, and only that, and leave the question of ceremonies to the clergy, if we need them.

Let us rather entrust our bodies to the Inspector of Nuisances till some proper provision can be made by the State. With regard to the time allowed to elapse between death and burial in this country, we are generally in agreement with the customs of Greece and Rome, to await the period of physical decay. In Germany forty-eight hours only is allowed, Spain and Portugal five or six hours, France twenty-four hours. In other countries the time is largely dictated by the climate.

FRETTED MEMORIAL-CARD MOUNT.

This Victorian atrocity, printed in black and silver, was supplied by the undertaker. The memorial card was attached, the whole intended to be framed and glazed (illustration approximately half full size). Note the traditional symbols of grief—the inverted torch, palm of martyrdom, broken column, ivy and weeping willow.

CHAPTER III

PREPARATION FOR BURIAL, COFFINS, "GRAVE-GOODS," SUTTEE

In order to follow the various burial customs as clearly as possible, we will consider them in their natural sequence.

Death has taken place, with or without such a supernatural warning as we have noted in a previous chapter, and precautions have been taken (we will hope) to ascertain that what was once a human being is now a " lifeless corpse "—an expression that we may use without tautology. Whilst the word " corpse " is now accepted as denoting a *dead* body, it was at one time as often used in describing the living; of which Trench gives the following examples :[1]

"A valiant *corpse* where force and beauty met." [2]

" Women and maids shall particularly examine themselves about the variety of their apparel, their too much care of their *corpse*." [3]

When the soul or personality goes away, leaving the body behind, it severs all association with the remains, which become a public charge, with an implied obligation on the relatives. Should they, however, for one reason or another refuse it burial, any stranger may undertake that duty, and recover the cost from the estate of the deceased by law.

[1] Trench, " Select Glossary."
[2] Surrey, " On the Death of Sir R. Wyatt."
[3] Richeomes, " Pilgrim of Loretto."

FUNERAL CUSTOMS

The only way that a person in this country can assure his wishes being carried out in respect of a particular form of burial is by leaving his property to friends or relatives conditionally upon his expressed desire being respected. Although it is of course still open to such a person to refuse the legacy and act in the matter according to his lights. This is not infrequently done in cases of a difference of religious opinions. An amusing case of avarice *versus* religious convictions will be found in a chapter on cremation.

It cannot too strongly be insisted upon when we compare the practices of the past with the present, that the very customs to which we cling so unreasonably, are for the most part unworthy remnants of superstitious rites, and not anything dictated by any form of Christian religion to which we may subscribe. This is important, because we can readily trace the continuity of such usages in the absence of any sort of authority for what we do—to the accepted and erroneous belief that they are associated in some way with articles of a faith, which it would be impious to rough-handle, thus they have been handed down from generation to generation, impervious even to ridicule and carefully fostered by the Dismal Trader.

Let us look, for instance, at the demands of the Roman Catholic Church, as representing a body of Christians who, employing an elaborate ritual, might impose such customs upon their followers.

(1) That the body be decently laid out.

(2) That lights be placed beside the body.

(3) That a cross be laid upon the breast, or failing that, the hands laid on the breast in the form of a cross.

(4) That the body be sprinkled with holy water and incensed at stated times.

PREPARATION FOR BURIAL

(5) That it be buried in consecrated ground.

Here we have certain observances, decreed, which have no relation to mourning weeds, floral offerings, funeral repasts, plumed hearses or tombstones, whilst as far as ceremony is concerned they merely apply to the dead those rites which are (rightly or wrongly) enjoined for the living. The wearing of the cross—for example, the recognized symbol of the Christian faith, the use of lights, incense and holy water are but the common practice of Catholicism. There is one thing which the Catholic Church does *not* allow, as being historically against the Christian practice—and this is cremation.

If we go back to the earliest Christian times we find certain decrees issued in relation to the burial of the dead, but still no mention of the "trappings of the trade."

In the days of Constantine, companies of functionaries were established, with definite duties of charity to the dead. They worked in groups under the general supervision of the Decani or overseers. Some were charged to "prepare for the religious procession," others to "carry the bier," whilst it was the duty of yet another group to "lift the body and dig the grave." Laws were also made at the same period to secure all expenses against overcharge. Every person who needed it was to have a coffin without payment, whilst even the poorest were to be followed to the grave by a crossbearer, light-monks and three acolytes. The funeral banquet, an abuse which on various pretexts was creeping in, was also banned by the Church.

The Council of Auxerre forbade the ceremonial kiss given to the dead by the priest, and the practice of dressing the body in rich garments.

Certain Jewish customs were adopted by the Church as "pious practices" (as distinguished from

c

articles of faith) because of their association with the burial of their Divine Founder. An instance of this is the ceremonious cleansing of the body after death. St. Chrysostom writes of this as being "hallowed in the person of our Lord"[1] (whose body was washed as soon as it was taken from the Cross). To the Christians this Jewish custom (the special obligation of a son to his father's body) signified that the dead, freed from the stain of sin by the Sacraments, might be received into Heaven "where no unclean thing may enter."

The charitable St. Martin took particular care to search out the dead bodies of the poor and destitute, and we are told, "Never failed of washing them with fair water."[2]

Jewish funeral customs are sufficiently interesting to call for special consideration, and it would not perhaps be generally supposed that simplicity was the keynote enjoined for a people who notoriously love display, nor can we fasten on them our stupid pagan survivals.

It is strictly ordained that there must be no adornment of the plain wooden coffin used by the Jew, nor may flowers be placed inside or outside. Plumes, velvet palls and the like, are strictly prohibited, and all show and display of wealth discouraged; moreover, the synagogue holds itself responsible for the arrangements for burial,[3] dispensing with the services of the "Dismal Trade." Fixed and reasonable charges are made for services rendered. For anything like this admirable commercial "undertaking" we must look in our own country to the olden days of the trade guilds. The guild supplied a hearse, such as will be presently

[1] "Eighty-fourth Homily on St. John."
[2] Pierre Muret, Trans. P. Lorraine, "Funeral Rites, Ancient and Modern."
[3] Leopold Wagner, "Manners, Customs and Observances."

PREPARATION FOR BURIAL

described, also a pall, bier, candles, etc. These articles were collectively owned, and held always at the disposal of those of the fraternity who might have need of them; they might, moreover, be borrowed by the members for the use of friends, in which case a toll was taken of a certain quantity of wax, which would be made up into candles as required. In some parishes in England to-day a bier and a pall are still kept for the use of parishioners, to which was added at one time a coffin in which the shrouded body was carried to the grave, and from whence it would be removed at the grave side, the coffin being returned for a further occasion.

No doubt the origin of the custom of washing, anointing and clothing the corpse in garments suitable to its rank was instituted in the dim ages, when it was believed that the departed required such attentions to enable them to appear at their best in a future material state. Handed down to later times the Christian put his own interpretation to the practice which he had adopted.

The primary doctrine of the Resurrection of the *body* somewhat crudely interpreted presupposed the resurrection of the clothes by the old force of associated ideas. This led to a continuance of a tradition which we have by no means forsaken to-day. Thus we still array in their robes of office, kings, monks, nuns and priests, as well as soldiers, statesmen, and others who wear a distinctive dress, whilst on the Continent great satisfaction has been derived from the thought of appearing before the Creator in the inevitable evening dress, apparently with a view to impressing Him with a sense of the social standing of his creatures so arrayed. As a somewhat happy contrast to this, one is inclined to admire the humility of the Greek church, whose "religious" are buried naked, with the exception of a hair cloth, as a sign of a life of penance.

In the matter of dressing the dead, the same customs do not apply everywhere—some only cover the body with a winding sheet, with the exception of the priests, who are robed in their "ecclesiastical ornaments," as the bodies of the martyrs were ordered to be arrayed in a "fair surplice." Pope Gregory even finds fault with some of his predecessors for having such honours done to their bodies, which were the special privilege of the martyrs. In Italy the dead were wrapped in the cloaks they wore in life, "which was considered honourable and done in the first century."[1]

Muret further reminds us that it was "an ancient Christian custom to perfume the body in commemoration of the spices in which the body of the Saviour was wrapped, and that the pagans, who much prized perfume and used it in their religious rites and copiously on their bodies, much chided the Christians for wasting precious ointments on their dead at the expense of the living."

In China, where rank is so deeply respected, the clothing of the dead is a very costly and elaborate proceeding. According to social standing the corpse must be provided with anything up to the fifty suits due to a ruler, for whom upper and lower garments are used. The student comes in for a rich assortment of black silk robes in recognition of his learning, which is held very honourably by the Chinese.

It is hardly necessary to add that despite the liberal contributions of friends, known as "helps," a family is frequently ruined, as is sometimes the case in our own country, in paying what are supposed

[1] Pierre Muret, Trans. P. Lorraine, "Funeral Rites, Ancient and Modern."

PREPARATION FOR BURIAL

to be "proper marks of respect" to their deceased relatives. Whilst the most expensive thing about a man in China is his funeral, the least expensive is that of a child. During the old regime, parents frequently wrapped the dead infants in lengths of matting and laid them at certain street corners, where a man passed with a black cart drawn by a black cow every morning, and collected them for burial.[1]

In early days in England the bodies of the poor were committed to the grave practically naked, or at best wrapped in a shroud of linen, and only the prosperous were allowed to be "chested," as it was called. Cox mentions a curious instance of this as late as 1608, when one John Skerry, "a poore man that died in The Place Stable (Poyning, Surrey), and being brought half naked with his face bare, the parson would not burye him soe, but first he gave a sheete and caused him to be sacked therein, and they buried him more Christian-like, being much grieved to see him brought soe unto the grave, and at this time did one Thatcher dwell at The Place" (or manor house).[2]

In the year 1666 an Act came into force insisting that all persons should be buried in a shroud composed of woollen material in place of linen previously used.

It would seem that this new law was easily and frequently evaded, for in the year 1678 and again in 1680 it was found necessary to amend it; a provision was added that a certificate must be given by the relative of the deceased person, in the form of an affidavit, declaring that a woollen shroud had been used at the burial.

If we compare the population of England at

---

[1] Isaac Taylor Headland, "Home Life in China."
[2] J. Chas. Cox, "The Parish Registers of England."

that period with the population to-day, the impetus which this law gave to the paper trade, which it was designed to assist, is very remarkable. It will also give some idea of the value of the costly hard woods and metal which we consign to the earth every year. We are told that as a result of this law, it was computed that no less than 200,000 lbs. of rag were saved from corruption in the grave. In order to enforce the regulations, a heavy fine was imposed for non-compliance, but the gay decking of the corpse is a custom which dies hard, and persons of means were often found to pay the penalty rather than submit to what they considered an *indignity*. The parish churches were obliged to keep a special register of burials for the purpose, and an affidavit had to be made before a Justice of the Peace or a clergyman that the new law had been duly complied with. The certificate was signed by two witnesses. A bait was offered, consisting of a part of the fine, to any informer who could produce evidence that the Act in any particular case had been evaded.[1]

These laws were not repealed till the reign of George III, 1814.

In the year 1700 there appears an entry in the parish register of Eye, that the executors of one Thomas Deye were fined five pounds for burying a body wrapped in linen. Cox gives the following extracts from one of the special registers:

" Well wrapped in a shirt of woollen and was let down into his dormitory with that vestment about his corpse, to the great satisfaction of the law enjoining that habiliment as convenient for the dead."

" Francis Pickerings was shrouded only in a

---

[1] Capes, " Rural Life in Hampshire."

PREPARATION FOR BURIAL

winding sheet made of the fleece of good fat mutton."[1]

For the same reason that it was once the custom in Ireland to remove the nails from the coffin immediately before lowering it into the grave (in order that the dead might have no difficulty in freeing themselves on the day of Resurrection), so we find that the shroud or winding sheet was often loosened from the feet and hands, lest its tight folds should prevent a speedy egress at the all important moment. A special costume for burial was provided, and in some cases prepared during life, by the women, so that there might be no doubt about its being ready when required at death.

The Norwegian peasant makes her burial garment from a special material, and reverently hoards it up for use at her death, whilst not infrequently in this country poor women who are forced by circumstances to spend their last days in the workhouse take with them a nightdress and a pair of white stockings in order that they may appear "respectable" at their death.

The following is a description of a curious ancient Jewish dress for a corpse in the seventeenth century: A special pair of drawers was made by women who did this work as a charity. After this had been put on the body a skirt was added, a frill of fine linen, a taled or cloak, square in form with ribbons suspended, and on the head a white cap.[2]

That white stockings are still considered in certain spheres of life as fitting for the special use of the dead the following incident will show, which recently came to the writer's notice. A little girl, whose mother kept a small linen draper's shop in

---

[1] J. Chas. Cox, "The Parish Registers of England."
[2] Leon Modema, "Costumes des Juifs," Trans. Simon.

London, was invited to a children's party. Her scanty wardrobe contained a muslin frock suitable to the occasion, but her heart was set on a pair of white stockings to complete the effect. Having seen the necessity stocked for sale in the shop, she ventured to ask for the loan of a pair, a request that was angrily refused by her mother, who explained that they were sold only for the use of the dead.

In England, till the middle of the sixteenth century, it was ordained by the Church that if a child should die within a month of its baptism it must be buried in its chrisom. The chrisom was the prototype of the baptismal robe. It was originally made in such a way that the priest might readily anoint the infant with the chrism or holy oil used at baptism, with the sign of the cross between the shoulders and on the breast. This garment was worn till the seventh day to protect the places so anointed, or till such time as the mother was "churched." For the same purpose a band of linen was at one time bound round the head of children and kept there for eight days after confirmation, of which the white band often worn by boys round the arm when they are confirmed is a probable survival. In the event of the child dying before the stated time, it was known as a "chrisom" child, and it was decreed that it should be buried in its chrisom, bound round the body by swaddling bands, in place of the shroud. It might be mentioned here, that whilst we generally associate swaddling clothes with children, it was once a term used to describe the strips of material bound round the shroud of children or adults. There are a few memorial brasses to be found in our churches, depicting "chrisom children" shrouded in this curious manner.

The burial of children has always differed in

PREPARATION FOR BURIAL

some ways from that of adults. The Romans, for instance, buried them in the ground under the eaves of their houses, because it was thought that the infant spirit, being near its parents, would not "walk" as it otherwise might do if interred far from its home.

For the same reason, even to-day, we generally bury the body of a very young or unchristened child in the coffin of a woman adult, in order that the little ghost may not torment its parents with reproachful "lamentings"; for the origin of the practice has nothing to do with the mere economy of burial charges.

We saw that the Chinese wrapped their dead babes in old matting, but something very similar has been done much nearer home.

In France, some years before the revolution, De Braz tells us that the parents of a dead child used to make a little receptacle for its body by stripping the bark from a chestnut tree, which they bound round the infant with broom. So common was the habit that it became necessary to pass a law making the priest the responsible person to see that a practice which ruined so many trees was discontinued. The priest of each parish was instructed to announce the new regulations from the pulpit in the various provinces. The penalty for non-compliance was a very heavy fine.[1]

This bark shroud or coffin was an instance of the use of something which answered both purposes. Binding the body with reeds or sewing it up in the hide of an animal are other instances. The body of Henry I was salted to preserve it and sewn into an ox hide and brought to England for burial.

Cox reminds us that the book of Common Prayer certainly anticipates uncoffined burial, as the word coffin is not even mentioned, reference being made

[1] De Braz, "La Légende de la Mort chez les Bretons."

only to the "corpse" or the "body"—thus, "the earth shall be cast upon the body."

In Wheatley's book on the Common Prayer (1710) occurs the comment, "When the body is stripped of all but its grave-clothes, and is going to be put into the grave," etc.[1] A trace of interment without a coffin at the present day may be found in the traditional rites of the orthodox gipsy, who prefers to be shrouded in his best suit of clothes —turned inside out—and buried at the cross-road, or under a hedge with no other covering.

That "chested burial" was at one time considered as an attribute of wealth or social standing may be gathered from the following ancient regulation taken from the records of the historic town of Rye (Sussex):

In the year 1580 the City Fathers decreed that "no person who shall die within the Port of Rye under the degree of Mayor Jurat or common councilman, or of their wives, except such person as the Mayor shall give licence for and being paid to the Mayor for the use of the poor, shall be chested or coffined to their burial, and if any carpenter or joiner make any chest or coffin for any person to be buried (other than for the persons aforesaid excepted) he shall be fined ten shillings for every coffin so made by him."[2]

When a coffin was used for the poor it was only for the purposes of conveying the corpse from the house where the death took place to the graveside. There the body would be removed and placed in the grave, covered only by the shroud or winding sheet.

In Scotland, about the sixteenth century, a kind of combined coffin and bier was in use. It consisted of a wooden receptacle, one side of which was

---

[1] J. Chas. Cox, "The Parish Registers of England."
[2] "Records of the Town of Rye."

PREPARATION FOR BURIAL

hinged as a lid, from which the corpse was removed and lowered into the grave by means of ropes.

Andrews also describes the "death hamper," as it was called, where it was in use in some parts of the Highlands. Three pairs of loop handles were provided, through which iron bars were passed to enable it to be conveniently carried. After it had been lowered into the grave, it was turned over to relieve it of its load, and brought to the surface again for use on a future occasion.[1]

Simpler still was a contrivance once used in Brittany. It consisted of a top and bottom plank, one over and one supporting the body. Blocks of wood held them together, two being nailed close to the neck of the corpse, two under the arms, and two near the ankles, thus forming a rough crate without sides rather than a chest.

"To chest" or place the body in a coffin is an expression frequently to be met with in early English records. Thus we read in the Bible, "He (Joseph) dieth and is chested."[2]

In countries where earth-burial could be avoided, a coffin would be of little importance in preserving the body from decay, a natural or artificial cave being used in which the body would rest on a ledge or shelf, without any covering except the grave clothes.

We find the cave habit perpetuated in the use of stone coffins, many examples of which have been unearthed in this country. When suitable materials were not available from which to construct such a coffin, small slabs of stone were built round about the body as a protection such as we find in early Christian cemeteries.

The stone coffin was indeed more nearly related to the tomb, for owing to its weight it was not

[1] W. M. Andrews, "Bygone Church Life in Scotland."
[2] Bible, Gen. l. 26.

possible to conveniently carry it any distance, so that the body could be brought to the coffin and deposited therein.

Let us look for a moment at the origin of thus boxing the body instead of the simple practice of placing it, shrouded only, in direct contact with the earth. Undoubtedly it originated in the attempt to preserve the corpse as long as possible from decay, and the reason for so doing was in Christian countries anyway, the belief in a final material resurrection of the body.

We have seen that the poor looked upon the coffin as a luxury, which had, in some instances, even been denied to them by law. It is still regarded by meaner minds as a symbol of social status and respectability, and the undertaker finds in the poorer districts a ready demand for the polished oak and gaudy "furniture" which is the pride of his profession. In support of this the following true story was told by the late Canon Barnet.

Some slum children were taken for a day's outing to the country, and later, their experiences formed the subject of an essay at school. One little girl appeared to have been much impressed by the trees, and thus described the oak: "From the oak tree is made *coffins* and other *expensive articles*."[1]

We can hardly believe that even the most bigoted could suppose that burial without a coffin rendered the poor at a disadvantage in answering the Roll Call on the Day of Judgment, for we have an example from the most orthodox source to disprove this. The Trappist Monk wrapped only in his habit for a shroud, with his head and face protected by his cowl, is reverently committed by his brothers to the earth in the little cemetery belonging to their Order, without any coffin or other protection what-

[1] Canon Barnett, "Practical Socialism."

PREPARATION FOR BURIAL

ever, and this could hardly be the case if there was the slightest reason to suppose that its welfare in the future state should be imperilled. Undoubtedly the custom of preserving the body as long as possible from decay is one of those unauthoritative conventions which we follow without attempting to define our reasons or real feelings in the matter.

Needless to say the " Trade " is all in favour of a substantial and " beautiful " (?) casket, to cast into the grave, with such expensive furniture fittings and linings as can be thrust upon the relatives at a time when they are not in the spirit to bargain.

If we estimated the value of the oak, elm and other valuable hard woods which we commit to the earth every year, to rot and decay, to say nothing of the value of brass and other metal which goes with them, we must see how truly appalling is this waste. Our folly in this respect forms one of the soundest claims which the advocates of cremation put before us, from the purely utilitarian standpoint. Taking the annual number of deaths in England and Wales as something like 260,000—translate that into pounds sterling and you will have very largely under-estimated the value of the wood alone, which is used for coffins during that period. Prodigal as we are in our use of timber for various commercial necessary purposes, which we ruthlessly destroy and never systematically replant, we at least manufacture articles which may perhaps last for generations, whilst wood used for coffins, from a utilitarian standpoint, may just as well have been burnt.

Even in a damp soil a coffin made of oak or elm, with or without a leaden shell, will preserve the human remains for a very considerable period. Elm is largely used, both for economy and its peculiar properties of resisting the action of rot when in the ground.

In light sandy soils decomposition is a very much slower process. Some earth has the peculiar property of mummifying the body. The placing of antiseptic carbolic sawdust, etc., in the coffin greatly tends to preservation, whilst the use of india-rubber and other such expedients is the outcome of foolish sentiment which seeks to delay the reasonable and inevitable courses of Nature in reclaiming what she has lent to us. Not only are such practices illogical, but opposed to the laws of sanitation; nor are they warranted by any precept, civil or ecclesiastical.

Whilst preservation, including the ancient science of embalming, is (except in certain rare cases) unnecessary and objectional, we must not go to the opposite extreme and bury our dead with quicklime or corrosives, which might tend to render more difficult the detection of crime. Very large sums of money have been paid for costly coffins elaborately carved and silver mounted, whilst the use of velvet, swansdowns, paddings and pinking, show us a remnant of the hard dying belief that the dead are merely sleeping in their graves, and require such material comforts.

The orthodox Jew believed this very really, and also that the actual process of decay was in the nature of a punishment, the pains of which the dead were called upon to endure in satisfaction of sins committed during their lifetime. We are not therefore surprised to find secret efforts often made with a view to shortening this unhappy period. Earth was placed in the coffin, and holes bored in the wood to accelerate decomposition. Perhaps as a claim to special consideration the Jews sometimes made their coffins from the boards of a table at which the poor had been fed.[1]

[1] "The Jewish Encyclopædia."

PREPARATION FOR BURIAL 47

It has been said that the very customs to which we cling, that are objectionable, have no relation to any doctrine imposed upon us by our religious beliefs. The special preservation of the bodies of the dead, when carried beyond an occasional necessity (where certain diseases have produced an extremely rapid mortification) is all part of an ignorant literal conception of the doctrine of the resurrection of the body. That such a materialistic conception was once very general is easy to determine; for instance, teeth were often carefully preserved, as they were shed in the natural course of events, during lifetime, in order that they might eventually be buried with the body and, as dismembered parts, be readily available at the "Last Day." If such precautions were necessary the matter presents many problems, such as must have troubled the mind of the Sunday School scholar, who inquired in his perplexity where missionaries went to when they died, and being assured that they undoubtedly gained admission to the celestial state, the child asked "if cannibals went to Heaven also." The horrified teacher denied so liberal a doctrine. "Well, then, what happens to the missionary who gets eaten by the cannibals?" was the logical response.

Many cases are on record where a coffin has been purchased during the lifetime of a person of eccentric habits, and often served as a bed, in order that the owner might become accustomed to the use of the receptacle in which the body would repose during the long sleep. It is well known that Madame Sarah Bernhardt kept a coffin, and was photographed in it in her boudoir. Whatever may have been the motive of the celebrated actress, others have done the same thing, in the sense of self-repression, as the monks of some Orders daily dig a spadeful of the earth which is eventually to cover their remains, as an act of humility.

Evelyn mentions attending the funeral of a master shipwright, and he tells us "it was the custom of this good man to rise in the night and to pray, kneeling in his own coffin, which he had by him for many years."[1]

In China, when a son wishes to make a handsome and welcome gift to his parents, he presents them with a coffin, which is often to be found in the houses of the middle classes. It may be made of fine wood or cypress, and it is often very costly. The Chinese coffin is of tremendous weight, and according to a rule prescribed for persons of different degrees of dignity, the outer shell may be as much as eight inches in thickness, the inner shell six inches, and the innermost four inches.

The correct measurement of a student's coffin is six inches in thickness, and even the poor are buried in wood five inches for the outer and four inches for the inner shell. As a rule, plain white unvarnished wood is used for the purpose.[2]

In Mrs. Hugh Fraser's charming account of her travels in Japan, she gives the following description of the funeral procession of a Prince which she witnessed, and thus describes the conveyance of the body to burial:

"The bier was a lovely shape, like a small temple, all carved out of spotless white wood. It did not look like a coffin but like a closed litter, with beautiful chased golden mountings and fresh green bamboo blinds closing the litter windows. The roof rose at its corners in delicate ornament, and tassels of pure white silk hung against the blinds.

---

[1] Evelyn's Diary.
[2] Isaac Taylor Headland, "Home Life in China."

PREPARATION FOR BURIAL

"The bier was carried by fifty men by means of poles crossed and recrossed. This covered a double coffin made of white wood."[1]

The universal custom of burying articles of various kinds with the body has been responsible for our gradual enlightenment as to the habits and surroundings of those who inhabited the world before us, from the most remote periods.

It is from the tombs that we have discovered many historical facts which tradition had either misused or entirely forgotten. We are indeed richer to-day in our knowledge of the past than those who lived many centuries nearer to events. Not only articles buried with the body, but the bones and impressions left by the body in the soil long after the tissues had crumbled into dust, continue to reward the patient investigator with such information as enables him to piece together, not only the mode of life, but the actual appearance of the dead, whose burrows he uncovers.

In many cases traditions have been verified in a startling manner. Some parts of a suit of gilded armour were recovered in recent years from a place where tradition only had handed down a story through the centuries of a knight of great valour so equipped.

The origin of the practice of burying weapons and utensils with the dead is obviously the outcome of the belief that the departed spirit would require such material necessities in the "after life." Weapons of battle and the chase, domestic pottery and the like are most frequently recovered, owing to the time-resisting properties of the flint, bronze or glass from which they were generally constructed. Food, if buried, would quickly decay, but the

[1] Mrs. Hugh Fraser, "A Diplomatist's Wife in Japan."

50 FUNERAL CUSTOMS

earthenware pots or glass vessels in which it was stored, remain in evidence of the practice.

The discovery of a number of tusks at Llanbede (Vale of Conway) shows us that the wild boar once roamed through our forests, whilst such treasures as drinking horns, metal shield bosses and remnants of military equipment not uncommonly reward the labours of the excavator.

Apart from private collections, there is hardly a museum, however modest may be its aims, that does not contain numerous examples of such objects dug from the earth, and nearly always from the site of the graves of our long forgotten ancestors.

To catalogue these treasures would be altogether outside the scope of our subject, for we are rather committed to learn the reason of their presence with the dead than to study them as a matter of archæological interest. The axe for slaughter, the dagger or meat-knife, and the hammer for breaking bones, tell their own story. Such simple necessities as these we shall expect to find in plenty. That they should accompany the dead in their travels to the spirit-world is consistent with the belief which we know to have been held by all primitive peoples.

We find other objects in the graves which are yet more worthy of our notice, for they speak to us of superstitions which we may scorn in the light of our superior knowledge, but which we are not ashamed to perpetuate, largely because we have so dim a conception of the beliefs which we profess.

Ever since the exchange of goods by barter gave place to the more convenient practice of trading by tokens, money has been buried with the corpse. This habit has been common to all nations. If the hunter required his arrows and a spear with which to support himself in the future state, the trader would feel very helpless were he not buried with

PREPARATION FOR BURIAL 51

money with which to meet expenses and purchase his necessities.

Accustomed to be taxed on every possible occasion by grasping officials, even the cultured Greek took with him on his last journey coins with which to reward Charon for the safe conduct of his soul, over the dark waters of the Styx.

The Chinaman has much the same belief, and for safe keeping a coin is placed in the mouth of the corpse in order that it may be readily produced when the inevitable demand for a fee is made by some ghostly janitor.

Whilst Christian precept has found a spiritual meaning for many traditional practices, which, thus sanctified, have been carried forward from pagan times—as in the matter of the orientation of the body—it is to be feared that even these have become as foreign and meaningless to the modern mind as the pagan custom so continued. The matter of burying money with the dead is no exception.

The mediæval Christian writer finds " in the universal custom of closing the eyes and mouth of the corpse directly death has taken place the poetical thought that " the dead may look no more upon this imperfect life, now that they have seen the glory of the world to come "—and in closing the mouth " that they may taste no more of anything of this world, but rather use their mouths for praising God in Heaven." [1]

It is very doubtful if even the modern Christian sees anything of the sort in this traditional practice, but it is remarkable to note that the custom of placing coins on the eyes of the dead, which was very generally done a generation ago, is still to be met with. This is indeed a relic of the primitive

---

[1] Pierre Muret, Trans. P. Lorraine, " Funeral Rites, Ancient and Modern."

superstition that money, so urgent a necessity in this life, cannot readily be dispensed with in the future state. Quantities of silver and copper coins have been unearthed at various times in English churchyards, and it need hardly be said how valuable a record these have been as a guide to the period at which interment took place. In China, at one time, money, clothes and other things of value were burnt as a means of passing them on for the use of the departed spirit; but so great was the expense that, in more recent years, imitations made of paper were substituted.

As the funeral procession of a Chinese dignitary passes along the streets, round pieces of paper with a square hole in the centre in imitation of the copper cash used in the country, are scattered broadcast. It is intended for the future use of the departed official, at whose shrine offerings of gold and silver paper ingots will later be made. With the same intention, coins, jewels and precious ointments were lavishly placed to be burnt on the funeral pyre of the Roman of position.

The hammer has thus been mentioned as one of the objects commonly buried with primitive man, and we find this custom continued under another guise, namely, that the dead may use it to announce their arrival by " knocking with it on the gates of Purgatory." [1] This quaint belief is still to be met with in Ireland.

At the funeral of Zachariah Smith, a gipsy who was buried in Yorkshire a few years ago, in the traditional manner of his tribe, the following articles accompanied him for his convenience in the future state: An extra suit of clothes, his watch and chain, four pocket-handkerchiefs, a *hammer* and a candle.[2]

[1] Walter Johnson, " Byways in British Archæology."
[2] Rev. Hall, " Gipsy Customs."

PREPARATION FOR BURIAL

Possibly with the same idea, that of announcing his arrival, it was a practice in Scotland to put a bell under the head of the corpse, and on the breast a vessel containing salt typifying immortality, and bread, the corruptible body.

Like the pages of history the graves of the dead sometimes give us touching evidence of frailties common to all mankind. What matter the achievements of King Alfred, as warrior, lawgiver or scribe! Enough that it is recorded of him that he burnt the scolding widow's cakes, and in so doing endeared himself for ever to the youthful mind. So in delving amongst dry and forgotten bones we shall sometimes find trinkets and treasured personal possessions—vanities which bridge the centuries and strike a deeply sympathetic chord of kinship in our hearts.

The skeleton of a mother of our race folding fleshless arms round the little bones of the child she bore, or a skull remarkable amongst a thousand others, the arrow-head still resting where it found its mark. What could be more human than the Swedish custom of burying a looking-glass with unmarried women, in order that they might arrange their loosely coiled tresses to appear to advantage on the day of Resurrection. The fact that married women braid their hair rendered unnecessary any such precaution in their case.[1]

In the Egyptian tomb, happiness in the after life of the children was assured by burying with them the toys with which they had played during their earthly sojourn.

In examining the spoils of the graveyard, we must distinguish between such things as were

[1] England Howlett, F.S.A., "Burial Customs" (Curious Church Customs and Cognate Subjects). Edited by Wm. Andrews.

intended for the use of the dead and articles committed to the earth as symbols only, such, for instance, as wheat—a very ancient token of resurrection—or the scarab beetle so frequently found in Egypt, and still more frequently manufactured for the tourist trade. The connection between the scarab and resurrection is not at first apparent, for it is based on a misconception. This insect was popularly supposed to create its kind from the earth. It may still be seen working in the sand as the early Egyptian saw it, rolling up little balls of dung, which, presently bursting, releases its progeny *created* from the earth, as the poetic Eastern mind supposed, having overlooked the simple fact that the beetle had laid a tiny egg, round which the dung was moulded, thus providing a hot-bed for the purposes of fertilization.[1]

Wheat, frequently buried by the Egyptian, is plentifully found engraven on the early Christian monuments, for to the Christian mind it holds a double meaning. Whilst the germ of life it contains is significant of resurrection, as the basis of bread, it was ever associated with the Sacraments. In quite recent years in England, it was the custom to distribute a sheaf of corn amongst the mourners at a funeral.

It was once a common practice to place an hour-glass in the coffin to represent the "running out of the sands of time." Howlett thinks it probable that little hour-glasses were distributed amongst the mourners, to be thrown into the open grave.[2]

Perhaps one of the most remarkable instances of the hard-dying belief that the soul requires material assistance in the after life is a Russian custom of

[1] Grant Allen, "Nature's Workshop."
[2] England Howlett, F.S.A., "Burial Customs" (Curious Church Customs and Cognate Subjects). Edited by Wm. Andrews.

THE CAPUCINE VAULTS, PALERMO.

A THIRTEENTH CENTURY STONE COFFIN, CUT OUT OF A SINGLE BLOCK, RECENTLY UNEARTHED ON THE SITE OF MERTON PRIORY CHURCH, WIMBLEDON. IT CONTAINED THE SKELETON OF A MAN.

giving a parchment certificate of good conduct, which is placed in the hands of the corpse, to be presented as a credential to assure ready admittance into the realms of bliss.

Eventually the Christian Church forbade the interment of what were known as "grave goods" with the body, but an exception was made in favour of kings and priests, who were allowed to retain their robes and symbols of office.

Amongst the many rich finds which have been made in the tombs of Royalty, was the treasure discovered accidentally by a poor labourer in the resting-place of Childerie I at Tournay. Here was unearthed a cornelian Etruscan scarab, probably a valued amulet, a divining ball and a signet-ring. There were also recovered three hundred golden bees, with wings inlaid with a red stone, which it is supposed formed ornaments on the harness of his horse, the skeleton of which, together with that of his page, were lying near their royal master.[1]

The practice of giving the material necessities of life to the dead, in the belief that their requirements in the spirit world were the same as in the sphere from which they had departed, leads very naturally to the belief that the wife and slaves of the rich man should accompany him also. Hence we find that in the case of a person of rank or position it has been the custom in the past to slaughter not only the man's wife, but his page, slaves and personal attendants.

So deep was the belief of a material hereafter that we find no horror expressed, as a rule, on the part of the victims, who would consider it an honour to be selected to accompany their lord on his spiritual travels.

In the Congo, on the death of a native king or

[1] W. Jones, F.S.A., "Finger Ring Lore."

chief, it is the custom for twelve young girls to throw themselves into the grave that they may be buried with their master. So great is the competition for the favour that a fierce fight often ensues amongst the claimants, in which some are killed, the number of applicants being thus reduced.

In Mexico, at one time, they buried with the king his jester and dwarf for his amusement, a number of women for his material consolation, and a priest to act as guide in the spiritual realm. Sir H. Johnston tells us that when an important Lubu dies a young slave is obtained, and his neck having been broken by a blow, he is laid by the corpse, which it is his duty to attend. Such customs are still continued amongst uncivilized peoples, and were practised in China under the old regime.

The horrible rite of self-immolation was common in India as late as the year 1829, when "suttee" was abolished. Till that time the Hindu widow voluntarily perished in the flames of the funeral pyre at the death of her husband. That it was considered an honourable act may be gathered from the fact that the word is derived from "sate," which means "a virtuous life." Credit has been given to the British Government for suppressing this ancient sacrifice, but although it is true that the weight of the English law made it possible to stamp out the evil, it is claimed that enlightened native opinion first urged the Government to abolish "suttee."

The noble Hindu Rajah Ram Mohan Roy is said to have been the prime mover in this matter. Swami Abhedanana tells us that " self-burning of widows was not sanctioned by the Vedic religion, but was due to other causes." Some say that when the Mohammedans conquered India they treated the widows of the soldiers so brutally that the women

PREPARATION FOR BURIAL

preferred death, and voluntarily sought it. In order to have Scriptural authority for the rite of suttee, the Brahmin priests perverted the meaning of the Vedic text which thus describes the funeral ceremony of the ancient Hindus: " Rise up, woman, thou art lying by one whose life is gone. Come, come to the world of the living, away from thy husband, and become the wife of him who grasps thy hand and is willing to marry thee."[1] (Rig. Veda Bk. 10, Hymn 18, Verse 8.)

The Brahmin practice might indeed seem nearer to the original intention of the Veda, anyway, it enables them to keep up the tradition, but with humanitarian methods. When the body of their dead is lifted on to the unlighted pyre, the widow places herself by the side of the corpse in order to demonstrate her willingness to offer herself as a victim; one of the near relations then approaches, with a bow and arrow, as if to shoot her, but another interposes, saying: " Rise up, woman, thou art lying by one whose life is gone, come down to the world of the living, you who have shared his couch and have borne him children."

The widow then descends from the pyre, to which a torch is afterwards applied. If any further assurance is required that the widow has given satisfaction and done honour to her husband, the funeral oration should bring her comfort, for herein she is reminded that " she is not in reality a widow, who has gone unweeping to the pyre and who has been the wife of so virtuous a man." By this simple expedient everyone is satisfied.

In the year 1822 an English officer in India was present at the funeral of a person of rank whose wife was to be sacrificed in accordance with the custom of suttee. Seeing the preparations being

---
[1] Swami Abhedanana, " India and Her People."

made, he was much disturbed by the thought of the tragedy that he was about to witness. Approaching the widow, he asked her if she wished to be burnt to death, and she assured him that she did. Having partly disrobed and taken off her jewellery, at a signal given by the priest, she took an affectionate farewell of her relatives, and was led to where her husband's body was already being consumed. Scorched by the fierce heat of the flames, her courage forsook her, and the poor creature ran back and threw herself into a pool of water, from which she was dragged again to meet her fate. Three times she tore herself away and fled; on the third occasion the Englishman could stand it no longer, and with great difficulty he stopped the proceedings. Needless to say, the natives were much incensed by his interference, more especially as they believed that a scourge of plague would certainly follow so impious an action. Perhaps it was well that the poor woman died next day from the effects of her burns.

Where the actual practice of the sacrifice at the funeral has ceased to exist, we shall find it carried out in symbol. The Egyptians contented themselves by making clay images as a substitute for human lives, whilst the Chinese burn figures of paper.

Before we congratulate ourselves that such outrageous superstitions as these can find no echo in our customs—absurd as they may be—we might look with some suspicion at one or two of our observances. Such, for instance, as the fact that the widow follows immediately behind the coffin in the funeral procession, and is led to take a "last look" after the body has been lowered into the grave. It may be said that it is natural enough that the widow, as chief mourner, shall have a certain

PREPARATION FOR BURIAL

prominence on this occasion. That there is more in this than a mere matter of etiquette is demonstrated by the fact that a particular meaning has always been connected with her first place in the procession. An old Jewish tradition tells us that the widow followed next to the body of her husband "because woman brought death into the world."[1]

It is, however, unnecessary to labour the point in order to connect our modern funeral practices with the idea of sacrifice at the grave, for there is no doubt whatever as to the origin of a popular military custom—still observed—of leading the charger of a dead soldier to the grave.

Soldiers, leader, chief or king, the titles are inseparable, and from the earliest times such have been buried with special marks of honour, amongst which we find the sacrifice of the war horse at the graveside, and the interment of its body with its master, in order that it might carry him to victory in the spirit world.

Sometimes a sportsman is followed by his favourite hunter, which is in some instances buried with him.

Herodotus mentions the slaughter of slaves and horses, even the cruel practice of maiming or breaking the foreleg has been resorted to—in order that the painful limp thus produced might give to the unfortunate animal an appropriate appearance of grief. The Turks put mustard seed in the nostrils of the poor beast, in order that its tears may be taken by the stupid sight-seers as a token of grief at the separation.

Egotistical and selfish people are to be met with who leave special instructions that at their death their favourite animals are to be shot or poisoned;

[1] "Jewish Encyclopædia."

"as soon as possible after my death, my dogs shall be painlessly destroyed," is a recent example. It will be said in favour of the owner that the decree may arise from a natural and affectionate desire that the animal in question should be saved by this means from possible ill-treatment or neglect, but it will be found that such wills are nearly always made by those who have ample means with which to make a provision for the short lives of their pets.

Even if it be taken for granted that friends and relations are not to be trusted with the task, are there not institutions enough which cater for the wellbeing of animals left in their charge?

For such illogical reasons poor distraught mothers frequently murder their children. Is it not rather that consciously or unconsciously the old tradition creeps in that the spirit of the favourite must follow its master to the shades?

CHAPTER IV

WAKES, MUTES, WAILERS, SIN-EATING, TOTEMISM, DEATH-TAXES

DURING the period between death and burial (which varies according to custom and climatic conditions) it seems natural enough that the body of a deceased person should be kept under close observation, for one reason or another, not the least of which is a scarcely abandoned hope of a return to consciousness. The separation and sudden change of conditions which death has brought with it, will be but gradually realized. The friends and relations who have so recently been accustomed to tend the sick person, now that their ministrations are no longer required, will hesitate to leave their charge till the moment when the body must inevitably be taken from them for the burial.

Thus, "watching" the dead became a recognized institution. It was an old Jewish custom to place the dead in the sepulchre, which would remain unsealed for the space of three days, during which period the body was frequently visited by the relations in the hope that signs of a return to life would be found.[1]

In Christian practice the offering of special prayers for the deceased at a time when the soul might be considered as in need of consolation in

[1] "Jewish Encyclopædia."

passing into another state, suggested the gathering together of friends and relations, who in the actual presence of the body, would pray for the soul of the departed and console those who were afflicted by the loss. This was the origin of the "wake" or "watching."

Now there is no human necessity which has not nurtured a profession, and we find ample evidence of professional watching, not only in the past, but even existing to-day, as a recognized means of livelihood. So completely did the paid watcher take charge of the situation that in Scotland the thrifty poor were obliged to shorten the period between the death and burial of their dead, in order to reduce his charges. The social status of the bereaved family was largely estimated by the length of time they were able to hold out against the exactions of the watcher, but it was considered a point of honour to employ the services of this functionary.

"Lykwake" or corpse watching for payment is still practised by the Jews.

A case for damages recently came before the King's Bench (1916). A Jewish watcher claiming compensation for personal injuries sustained by the breaking of a rope in a lift in which he accompanied the "client" in his charge, from the ward where he died in an infirmary. It transpired in hearing the evidence, that two pounds or more could easily be earned per week in the profession, without taking into account gratuities contributed by grateful relatives.

Many extraordinary customs have resulted from the vigil in the chamber of death. Jusserand tells us that in the fourteenth century the watchers sought to enliven the tedious hours of duty by what was known as "rousing the ghost." This performance

WAKES, MUTES, ETC.

seems to have consisted of playing practical jokes to frighten the superstitious relatives, and in taking various liberties with the corpse. It may have originated in attempts to "raise" the dead, as it is suggestively called; in other words to call back the spirit of the departed by certain forms of witchcraft or "black magic," such as were frequently attempted in the Middle Ages. This abuse must have been very common, and the occasion of great scandal, for at the Council of York (held in the year 1367), "Those guilty games and follies, and all those perverse customs which transformed a house of tears and prayers into a house of laughing and excess," were expressly forbidden.

The Guild of Palmers of Ludlow permitted its members to perform the duties of the night-watching of the dead *only* on the understanding that they should "abstain from raising apparitions, and from indecent games."[1]

In the South of Ireland this folly, in course of time, developed into a recognized form of play or pantomime, acted at night by the watchers in the chamber of death. Here a sham battle took place between two of the younger men, one of whom was supposed to be eventually killed by the other, and then restored to life by a person taking the character of a "Sorcerer."[2]

In addition to the play, the more nervous of the relatives were scared by the actor, who would mimic the voice and gestures of the dead.

Much the same sort of thing was at one time common in Scotland, where the duel was no small matter of pretence, for the fighting frequently became very violent, and blood flowed copiously.[3]

---

[1] J. Jusserand, "English Wayfaring Life."
[2] Lady Wilde, "Ancient Legends of Ireland."
[3] J. G. Fraser, "The Belief in Immortality and Worship of the Dead."

64 FUNERAL CUSTOMS

It need hardly be said that such boisterous horseplay was sustained, if not instigated, by the liberal libations of various intoxicants and good cheer, which the house of mourning was expected to provide. Pancakes were considered as especially suitable to the occasion, and when, as was often the case in village communities, fifty or more persons undertook the vigil, it must have been no light matter to provide each with his accustomed share. The wake began to be looked upon rather in the light of an entertainment, and often one member from every house in the village would take his turn as a matter of right.

In Ireland bread, cheese and whisky were distributed at midnight, after which the fun began. At no time are the laws of hospitality more rigorously maintained than at the funeral, as we shall presently find, when we consider the funeral feast. It was quite as unpardonable a breach of etiquette to refuse any of the good things provided as it was to limit the supply to less than was dictated by custom. In Ireland even non-smokers were expected to take at least a ceremonial puff or two from the pipe of tobacco offered by the host.

Amongst other interesting observances, it may be noted that the watchers were expected to carry salt in their pockets, from which they ate from time to time. What they were *forbidden* to do was to "light one candle from another," or to "remove any of the ashes from the fire."[1] The use of salt may be thought in the circumstances to have been merely an encouragement to drink the liquors generously provided, but we find it constantly used for strictly ceremonial purposes in funeral rites.

In Brittany, where honey formed an important part of the midnight repast in the death chamber,

[1] Deeney, "Peasant Lore from Gaelic Ireland."

WAKES, MUTES, ETC.

a curious superstition existed. A little fly (quite distinct in appearance from an ordinary insect) was thought to appear on the lips of the corpse, from whence it would presently go to the jar of honey, from which it would take its fill. The fly was none other than the soul of the departed, fortifying itself before taking its long journey into the distant spirit-world.[1]

From the moment that the undertaker "undertakes" the funeral arrangements, he assumes an implied professional responsibility for the safe keeping of the body. This is the origin of the now obsolete practice of posting one or more of his miserable minions on the front doorstep of the house of mourning. Assuming that expression of deep melancholy which, together with a seedy frock-coat and a time-worn "topper," formed a part of his stock-in-trade, he mounted guard; supporting a dignified attitude by means of a crape-covered wand, which he held in his hand. Such a ludicrous sight was within living memory quite common in this country.

As we pass the dreary rows of suburban villas, now let out in unsavoury tenements—once the pride of an earlier generation—we may imagine the forlorn entrances, their knockers swathed in crape, and the now neglected doorsteps supporting the lugubrious mute. He was in fact the man in charge, representing his master. His presence produced a thrill of awesome excitement in the neighbourhood that gradually gave place to a wholesome ridicule, which finally chased the old carrion crow from the house of mourning.

Laugh as we will at the mute, he had a history and a pedigree which for longevity would put to shame the pretensions of many a noble "house."

[1] De Braz, "La Légende de la Mort chez les Bretons."

FUNERAL CUSTOMS

He was a direct descendant of the Roman mime, who likewise dressed in black, but wearing a portrait mask of wax—aped the mannerisms, not only of the deceased, in whose funeral procession he walked, but of the defunct members of the family. He was selected for the particular occasion in as far as he resembled in general appearance the person he was called upon to represent. When portraying the ancestors, it was intended to convey the idea that they had materialized in order to escort their newly deceased relative to the underworld.[1] The masks used for the purpose were carefully preserved as family heirlooms, and only publicly exhibited at funerals.

Professor Ridgeway traces the origin of the tragedy actor to such religious ceremonial rites. He was originally a medium of the spirit of the dead, and, as such, associated with the practice of the worship of the dead.[2]

To-day this historical figure has merged into the more useful, if less picturesque, bearer. Kattafin or " Shoulderer " as the Jews call him.

An amusing dispute arose in Paris (1913), where the *coque-morts* is still of some importance in municipal service. As an insight into the manners and customs of his kind, it may be worth quoting. It appeared that the City Fathers had received many complaints as to the unshaven and unkempt appearance of these officials supplied by the Department; the matter was solemnly debated, when it was realized that on their slender stipend such relatively expensive matters as hair-cutting and shaving could hardly be insisted on with any show of justice. On the other hand, it was decided that there was

---

[1] T. G. Tucker, " Life in the Roman World of Nēro and St. Paul."

[2] Professor Ridgeway, British Association, Newcastle.

WAKES, MUTES, ETC.

reason for the complaints of the citizens, whose petition was suitably acknowledged; forthwith it was decreed that these functionaries should be trimmed into respectability at the City's expense. That their dishevelled locks, a recognized sign of grief, should be thus trimmed off them, showed a want of knowledge of the history of funeral practices, for the Romans much prized such tokens of the abandonment of despair,[1] and even Biblical injunctions are not wanting.

Certain barber establishments in the city were commissioned to tend the *coque-morts* free of charge—then the storm broke! That one citizen should be thus favoured with municipal patronage whilst others were neglected cut at the most cherished traditions on which the Republic is based. The neglected barbers rose to a man and demanded a fair share of the trade. "Give *tickets* to the *coque-morts*," they demanded, "that they may extend their patronage to whom they will, rather than encourage a pampered minority." And so the matter was settled.

Even this equitable arrangement was found to have its drawbacks in practice, owing to a regrettable tendency on the part of the *coque-morts* to sell their tickets and go unshaven as before.

Women are more given to the display of emotional grief than is common amongst men, and they have for this reason been much in demand as "wailers"; in this capacity their professional shrieks have echoed down the ages. A generation ago they were frequently to be heard on the Continent, in Wales and Ireland. They too had followed the Greek and Roman to his tomb, crying and beating their breasts (for suitable remuneration), lest the attitude of studied self-repression, con-

[1] T. G. Tucker, "Rome the Imperial City."

sidered a correct deportment for mourners of rank, might be misinterpreted by the dead, who were believed to be ever ready to avenge the slightest sign of indifference on the part of those they left behind them. No doubt the harsh and discordant lamentations of these wailing women were much appreciated, their wild gestures seen by the flickering torchlight giving a certain dramatic atmosphere to the occasion, which would be dear to the Roman heart.

Not less effective the thrice repeated ceremonial farewell with which the wailers signalled the close of the ceremony. Even now, in Corsica, where emotions are quickly stirred, the wailing woman carries on her traditional duties with a fierceness which is only equalled by the efforts of her sisters amongst primitive people. Tearing their hair, rending their garments, and beating their breasts till the blood flows in their frenzy, they exhort the mourners to avenge such smouldering feuds and insults as death may have been the occasion of reviving. Like the Romans of old, three times they call the dead by name; their hair dishevelled and uttering unearthly shrieks, they circle round the body of the dead in measured caracole.[1] In the East the custom is still in evidence, where at Jewish funerals the frantic remorse which is assumed, is heightened, should it show any signs of flagging, by the banging of drums. This further custom is perhaps added as the fruit of a commendable desire to give full value for their fee, and in lieu of the common practice of self-inflicted physical violence —for this is forbidden in the forty-fifth " prohibitive commandment " which restricts the Jews from " lacerating themselves for the dead."

A less known but even more remarkable

[1] J. E Rossi, " Les Corses."

WAKES, MUTES, ETC.

functionary, whose professional services were once considered necessary to the dead, is the sin-eater. Savage tribes have been known to slaughter an animal on the grave, in the belief that it would take upon itself the sins of the dead. In the same manner, it was the province of the human scapegoat to take upon himself the moral trespasses of his client—and whatever the consequences might be in the after life—in return for a miserable fee and a scanty meal. That such a creature should be unearthed from a remote period of pagan history would be surprising enough, but to find reliable evidence of his existence in the British Isles a hundred years ago is surely very much more remarkable.

Professor Evans of the Presbyterian College, Carmarthen, actually saw a sin-eater about the year 1825, who was then living near Llanwenog, Cardiganshire. Abhorred by the superstitious villagers as a thing unclean, the sin-eater cut himself off from all social intercourse with his fellow creatures by reason of the life he had chosen; he lived as a rule in a remote place by himself, and those who chanced to meet him avoided him as they would a leper. This unfortunate was held to be the associate of evil spirits, and given to witchcraft, incantations and unholy practices; only when a death took place did they seek him out, and when his purpose was accomplished they burned the wooden bowl and platter from which he had eaten the food handed across, or placed on the corpse for his consumption.

Howlett mentions sin-eating as an old custom in Hereford, and thus describes the practice: " The corpse being taken out of the house, and laid on a bier, a loaf of bread was given to the sin-eater over the *corpse*, also a maga-bowl of maple, full of beer. These consumed, a fee of sixpence was given him for the consideration of his taking upon himself the sins of the deceased, who, thus freed, would not walk after death." He suggests the connection between the sin-eater and the Jewish scapegoat of the old Testament.[1]

We shall consider in its proper order the relations between death and the funeral feast, but there is an aspect of the matter which is closely allied to the idea of the transfer of a personality for good or for evil, by means of the consumption of certain food, as in the case of sin-eaters, or by actually partaking of such parts of the human body as are associated with vitality. Traces of this revolting cult are still to be found, but its roots are deeply buried in antiquity. It is not exactly what we mean by cannibalism, in the sense in which we commonly use the word, to imply the eating of the human flesh as food. We shall remember having read in accounts of travel that these savage orgies were accompanied by demoniacal dances, which were supposed to be manifestations of joy or "war dances" in token of victory over a fallen enemy.

These dances are probably a survival of religious rites, performed the world over, in honour of a human sacrifice offered to the great god Bel. "Cannibalism," says Garnier, "appears to have been initiated by Cronus (i.e., Saturn or Cush), Cronus being the originator of human sacrifices"; he quotes R. G. Hislop, who states that the word cannibal—our term for the eater of human flesh—is probably derived from Cahna Bal, i.e., the Priest of Bel. The eating of human flesh is still

[1] England Howlett, F.S.A., "Burial Customs" (Curious Church Customs and Cognate Subjects). Edited by Wm. Andrews.

WAKES, MUTES, ETC. 71

part of the religious rites of many of the Hamitic races of Africa.[1]

Totemism, animism and such cults are too large a subject to be dealt with in a few words. Briefly, they were related to early mysticism, and surrounded by all sorts of magical rites, which seem to have been recognized, and their practice strictly forbidden by Biblical injunction. Anyway, underlying all these practices, was the idea that by eating—let us say, the heart of a lion—the fierce courage of that beast would be absorbed into the nature of the participant. From this resulted the many tribal signs, each as are commonly known to us, as borne by the North American Indians, " Eagle Heart," " Running Bull " and the like. Irish and Welsh legends show that men were prohibited from eating the animal from which their tribe took its name, it was " taboo " and as such, was originally partaken of only ceremoniously, even the name of the animal being uttered, if at all, with special veneration. Further, it explains the worship of the golden calf—the swarming of mice, etc., mentioned in the Scriptures.[2]

The image of the tribal beast would be the mark of the tribe, and we shall find it painted on their tents, and borne into battle as an emblem.

It found expression eventually in heraldry; it represented personal qualities or attributes, " The Lion of St. Mark," or " The Eagle of St. Luke." It was related to tattooing.

It was the " taboo " of the Israelites which accounted the flesh of certain animals as unclean. We find traces of the cult in the funeral rites

---

[1] Col. J. Garnier, " Worship of the Dead."
[2] See Stanley A. Cook, " Israel and Totemism "; Robertson Smith, " Kinship and Marriage "; Haddon, " Totemism," British Association, 1902; Elton, " Origins of English History."

of the ancients, and for that matter even in our own.

Mr. William Beaver, the resident Magistrate of the Western Division of New Guinea, recently reported a case of this form of sorcery which came within his jurisdiction. A number of sorcerers surrounded the hut of a native at night, whom they proceeded to bind by placing a spell on him. This was achieved by pointing a human bone towards him. The native by this means was rendered helpless, when he was murdered and his body buried. Later, it was removed from the grave and certain portions of the body were distributed and eaten ceremoniously.

To cast a spell on an enemy by pointing a human bone at him is a well-known form of magic; it is practised by all tribes of the Itchumundi nation. For this purpose the fibula of a dead man's leg is used. After being scraped and polished, it is painted with red ochre and attached to a cord made of human hair. A sorcerer so provided is greatly to be feared, and it is believed that anyone toward whom the bone is pointed will surely die.[1]

The following is another instance of the survival of the notion that the power of an individual may be transferred by the consumption of certain portions of his body. Sir H. Johnston thus described the death of a Subu chief: " The wailing women dance in front of the hut where the body lies, striking each other with hatchets as they dance. Meanwhile, the wives of the chief squat round the corpse, keeping up a ceaseless lamentation. After some days spent in this manner the stiffened limbs of the chief are forcibly bent, and

[1] Irne Toye-Warner, F.R.A.I., " Black Magic " (*Occult Review*, August, 1916).

the body is then placed in a wicker coffin and mounted on the higher of two steps or stages prepared for its reception. The lower stage supports an earthenware vessel in which the fluids from the body are collected. In this manner it is left for several weeks; the horrid contents of the jar are eventually used by the witch doctor for magical rites."

Eating the flesh of a corpse to become associated with its virtues was a common Australian practice; in some cases the mourners were smeared with the fluids from the body, and when the remains were cremated the ashes were used in a like manner. If a further instance of the custom is necessary to show that it is by no means extinct, we may recall an incident which happened in China in the year 1912. One of the leaders of the rebellion was executed in Nankin; after being shot, his body was opened and his heart extracted. It was cooked in accordance with the rites practised in the Ming Dynasty. This highly prized portion was afterwards cut up and distributed amongst the soldiers who had carried out the execution, in the belief that the courage and skill of the chief would be passed on to them by this means.

That we have at least known of such things in the British Isles, if only in legend, is shown by a fantastic story told in Scotland of a certain Dr. John Fian, Geillie Duncan and others meeting the Devil at North Berwick Kirk—of black candles round the pulpit, from which his Satanic Majesty called the roll and preached a sermon, and of the "rifling of three graves for the purposes of magical cookery."[1]

It will be obvious to anyone who has examined a mummy in a museum that the body has been

---

[1] Wm. Andrews, "Bygone Church Life in Scotland."

deprived by a process of embalming of those fluid elements which go so largely to make up the construction of our bodies. The fluids having been drawn off from the arteries and cavities, antiseptic liquids would be introduced to render the body immune from the ordinary courses of mortification and decay. These fluids taken from the body were used for certain ceremonial purposes. Of such unsavoury ingredients medicines were concocted in the middle ages, whose curative properties lay in their supposed magical power. To distinguish them from the more legitimate, if equally experimental nostrums which are prescribed for the cure of *our* ills, the physician placed the sign of the cross on the prescription, as an earnest that the curative elements in his medicine did not depend on any supposed powers of sorcery. This sign, which has long since lost its meaning, is used on prescriptions to-day; curative charms of one sort or another are still to be found—" charming " warts, for instance, is still held to be efficacious.

Medical science once made use of certain powers attributed to the dead body—as the quotation of Kipling reminds us:

> " If it be certain as Galen says,
>   And sage Hippocrates holds as much
>   That those afflicted by doubts and dismays
>   Are mightily healed by a dead man's touch." [1]

It was generally believed that certain forms of disease, particularly ulcers and cancerous growths, might be effectively healed by being touched by a dead man's hand, as " King's Evil " was held to be cured by the hand of the King.

[1] Rudyard Kipling, " Our Fathers of Old."

WAKES, MUTES, ETC.

This remarkable superstition is met with in many forms; in Scotland, for instance, it was thought to be necessary in order to avoid the possibility of being haunted, that those who took part in the funeral rites, must not only see the body before it was shrouded or borne to the grave, but also *touch* it. It was further held that the corpse of a murdered man would not decay till it had been ceremoniously " touched."

Looking through the records for a trace of such customs in our own country, we find a very significant old Cornish belief that children should be made to kiss the dead, in order that by so doing they might receive from them the gifts of long life and physical strength.[1] Even now amongst the lower orders of society we find that kissing the dead is looked upon as a pious necessity, an unwholesome habit which might well have a deeper meaning than the mere promptings of affection.

Whilst with all our pagan survivals, we can hardly be accused of such revolting practices as have been described, we can certainly find a trace of totemism in the hatchment. If we seldom see it in use, it is no fault of the " Dismal Trader," for whatever there may be lacking in his shop window as a sign of his calling, there you are certain to find the emblazoned hatchment, by which means he seeks to impress the public with a sense of the rank and social importance of his clientele—full well he knows the world to be a snob, and no one trades upon the fact more effectively. Even the poor seamstress disguised under a French name and claiming to be a " Court " dressmaker, is a poor second.

Properly the hatchment—of which the word

[1] M. A. Courtney, " Cornish Folklore."

achievement is but a corruption—is the arms or escutcheon of a person granted to him in recognition of some personal prowess. In Herald's College it will still be referred to as "achievement." In the form in which we find it exhibited in the undertaker's window, it is framed and ready to be hung at the death of a distinguished patron on the front of his mansion, to notify the fact of his decease; from the house it would afterwards be removed to the church where the body has been interred.

The arms are emblazoned on a diamond-shaped "field." To denote the death of the master of the house, the right half of the device would be sable or on a black ground, but in the event of the death of his lady, the left half will be "argent" or silver, the "field" being reversed. For a widow, widower or unmarried person the whole of the "field" will be sable.[1]

The custom of the use of the "achievement" is readily traceable to the totem stage of society.

Whilst looking at the hatchment displayed in the undertaker's window, we shall probably have noticed amongst the trappings of his trade, a number of tall brass candlesticks reposing prominently in a glass case, and they serve to remind us of the very important part which candles have played in all ages in the observance of funeral rites. The word funeral, properly speaking, denotes a torchlight procession, for it is derived from the Latin "funeralis" from funis, a torch. It was at one time the general practice to bury at night by torchlight, and long after this was discontinued, torches or candles were carried in the funeral procession and were placed about the body, from the moment of death till the time of burial.

The reason for this is worth some consideration.

[1] Wilfred Mark Webb, "The Heritage of Dress."

The Christian, whilst condemning the habit of burial at night as a pagan practice, and if only for that reason to be avoided, sees in the flickering flame a symbol of the " light of faith," but this hardly goes to the root of the matter. An old chronicler, in claiming the lighted candle as an " Emblem of Joy, Heaven and Life " says, " Secondly, we make use of lights to put all the powers of darkness to flight,"[1] but we shall be nearer the truth with all respect to his pious aspirations, if we reverse the order of his thoughts, for it is clear that the purpose of surrounding the body of the dead with lighted tapers was primarily to scare the evil spirits from an attack on the now helpless " sleeper."

We are told that in parts of Ireland twelve reed canes were used in olden times in place of candles to scare the devils from the departing soul, for it was supposed that a " circle of five was an effective protection from the powers of darkness."[2]

Darkness has always been held to favour the conditions in which ghosts of the departed may materialize. The subtle psycho-plastic matter of which the apparition is compounded—a dough-like substance, which the modern investigator claims not only to have handled, but to have actually weighed and examined under the microscope, will not readily withstand the action of light. J. Hewat McKenzie tells us that " the necessity for darkness during materialization is in harmony with the creation of all animal and vegetable structures, as the former are built in the darkness of the womb of the animal body and the latter within the darkness of the soil."[3]

[1] Pierre Muret, Trans. P. Lorraine, " Funeral Rites, Ancient and Modern."
[2] Lady Wilde, " Ancient Legends of Ireland."
[3] J. Hewat McKenzie, " Spirit Intercourse."

That our forefathers held the funeral light as a very important matter we shall see from many old customs.

Symbolically, the lighted torch has ever been an emblem of life—and extinguished—as of death. Poets have compared its flame, blown hither and thither by the adverse winds of fate, to the uncertainty of human life.

The American Indian, mourning for one of his tribe, will kindle a torch from "holy fire" and brandishing it three times round his head, extinguish its flame in water, in token of death, a custom which reminds us of the Roman usage of extinguishing the lighted flambeaux carried in the funeral procession of the mourners in the earth which would presently cover the remains.

One of the principal tributes which it was customary to pay to rank and position was a great burning of candles, and the more wax consumed the greater the honour it was considered had been paid to the dead.

The amount of wax required for the use of the Church was very considerable, as its consumption was not necessary for ceremonial purposes only, but also for lighting the edifice. This was met by a charge, and like many other contributions in the past, it was paid in kind. Twice a year "waxcot" was collected; the word is derived from the Saxon "sceat" which means a contribution, thus waxceat, corrupted in course of time to "waxcot," was a contribution in kind to the Church for the altar and other lights. We meet the word again in the expression "scot" (or sceat) free—signifying tax or contribution free. In addition to this imposition it was also customary for a person to leave a sum of money by will to provide candles for use at their funeral, and to be placed round

WAKES, MUTES, ETC.

the tomb on the anniversary of the death. Not infrequently a hive of bees would be offered for the same purpose, or for some other specified use. Dr. Gasquet quotes the following example: "At Bromley, Margaret White, widow, who died in 1538, by her will gave one hive of bees to support the light of All Hallows, and one hive to support the light of the sepulchre, and a third to the light of St. Anthony."[1]

The composition of the materials for church candles is stipulated and rigidly adhered to. Bees-wax is specially used in the manufacture of the dark yellow candles connected with the services of the dead, and during one of the ceremonies which the Catholic Church performs during Holy Week, a special prayer is said for the bees, whose industry provides the lights for the ensuing year.

Whilst on the subject, we may call to the mind the curious custom of "telling" the bees of a death in the family. If this precaution should be neglected it has been thought that they would at once abandon their hives—never to return. The proper method of procedure is to knock at the hive with the door key of the house, an instrument we shall find used by the "bidder" in giving invitations to a funeral. The hive is then tied round with a band of crape, whilst the little inmates are solemnly informed of the catastrophe.[2] Good tidings were also told to the bees, as Kipling reminds us:[3]

> "Marriage, birth or buryin',
> News across the seas,
> All your sad or merryin',
> You must tell the bees."

[1] Dr. Gasquet, "Parish Life in Mediæval England."
[2] Canon Atkinson, "Forty Years in a Moorland Parish."
[3] Rudyard Kipling, "The Bee-boy's Song."

FUNERAL CUSTOMS

In addition to "waxcot" various other contributions were exacted in pre-Reformation days of the nature of the tithe which is still levied. Harassed during life by taxes and assessments of various kinds, even death did not bring a relief from their responsibilities. When our forefathers stepped for a moment from the dull course of their daily routine in satisfaction of some human necessity, they called attention in so doing to their otherwise neglected existence, and at once *someone* would demand a tax. At marriage the "merchet" was paid to the lord of the manor, who would be down again on his unfortunate tenant for the collection of "heriot" at his death, when to the Church "mortuary" would also be due.

Heriot was originally a due under the feudal system, and consisted of the return to the feudal lord of the horse and military equipment with which the vassal had been provided, in order that he might serve his master in battle or private feud. It was one of the many "good old customs" sanctified by age, and retained for the sake of revenue, long after any excuse for its existence could be claimed; when war horses and armour no longer provided were obviously not there to be seized, a farm horse or a cow would be demanded from the relatives, who were reckless enough to enjoy the luxury of having the head of the house taken from them by death.

In the fourteenth century the lord of the manor claimed the best possession of a deceased tenant, whatever it might be, and so long as he left not less than three head of live stock the Church was allowed to take what was judged to be his second best possession.[1]

Capes gives an instance from Sudshot, showing

[1] G. C. Coulton, "Chaucer and His Times."

WAKES, MUTES, ETC.

that in the early fourteenth century the heriot had sunk to a hen and two pence, because the deceased had no animals at all.[1]

Mortuary was paid to the Church at death, and it was supposed amongst other things to make reparation for anything due to the Church, which had either been overlooked or wilfully neglected. The matter was, however, regulated by an Act in 1529, which forbade the toll on the goods of a deceased person when their total value did not exceed ten marks. A sliding scale of charges upon the property of the dead was fixed for goods of a value over that amount. In its last stages the mortuary became associated with a charge made for a funeral sermon, and this imposition ceased altogether at the end of the eighteenth century.

[1] Capes' "Rural Life in Hampshire."

CHAPTER V

BELLS, MOURNING

THE " passing bell " is the herald of death, but the custom of ringing it has largely been abandoned in this country. Its object was to call attention to the fact that a soul was " passing " into the next world, and asked your prayers. More than this, it was believed that the ringing of the bell frightened the ever-present evil spirits, who would be making a special effort at the moment of death to obtain possession of the soul. It was at one time a common practice to ring the church bells during a thunderstorm, for Wagner (quoting Jurandus) says, " It is said that the wicked spirits that be in the region of the air *fear much when they hear the bells*, and this is why the bells be aringing when it thundereth, to the end that the foul fiend and wicked spirits should be abashed and flee, and cease from moving of the tempest." [1]

A special bell was reserved for this purpose, known in Scotland as a " mort-bell," and another called the " soul-bell " tolled after death had taken place. It was possible to tell by the sound of the " soul-bell " if it was rung for an adult, or for a child, for in the former case the tenor was sounded and in the latter, the treble. It was, moreover, customary to distinguish the sex, by tolling three

[1] Leopold Wagner, " Manners, Customs and Observances."

BELLS, MOURNING

times for a man and twice for a woman, followed, after a pause, by a stroke for each year corresponding to the age of the deceased. Nowadays a bell is sometimes tolled twenty-four hours after a death, but is seldom heard till the procession is in sight of the church, when its solemn note at minute intervals denotes the arrival of the body for burial.

Amongst other old customs, the practice is recorded of ringing three times before the gravedigger disturbed the burial ground for a new grave,[1] whilst Howlett speaks of " ringing home the dead," for he tells us that in Shropshire the bells *chimed* till the procession reached the church, when the minute bell was tolled, and at Hatherleigh in Devonshire a lively peal was rung after the funeral, as elsewhere is usual for a wedding.[2] In this, we are reminded of the cheerful strains of the military band which plays the soldiers home from the funeral of a comrade.

The will of a lady who recently died in London contained the following provision. After stating that her body was to be buried at Burford, Salop, it read: " I direct that when my coffin enters the churchyard there, the church bells shall ring in a joyful peal, according to an old Salop custom." [3]

The earlier practice is a relic of the days of communal life in village or hamlet, where the joys and sorrows of the individual were commonly shared—where the parish church was, moreover, the common centre of all activities, a place of record, law and order, as well as of worship, to which, in time of stress or rejoicing, all thoughts were turned.

---

[1] M. A. Courtney, " Cornish Folklore."
[2] England Howlett, F.S.A., " Burial Customs " (Curious Church Customs and Cognate subjects). Edited by W. N. Andrews.
[3] *The Star Newspaper*, July 7th, 1917.

FUNERAL CUSTOMS

Modern life, tending to separateness, has done much to destroy this feeling of kinship, and many old customs have been lost in consequence. To-day, it is true that the passing bell might toll unheeded—if it could be heard at all, above the hooting of motors or the grinding of machinery—and few would stay a moment at work or pleasure to " wing " a kindly thought to a soul passing to Eternity.

Gasquet, writing of the times of the old Trade Guilds, speaks of their employing a bellman to announce not only the death and burial of a departed craftsman, but his anniversary. He quotes the following, " The Sacrist was reminded to send the bellman round about the city, to proclaim the ' obit-day ' of one Richard Chapman, and every year his will. At each street he was instructed to ring his bell and say, ' For the sowles of Richard Chapman and Alys his wyf, brother, syster of Corpus Christi Gylde to-morne (i.e., to-morrow) shall be theyre yereday " for which service he was to receive one penny. His object was to call the various members of the fraternities and societies to attend funeral and anniversary masses, and pray for the soul of the brethren. The hand-bell used was called the Rogation bell, from its use in calling people to church. It was rung in funeral processions, from the house of mourning to the church. The ancient Romans also made use of a bellman to announce death.[1]

In some country villages in England and Scotland an official known as the Bidder may still be met with, whose duty it is to " bid " to the local funerals by knocking at the house doors with a key; in the towns he would ring his bell.

Murray, quoting a statistical account of Scotland

---

[1] Dr. Gasquet, " Parish Life in Mediæval England."

BELLS, MOURNING

compiled at the end of the eighteenth century, thus gives the form of his announcement, "You are desired to come to such a one's burial to-morrow against ten hours." No person was invited by letter in those days, and although the mourners assembled "against ten of the clock" the corpse was never interred till the evening, so little did they value time. The prescribed form of announcement by the parish beadle, perambulating the streets with his bell, was as follows: "All brethren and sisters, I let ye to wit there is a brother departed at the pleasure of the Almighty—here he would lift his hat—called ——. All those that come to the burial come at —— o'clock. The corpse is at ——."

In the funeral procession the beadle walked before the corpse, ringing his bell.

Almost all the quaint customs, traces of which we shall discover in many countries, will be found in Brittany generally garnished with picturesque additions of its own.

De Braz gives the following account of the method adopted by the good people of Pol-de-Leon in "bidding" to a burial. "Should the deceased be a man, then four old men, or if a woman, four old women from an almshouse make a circuit of the town, in either case preceded by two barefooted orphans, ringing a bell. Here and there at a point of vantage—the bell having ceased—the children in doleful voices recited these words, "We recommend to your pious prayers —— who has died to-day and whom we shall bury to-morrow. Take notice therefore, such of you as are faithful, to pray for his soul." This oration was concluded by the usual ejaculation, "May he rest in peace."[1]

We can hardly imagine in these strenuous days,

[1] De Braz, "La Légende de la Mort chez les Bretons."

how it was possible, not only for relatives and personal friends, but for the neighbours generally, to leave their work, sometimes for days at a time, to take part in these funeral celebrations. At the summons of the " bidder " they flocked to the house of mourning, in many cases bearing with them certain specified contributions to the funeral feast.

To-day, when we telegraph our condolences and telephone to the florist for a " wreath," we are clinging tenaciously to the principle if not observing the actual customs of other times, but in nothing are we more conservative than in our ludicrous persistence in wearing mourning " weeds."

In the same way that we have found the word " corpse " to have originally signified the body of the living, now used to denote the dead; so the word " weeds " at one time accepted as applying to garments generally, is now used to describe the ceremonial dress of mourners, in particular that worn by the widow.

" A hapless pilgrim moaning his abide,
Poor in his view, ungentle in his *weed*,"

is an illustration of this.[1]

Mourning clothes were also known as " doole," a word equivalent to " dole " expressing a " portion " or " pittance." Derived from the Latin " doleo " to grieve, it therefore carries a double meaning which very well expresses the sense in which the word " doole " was accepted as " something given away in relation to grief," for we find that it was the custom for the relatives of the deceased to present mourning garments to their relations, to the clergyman who conducted the burial service, also to intimate friends, and, by way of charity to

[1] Thomas Chatterton, " An Excelente Balade of Charitie."

BELLS, MOURNING

certain poor retainers and others who attended the funeral. The following verse of Ben Jonson's, quoted by Ditchfield, in an admirable book which throws rather a fierce light on "The Old-time Parson,"[1] shows that "doole" was one of the many pickings which fell to the parson's lot, and gives more than a hint at some others.

> ". . . draws all the parish wills,
> Designs the legacies and strokes the gills
> Of the chief mourner; and whoever lacks
> Of all the kindred, *he has first his blacks.*"[2]

A few years ago, the writer was shown a drawerful of wide black scarves, presented to the Vicar of a Yorkshire country parish on the occasion of many funerals at which he had officiated. This is a survival of the custom of giving "doole."

The expense of providing mourning must have been very considerable, but a foolish display of wealth to uphold the family honour is a very old human failing, particularly at the time of death. What is merely a vulgarity in the rich is apt to have serious consequences when indulged in by the needy, whose natural love of ostentation and display is carefully nurtured by the "Dismal Trade."

The mourning garment was originally a sort of loose black cloak, very much the same as that worn by nuns. It was designed to entirely cover the ordinary attire, and would be made up in a few general sizes, as it would have been obviously impossible to produce garments to *fit* a variety of persons at short notice.

Evelyn wrote in 1695: "I saw the Queen

---

[1] P. H. Ditchfield, "The Old-time Parson."
[2] Ben Jonson, "The Magnetic Lady."

88 FUNERAL CUSTOMS

(Mary) lie in state," and continued, "Never was so universal a mourning. All the Parliament-men had cloaks given them, and four hundred poor women," etc.[1]

We learn that over nine hundred black gowns were distributed at the funeral of the Earl of Oxford, who had been heavily fined by Henry VII for an excessive display of power and wealth, as exhibited by the rank and number of his retainers.

Froude, writing of Edward VI's reign, gives some interesting particulars of an attempt to restrict extravagance in the matter of "doole" at the funeral of Lady Seymour. For reasons of State, a great public funeral was thought to be inadvisable. The matter being put before the Lords the following pious conclusions were arrived at. " The Lords weighed with themselves that the wearing of 'doole' and such outward demonstration of mourning not only did not profit the dead, but served to induce the living to have a diffidence of the better life to come, to the departed in God, by changing of this transitory life, yea, and divers other ways did move and cause scruple of coldness in faith unto the weak." They further reflected, " besides, that many of the wiser sort, weighing the impertinent charges bestowed upon black cloth and other instruments of those funeral pomps, might worthily find fault with the expense thereupon bestowed. Considering, therefore, how at present the observation of the time of outward mourning and wearing of the 'doole' was far shortened and omitted, even amongst mean persons, from that it was wonted to be; considering further how private men should reserve their private sorrows to their own houses, and not diminish the presence of their Prince with doleful tokens—the

[1] Evelyn's Diary

Council dispenses the Duke (of Somerset) for wearing of 'doole' either upon himself or upon any of his family, or the continuing of other personal observances, such as heretofore were had in solemn use, as serving rather to pomp than to any edifying."

Froude justly remarks, " that if these injunctions were sincere, they were hastily adopted, and as soon forgotten, for in the following March, Wentworth, the Lord Chamberlain, was interred in Westminster Abbey where there was *great 'doole'* and a *great company."* [1]

Mourning in the days of the Stuarts was a serious business and lasted for a very long time. Lady Fanshawe, in her will, requested that her son and daughter should wear it for three years after her decease, an injunction from which they could only hope to escape by marriage.

Even in this period of rigorous etiquette, there were those of better disposition, for we learn that Lady Sussex, despite the fact that she had spent four hundred pounds (worth very considerably more in those days) on her husband's funeral to express her " love and valy of him," declined to accept " doole " from her relatives at the decease of a member of the family, as she was living in retirement and saw no one.[2]

In view of the sacred association of man and wife as expressed by the bond of marriage, considered as it was as indissoluble and sacramental, we shall expect to find the mourning of a widow for her husband as bound by special conventions, and this especially so in days when the thought of a second marriage for the woman would be looked upon with great disfavour and suspicion. It was for this reason that we find it a common practice for the widow to retire to a convent or to become

[1] James Anthony Froude, " The Reign of Edward VI."
[2] Elizabeth Godfrey, " Home Life Under the Stuarts."

what was known as a "vowess" living in strict seclusion, and devoting the remainder of her days to prayer and good works, both of which in her happier state may have been neglected—and enshrining in her heart the memory of such admirable qualities as her husband may have possessed. Putting all finery aside, the widow adopted the sombre habit and veil of a nun. It was the custom for a dowager of position to retire to the dower-house. "Dower," it should be explained, is that portion of a husband's estate which falls to his widow (the dowager) at his death, passing at her death to his heirs. Hence the wealthy widow became a dowager or person so endowed, and it was a common practice for a family of position to provide a special house on the estate for her residence, leaving the ancestral home to the heir, as a cradle for the next generation. In her unquestioning acceptance of self-effacement as a natural consequence of her widowhood, we see the shadow at least of the horrible practices of earlier times, which might well have condemned her to be actually sacrificed, and her body buried with that of her lord and master, for his comfort in a future state, a sentence commuted in more enlightened times to a form of lifelong imprisonment.

To the old-time widow, except perhaps in the case of a very young woman, the thought of a second marriage would be repugnant. To-day it is not uncommon to meet with people who have "a feeling" that second marriages are in the nature of ungodliness.

In the sixteenth century, regulations were made, restricting the use of mourning as to quantity and dictating also the quality of the materials, and the exact manner in which the garments were to be fashioned.

BELLS, MOURNING

The chief point of interest in the mourning habits of woman in the Middle Ages was the wearing of the barbe, a long pleated arrangement, often represented on memorial brasses. For those above the rank of Baroness the barbe was worn above the chin, and in the lower estates it was fastened below the throat. It consisted of a piece of fine linen.[1] The term is derived from the Latin "barba" or beard. It is to the convent also that we must look for the origin of the widow's cap, and particularly for the veil or "streamers," the survival of the veil once covering the face, but now thrown back and diminished in size. The grotesque widow's bonnet is still sometimes seen with a shortened veil covering the face, the lower part of which it conceals, beneath the deep hem of double crape.

In the windows of certain small shops in the Jewish quarter of any city may be found curious brown matted wigs which are sold to the orthodox Jewish matron, who still cuts off her hair when she marries, in order to render herself no longer attractive to men in general.

In Egypt, Greece and Rome, both men and women cut off their hair as a sign of mourning, in which circumstances the men wore wigs and the women caps. So, too, in "taking the veil," the nun sacrifices her tresses—the symbol of her personal vanities—a custom followed by the widow, but at a later period she adopted the widow's cap, closely covering her head to disguise the fact that whilst she admitted the principle, she was no longer prepared to part with her hair. The wearing of white cuffs probably also came from the convent. Webb says, in referring to the matter, "The white cuffs of the widow recall those of the nurse,

[1] Ashdown, "British Costumes of the Fourteenth Century."

and similar ones are used by some members of the legal profession as part of their mourning."[1]

A black crape "weeper" was worn at one time by men, as a token of mourning, bound round their hats and hanging down their backs. At the funeral of a child or a young girl, white took the place of black as an emblem of purity. The "Trade" still carries on the tradition when "extras" are provided.

The origin of the custom has a significance of its own.

Wagner attributes it to a survival of the "Liripipe," a long-tailed tippet depending from the hood worn by men in this country during the Plantagenet period. In the reign of Henry VIII the hood was exchanged for the hat, but the tippet was retained in the form of the hat-band.[2]

Of late years the mourning "weeper" was shorn of its tails and width which a few years ago reached within an inch of the top of the silk hat, became gradually reduced, till it ceased to have any special significance.

The following custom was very general in Switzerland thirty years ago. The men mourners in the funeral procession carried their hats under the left arm. Round the hat a "weeper" was tied, two yards in length. Over the brim a deeply bordered handkerchief was spread in the centre of which reposed a lemon, which was eventually placed ceremoniously in the grave, presumably as a token of the sharpness of grief.

A curious old French custom insisted that men should wear long black coats and a special form of headgear to which a kind of coif was attached which partly hid the face; whilst their women-folk

---

[1] Wilfred Mark Webb, "The Heritage of Dress."
[2] Leopold Wagner, "Manners, Customs and Observances."

BELLS, MOURNING

used a covering for the head and neck, made in two pieces of material, the widow of the lower classes retaining it till her death unless she married again.

In common with so many of our funeral customs, the use of black for mourning garments is connected with the deep-rooted dread of the return of the dead. It was believed that when cloaked or veiled in sable hue human beings were invisible to the spirits and thus free from any possibility of molestation.

Whilst black has been generally used for the purposes of mourning, it is not universal. Symbolical of night, the absence of colour seemed best fitted to express a soul abandoned to grief, the most respectful, and therefore the safest attitude for the living to adopt towards their dead, whom they wished above all things to propitiate.

In the year 1498 Anne, Queen of Charles VIII of France, dressed herself and surrounded her coat of arms with black on the death of her husband. This was considered an innovation, as white had previously been used by the French Queens. It could hardly have shocked the rigid etiquette of the Court as much as the action of Louis XI, who, a few years previously, forsook the customary purple of mourning for a hunting suit, half red and half white for the *sake of simplicity*.

So absurd were the restrictions before the fifteenth century that a widowed queen was not allowed to leave her apartments, which were heavily draped in black, till a year or more after the death of her royal spouse.

The order of mourning was revised by Mary, Queen of Scots, who was known as the White Queen, because she mourned in white the death of her husband, Lord Darnley. White weeds were also used by the ladies of ancient Rome in China and Japan.

In the Stuart period, beds draped entirely in black, with bedclothes to match, were considered as a proper accompaniment of mourning. This gruesome paraphernalia was lent to relatives and friends when they had need of it. At the death of Lord Sussex, Sir Ralph Verney sent a black bed and hangings to the widow, but later, she announced her betrothal to her third husband, the Earl of Warwick, and in so doing, asked what she should do with the now inappropriate piece of furniture, which she seemed anxious to be rid of, in view of her altered circumstances. When Sir Ralph was left a widower the family bed was unobtainable, for he was travelling about at the time; he, therefore, had to content himself with such solace as he might obtain from a black nightcap, a black brush and comb, black velvet slippers, etc.[1]

Amongst the colours used to express grief, perhaps yellow, a symbol of decay, is the most common. It was used by the Egyptians amongst others. With it, the native of Central Africa paints his body as a sign of mourning, as the Australian paints himself white and the American Indian with black. In Brittany the widow's cap was of yellow or a light brown—the hue of withered leaves—which is also the prevailing colour in Persia.

Blue or violet is the "doole" of the Turk, the former being used in France and Belgium in connection with the death of a child, as representing not only the celestial blue of the heavens, but also the traditional colour worn by the "Mother of the Saviour" at Golgotha. Violet or purple, with which the Roman soldiers clothed the Saviour as

[1] Elizabeth Godfrey, "Home Life Under the Stuarts."

BELLS, MOURNING

"King of the Jews," is the colour adopted by the Christian Church as a sign of penance and mourning, and with which the pictures and ornaments of the Catholic Church are veiled from Passion Sunday till Easter. Black vestments are, however, used in masses for the dead, and on Good Friday.

In the more remote English country villages, we may often see special mourning and wedding garments—a weird assortment of past fashions, which are only brought to light on the occasions of family ceremony from the press where they lay embalmed for generations in camphor or lavender.

The sight is surely not relatively more ridiculous than the orthodox frock-coat or "cut-away" worn in conjunction with a pair of evening dress trousers.

Knowing the value set on ostentatious displays of grief, we are not surprised to find the black bordered handkerchief still in use, particularly during the funeral procession, and at the grave, where it is calculated to produce an effect which is an apology for the absence of the historical "wailing women."

It is in the highest, and again in the lowest grades of the social scale (always the last to be touched by the tide of progress) that mourning is insisted on with a rigour which is simply fanatical.

In the case of the poor one is left wondering where the money comes from to pay for the luxury of grief.

When the cold hand of death is laid on the small wage-earner whose family has subsisted from week to week on his slender takings, often enough the last shilling in the house has been gone to provide some urgent necessity during his illness.

Hardly is the toil-worn body cold when the whole family, as if by some miracle, appear in new black dresses, and the widow is swathed in the

FUNERAL CUSTOMS

customary crape. How is it done, we ask in astonishment, in view of the fact, that to refit any one member of the family in ordinary circumstances at a short notice would be considered as a financial problem quite outside the scope of their resources. Well, it *is* done, *somehow*. You may see the " impossible " performed a hundred times a year in any poor neighbourhood. Of course there are burial clubs (as there were in Ancient Rome), and there are pawnshops, ready-made clothes and cheap materials, but insurance is too often an impulse in times of comparative prosperity and subscriptions are allowed to lapse during the first period of adversity. The pawnshop has already absorbed anything pawnable, else how could the family have lived through the expensive days when the wage-earner was " off sick."

Knowing the proverbial generosity of the needy, it may be supposed that some kindly neighbour has come to the rescue, but this source of supply will be resorted to only as a last desperate expedient, for according to the fierce code of honour prevailing in the district, this is a time for display, not for borrowing, and who knows better than the widow that a score of coldly criticizing eyes are watching events through broken Venetian blinds and dirty Nottingham lace curtains, which screen something yet more sordid, in order to see how the Joneses or the Williamses come through the ordeal. What will the Church do for Widow Jones—the Church that married her—and has not seen her since?

If we add to such a situation real grief, real despair and much untutored sentimentality, we have a pretty problem, and one that has to be faced *quickly*, for you can't keep a corpse waiting too long. Well, it rests between the moneylenders

"HONOURING" THE DEAD.

A modern funeral *with Extras*. Note the Feather-Pages, Outriders, Mutes, Wands, Batons—*and the District*.

BELLS, MOURNING

at a penny a week interest on the shilling, and such terms as may be made with various branches of the " Dismal Trade."

Go down into the slums and see how generously this folly is catered for—a question of business, perhaps—of supply and demand.

If there be any consolation to be gained in this sorry matter, it is in the contemplation of certain promises made to those who " do business " with widows—and to those who " grind the face of the poor."

Many instances might be given to show how hard it is for an enlightened individual to stand up against the weight of conventional ignorance at a time when affliction has rendered resistance most difficult. The following are two instances from personal experience.

A superior servant, a mere girl, married a house painter. Within a year of the event, the husband fell from a ladder and was killed.

The poor little widow bought a cheap black dress and a very simple black straw hat to wear at the funeral. Her former employer, who had much commended this modest outlay, met the girl a few days later swathed in crape, her poor little face only half visible under a hideous widow's bonnet complete with streamers and a veil. Asked why she had made these purchases she explained that her neighbours and relations had made her life unbearable because she did not want to wear widow's weeds, and at last she had to give in. " They said that if I would not wear a bonnet, *it proved we were never married*," she sobbed.

In other stations of life many a brave attempt to break down these horrid conventions has been over-ridden by some ghoulish relations on a plea of want of respect to the dead.

G

FUNERAL CUSTOMS

The scene of the following incident was a house in one of the "best parts" of a well-known London suburb.

A death had taken place in the family, and it had fallen to the lot of the eldest daughter to make the arrangements for the funeral.

She asked for a plain elm coffin without any ornaments.

"Elm," said the horrified undertaker, "but you can't have anything but polished oak *in a road like this*."

CHAPTER VI

FUNERAL FEASTS AND PROCESSIONS

WE have seen that certain parts of the body have been eaten in the belief that by this means such special virtues as the dead may possess would be transferred to those who thus participated; and we must bear this ceremonious cannibalism in mind in considering the funeral feast proper, for there was originally a connection. We must also remember the important fact that food has been offered from the earliest times at the grave, for the sustenance of the dead in their spiritual state. Superficially it would strike us as incomprehensible that even the most untutored mind could have supposed that the food so thoughtfully provided was actually *consumed* by the departed shade, in view of the fact that it still remained to moulder on the grave. This is a misconception of a point of view.

Wallis Budge mentions that in many places in the Sudan to-day, meat and drink are still brought to, and laid on the graves, that the dead may partake of them at their pleasure, but he reminds us that the ceremonies performed by their priests are believed to change the material substance of the offerings into a spiritual form, and of *this* the dead partake, leaving the material elements to be consumed by the priest and the relations, by which means they are brought into communication with their dead.[1]

[1] E. A. Wallis Budge, M.A., " Liturgy of Funeral Offerings."

It is probable that the earlier funeral feasts were nothing more than a distribution of the food offered to the dead, after they had obtained—as it was supposed—supernatural nourishment from it.

Some echo of this may be traced in the Bulgarian custom of feasting in the cemeteries on Palm Sunday, when the remains of the good things provided are left on the graves for the dead.

The most ancient Egyptian ceremonies were connected with offerings to the dead; wine, sweet beer, cakes of various kinds, fruit, scented oils, the heads of bulls and a variety of ceremonial garments were used for the purpose: so too by the Romans, whilst to-day the Chinese and the older civilizations hold fast in one form or another to the belief that the spirit needs some form of nourishment.

Once again in this practice we shall find the old terror of being haunted by the ghost asserting itself. The *Bodo* of India carry the dead man's share of food and drink to the grave, saying, " Take and eat, heretofore you have eaten and drunk with us, you can do so no more; you were one of us, you can be so no longer; we come no more to you—*come you not to us*." After this recital, in order to make the changed position still more definite, each mourner throws on the grave a thread bracelet, which he breaks off his wrist, saying, " Take that, the tie between the dead and the living is snapped." A similar ceremony is performed at the funeral feast in the Solomon Islands, where a portion of food is thrown into the fire, and the dead are thus invoked, " This is for you," and even at the daily meal a certain portion is set apart for their use.[1]

Pagan usage, sanctified by Christian interpretation, has frequently been carried forward to our

[1] Edward Clodd, "The Story of Primitive Man."

FEASTS AND PROCESSIONS 101

times, and it is interesting to note that when the Trappist monk is taken by death from the Community, his meals are still served for him in the refectory for thirty days after his decease; being given afterwards to the poor.

To the superstitious mind, a food offering should properly be served at the burial-place, otherwise a danger would be incurred by inducing the soul to wander back to its former haunts—a thing above all which mankind has sought to avoid by many a childish subterfuge.

In countries where the sacrifice of animals formed part of the religious rites, it frequently took place where the dead were buried, in order that they might have their part in the consumption of the meat thus provided.

Where the belief exists, as in China, that the dead have a duality of souls, one of which remains in the grave in order to receive the offerings of the living, the importance of the food supply is seen, for it is imagined that the soul would starve if not regularly nourished, in which case, of course, it would not fail to make its appreciation of the fact unpleasantly patent to the careless relatives.

In ancient Egypt, a regular portion of each man's estate was set apart for the use of the dead.[1]

For the purpose of feeding the dead, a tube or channel was sometimes used, connected with the mouth of the corpse, through which food was passed.

Such practices throw some light on ancestor worship, and the severe test of enduring affection it imposed on those who had not only to reverence their parents during their life but also after their decease, the latter being considered as

[1] E. A. Wallis Budge, M.A., "Liturgy of Funeral Offerings."

a higher virtue, and the supreme test of filial affection, as being the more difficult of accomplishment.

In this country, at least as late as the days of the Stuarts, it was a common practice for the mourners to drink wine from a cup placed for the purpose on the coffin, and in so doing to enter into a kind of communion with the dead.

In the obsequies of all times, some form of feasting stands out prominently as an important and necessary part of the ceremonies. There are always so many excuses to be found for celebrating any special occasion by eating and drinking that we may easily overlook the fundamental idea in accepting the practice as an ordinary form of hospitality. At first sight it does not seem unreasonable to account for the provision of a repast for the mourners as being a natural courtesy shown to friends and relations gathered together in order to take a last farewell of the departed. Knowing as we do that in days gone by travelling was not only a very difficult, but often a costly and even dangerous undertaking, it would appear rational enough that a substantial meal should be provided for the necessities of the guests.

Before the introduction of such conveniences as post or telegraph, several days might well elapse before those relations living at a distance could be advised of the death, and several more days would be taken in travelling to the house of mourning, so that relations might have to be entertained for some considerable time before the family could be assembled, and the burial take place. Much as it may have been contributed to the continuation of the usage, hospitality was certainly not the origin of the funeral feast.

The special object of the gathering was largely

for the purpose of offering prayers for the soul, in the actual presence of the body, till the burial.

Even if we credit the early Christians with enlightened motives in adopting Jewish and pagan customs such as shrouding the corpse with scented oils and spices, which much annoyed the pagan mind, it is significant to note that in the fourth century the charge was levelled at them that " ye appease the dead with wine and meals," which even now hardly ceases to be true.

Whilst the wake or watching was closely associated with special prayers for the dead, it had a further significance. We know in our own time how frequently the question of the manner in which the dead may have disposed of their possessions becomes a matter of excited interest, and we know also how old feuds which have smouldered for a generation or longer, may be fanned into flame by the unexpected turn of events, and especially so when by a sudden illness, or as the result of an accident, the natural order of the older generation dying off before the younger, is rudely broken. In such cases, priority of claim or complicated legal issues suddenly appear in a new light, strengthening hopes of inheritance, which had but a few hours previously seemed but very remote, or destroying anticipations, which, humanly speaking, had been held for long years to be certainties.

If such is the case in these more or less moral and law-abiding times, when the factor of foul play is practically eliminated, we must realize that in the past, when family quarrels were considered as honourably settled by deeds of violence, when the sacredness of human life was not allowed to stand too often in the way of illegitimate desires, in such circumstances the house of mourning might well become a pretty bear-garden, and the gathering of the clans the prelude to a furious faction fight. In those rough times, we should find death (especially if it came unexpectedly) looked upon by one side of the family, with ill-disguised suspicion.

Thus the ceremonious viewing of the body by friends and relations before the burial—a custom to which we still unthinkingly subscribe—was originally an obligation, in order that those who were present at the death might clear themselves of any suspicion of complicity in foul play. Those who attended the funeral came quite as much with a view to satisfying themselves that murder had not been committed, and that the estate should be faithfully divided, as from any pious interest in the spiritual welfare of the deceased.

There is yet another purpose for the funeral gathering which must not be overlooked.

The funeral repast was at one time known as the " averil " at which a special form of crisp bread or cake and ale was provided. This was of the nature of the simnel cake, or the " soul bread," still used in Belgium at the funerals. The word averil or arvel means " heir ale " or succession ale, from which we see that the feast was once considered not so much as a commemoration of the dead but as a banquet to welcome the new heir to the title or property—" The King is dead, long live the King "—or in lesser measure, the Squire is dead, let us welcome the young master who succeeds him.

As we have seen in other instances, the Christian mind in adopting the funeral repast puts its own interpretation on the custom, and distributes food and drink freely on such occasions in the larger spirit of hospitality, giving at the same time alms as well as provender to the poor, and to those who were in need of support.

FEASTS AND PROCESSIONS 105

Considerable sums of money were often left by will to be spent in this manner at death amongst relations and dependents, on the expressed or implied condition that the pious prayers of all who participated should be offered for the repose of the departed soul.

Whilst the rich might well purchase prayers in this manner in exchange for a liberal hospitality, the poor were not behind in such measure of display as they could afford, but they might well experience difficulties in provisioning their larders to meet so large a call upon their humble resources, so we find that in many countries it has been a usage for the mourners invited to bring with them an offering of food to augment the feast.

Now this gift of the guest to the house of mourning where it still exists, is generally in some form or symbol as is also the gift of the house of mourning to those attending the burial.

The averil as a rule was (to put it plainly) an unrestricted "gorge," wherein the honour of the bereaved family was thought to depend much upon the quality and above all upon the quantity of the good things provided, both liquid and solid, which is very much the view held at the present time in the lower orders of society. It was sometimes the custom for the women to eat separately from the men, who were inclined at the promptings of the liquor to forget their grief and become amorous over their cups.

Even the beast in the stable was not forgotten, which had contributed its labour in bringing the guests many weary miles to the feast, for it was against the canon of etiquette that the guest should carry with him the necessary fodder; the provision of which entailed another considerable expense on the host. In the days when travelling by road was inevitable, the stabling capacity in such an event would be taxed to the uttermost.

Some interesting details as to the consumption of food on such an occasion is quoted by Capes from a record of 1309, when the provisions were as follows:

" One and a half butts of cider—five pigs—one hare—five sheep—thirteen hens—nineteen geese—one and a half gallons of oysters—two hogs—nine capons—one and a half carcases of beef—four 'bacons' besides wine, ale, eggs, bread given to the poor and friends, and a fee of sixty-six shillings and eightpence to the Chaplain. Fifty pounds of wax was also used—presumably for candles."[1]

At the funeral of one Oliver Heywood of Thoresby (seventeenth century), the averil consisted of cold posset, stewed prunes, cake and cheese. An averil in 1673, which was considered as " rather shabby " according to the notions of those times, provided " nothing but a bit of cheese, a draught of wine, a piece of rosemary and a pair of gloves."

Amongst the poor, the mourners only expected to be provided with a special roll of bread, baked for the occasion, whilst the cost of the liquors consumed—rum, ale, or a mixture of both, known as " dogs nose "—was defrayed by a fund collected on a plate placed for the purpose in the middle of the table, to which all present contributed.

At the averil of one Charnock, things were done fairly well; eighty people were bidden to the feast, which cost four shillings and sixpence per head. The bill, we are told, was " defrayed by a friend."

Fights were frequent in these rough days, and we read that " gourging," " pawsing " and biting were common methods of settling family disputes

[1] Capes, " Rural Life in Hampshire."

FEASTS AND PROCESSIONS 107

when the liquor had roused the mourners to a sense of injustice.

Mrs. Gaskell, in her "Life of Charlotte Brontë," in describing the Yorkshire villages at the period, tells us that "the custom of averils was as prevalent as ever, and that after the burial had taken place, the sexton standing at the foot of the open grave, announced that the averil would be held at the 'Black Bull' or some other local hostelry where the mourners and friends repaired."[1]

Andrews, writing of Scotland in the last century, tells us that "there was a lamentable amount of ale and whisky drinking before and after the funeral. The company began to assemble two hours before the time appointed for the corpse to be carried from the house. If the deceased was a farmer, each of the guests was offered a glass of whisky at the gate of the farmyard and another on crossing the threshold. On entering the guest-room, a portion of shortbread and another glass of whisky were handed to him, a reverential silence being observed for a time, after which, conversation was carried on in whispers. When all the guests were assembled, the minister came, and a religious service was held, which lasted about three-quarters of an hour. This was followed by handing round cheese, oatcake and whisky, and afterwards shortbread and more whisky. Then the coffin was carried out, followed by all those who were sufficiently sober to walk straight."[2]

Most of the accounts of state and official funerals met with in old records make much of the quality of the fare provided, in some such terms as "and this (the burial) done—to the place where there was a grete diner."

[1] Mrs. Gaskell, "Life of Charlotte Brontë."
[2] W. M. Andrews, "Bygone Church Life in Scotland."

108 FUNERAL CUSTOMS

Prunes have been mentioned as an averil dish. They are accepted for the purpose on account of their black skins, which give a note of mourning appropriate to the occasion. In Belgium, where we still find many survivals of the funeral orgie, the cakes are coated with a dark coloured chocolate icing, and are served on black paper mats with fretted " cut out " edges, whilst custom dictates that only white wine shall be served in order to avoid the introduction of colour.

It has been stated that the Jewish religion discourages any form of funeral display, and in contrast to the lavish hospitality of the averil, the guest of the orthodox Jew is only offered such cold comfort as may be obtained from hard-boiled eggs and salt. Apart from its sustaining properties, the egg, like our " Easter egg," is used as a symbol of regeneration, whilst the salt as a very ancient token of incorruptibility, has been very frequently used at Christian burials.

An interesting survival is mentioned by Howlett, who states that, " in Cumberland, the mourners are each presented with a piece of rich cake, wrapped in white paper and sealed, a ceremony which takes place before the ' lifting of the corpse,' when each visitor selects his packet and carries it home with him unopened, and in some parts of Yorkshire, a paper bag of biscuits, together with a card bearing the name of the deceased, is sent to the friends." [1] In this we clearly trace the custom alluded to, of obtaining prayers in exchange for a material consideration, whilst the more substantial gift of a flagon of ale and a cake given to the officiating minister in the

---

[1] England Howlett, F.S.A., " Burial Customs " (Curious Church Customs and Cognate Subjects). Edited by Wm Andrews.

FEASTS AND PROCESSIONS 109

church porch (the priests' lodging was frequently built over the porch in olden days) would be considered as partly in payment for services rendered and probably also for the merit of his special prayers.

In the Greek Church (Macedonia) the "Pappa" or priest, who conducts the funeral service, receives a present of a dish of corn, cooked in a particular manner with sugar. This delicacy of corn symbolizing resurrection, and sugar the symbol of heavenly bliss, is made and presented to the priest by the women of the house of mourning on the third, eighth and thirtieth days after the death, and again on the first and third anniversaries, in order that the departed soul should be remembered in his prayers.

In Norway the guests bring with them an iced cake on the sugary coating of which the initials of the deceased are inscribed. These cakes are carried in painted wooden baskets and presented to the widow or nearest relative, who sits in state at the entrance of the house to receive the offerings. In return the guests are regaled with wine and coffee in token of welcome—a huge feast follows.[1]

The Chinese offer "helps" both of food and clothing, etc., of substantial value, and the same practice is common amongst African tribes.

We need go no farther than Ireland in order to see a wake, which still retains the character of what was at one time common in this country. It is particularly reminiscent inasmuch as it has for its purpose the calling together of friends and relations to pray for the soul of the departed. The wake is as of old, the meeting-place where half-forgotten family dissensions are apt to come to light. It is an opportunity for a lavish display of hospitality, often far above available means, in

[1] Beatrice Harraden, "Katherine Frenshaw."

order that the honour of the family, however tarnished in other respects, may be publicly upheld. The wake appeals to the Irish peasant as an opportunity to indulge in a "good time," when whisky, snuff and tobacco will be pressed upon the guest, in return for a prayer for the departed; in fact, for the time being, the house of mourning has all the advantages, and none of the disadvantages, of an inn. That drunken riots may take place in such circumstances we may well believe, though as a popular gibe in fiction, perhaps something has been added to the Irish wake by way of picturesque embellishment. Excesses, it might be mentioned, are strongly discountenanced by the Church, whose priests are forbidden to attend a wake where drinking is likely to take place, and as a further measure to restrict abuses, the body is ordered to be buried much sooner than is the case in this country.

Whilst in England to-day the formal funeral feast is frequently to be met with in country districts, it has become, generally speaking, an uncertain event, but there yet exists even amongst more enlightened people, an uneasy " feeling " that something of the kind is expected of them, and that wine and some sort of light refreshment should be provided on the day of the burial. Let it be said for their assurance that beyond the reasonable necessities of some hungry relation, the funeral feast is one of a series of degraded superstitions which follow in natural sequence after death, and that where it is retained, it is in ignorant fear of committing some milder form of sacrilege.

Enough has perhaps been said for us to realize how our funeral repast, ranging from a matter of wine and biscuits to a good square meal, is only a survival of all kinds of pagan practices,

FEASTS AND PROCESSIONS 111

which have no place whatever in modern life—another bogie which we carry along with us, fearing to let it drop lest it should rise up again and mow at us, or that our revengeful dead will rise to haunt us for showing a want of respect to their memory.

There are various customs connected with food and the dead, not necessarily in the sense of the feast.

In the seventeenth century in Scotland any milk, onions or butter which happened to be in the house at the time of death were thrown away, as it was thought that in some manner the spirit would enter and corrupt them.

In Brittany, butter was purposely placed on the table when a person had died from cancer, in the belief that the disease would enter the butter which was afterwards taken outside and buried. In Brittany, milk might remain in a room with the dead, but water standing in a jug must be removed, lest the wandering spirit should be drowned in it. The opposite view was taken in other places, when water was purposely left in the death chamber, in order that the spirit might wash and purify itself and thus leave the milk alone—a very important matter at the farm. Water also played a part in the obsequies of the Greeks, who placed a supply in a jug on the grave of an unmarried man, to show that he had not had the nuptial washing—marriage ceremony—as also to indicate that he left no heir. In the funeral procession the jug was carried by a youth.[1]

On the Continent we may sometimes find a cup-like receptacle on the grave in which holy water is now placed. This is a direct survival of

---

[1] Guichard, " Funérailles."

that used on early graves for the purpose of food offerings being made.[1]

Let us conclude our consideration of the funeral feast with a story which comes to mind of a country funeral, where the undertaker's mutes were pressed into service to act as waiters during the inevitable repast. One of the guests, a local magistrate, whose sense of duty had led him to join a rather mixed company, was startled during a pause in the dull conversation—which had been carried on in hushed tones round the table—by the mournful voice of a mute, who whispered in his ear, " Excuse me, sir, *the corpse's brother* takes wine with you."

The procession conducting the body to the grave has always offered a welcomed opportunity for the display of pomp, circumstance and ostentatious grief, so prized by vulgar minds.

The average man or woman can claim public attention only at marriage and burial, and on each of these occasions a nonentity becomes the centre of attraction in a ceremonial procession to and from the church.

The Roman citizen dearly loved to garnish the funeral cortège with all kinds of theatrical embellishments, and once again we can trace in the custom the old dread of the return of the avengeful spirit, should anything be left undone which might give honour to the susceptibility of the dead.

That retribution would follow, as a natural consequence of neglect, was the one certainty recognized by a people whose gods were so numerous and religion so involved that only their priests knew anything about either.

Marshalled by the Dismal Trader of the period,

---
[1] Ed. Clodd, " The Story of Primitive Man."

ILLUSTRATIONS FROM GRECIAN POTTERY.
Fig. 1.—Note method of constructing funeral pyre.
Fig. 2.—Note wailing women, uncoffined body carried on bier.

who was appropriately dressed in black, the body was conducted from the house on the third day after death. The corpse had been washed, anointed and dressed in the ceremonial toga and placed without pall or shroud on a bier, around which incense was burning. In the case of a citizen of rank, the servants of the household acted as bearers.

Wailing women were in the procession, giving vent to professional emotion, as a foil to the studied calm of the mourners, whilst the mimes followed after, wearing the ancestral marks described elsewhere.

The relatives were placed in strict order of precedence, the heir walking immediately behind the bier, his hair dishevelled, the folds of the dark grey or black toga which he wore held before his face in the approved manner of the old tragedian (who learnt the trick from him)—for the rest, there were the musicians, torchbearers and lictors. At some public place the procession would halt for the funeral oration, which was considered as a most important part of the proceedings, and from thence it wended its way outside the city walls to the pyre.

The special prominence given to the servants of the household is a relic of the days when they were slaughtered at the graveside. In China they walk in front of the body, and are sacrificed in figure by the burning of paper effigies.

The wax masks used by the Romans remind us of the curious wax figures which are familiar to those who have visited Westminster Abbey, where the "ragged regiment"—as it is called—forms a feature of much interest to sightseers. These now dilapidated portrait models represented at their funerals—Queen Elizabeth, Charles II, William III and Mary, Queen Anne, John Sheffield, the

Duke of Buckingham, the Duchess of Richmond, William Pitt, the Earl of Chatham and Lord Nelson.

They were either placed on the coffin or carried in the procession, a custom which was introduced towards the end of the fourteenth century in the case of royal or noble persons. The figures were left after the burial to mark the place of interment, till such time as a monument could be erected over the vault.

In the Chinese funeral procession a banner is borne before the body inscribed with the name and titles of the deceased, whilst the insignia and arms of those of position are carried on a cushion, a practice common in all countries.

In England, in the Middle Ages, the horse and armour of the knight preceded the corpse, the horse afterwards being claimed as a " mortuary " due to the church where the funeral mass was celebrated. The armour was either given to the next-of-kin or placed over the tomb, as in the case of Edward, the Black Prince, whose surcoat, shield and helmet, which were carried in the funeral procession, according to the instructions in his will, repose in his tomb in Canterbury Cathedral.

The sword, helmet and baton in the case of a Field-Marshal, are to-day placed on the coffin of the warrior, whilst his orders and medals are carried, as a rule, on a cushion in the procession.

Even in modern Italy we still find traces of mediæval processions, such as Lady Dorothy Nevill describes as having seen in Verona, which recalls something of the old Roman pageantry.

Passing through the streets one day she met the coffin of a poor man's child being carried to the church; it was attended by a number of little boys bearing torches—a remnant of the days when burials took place at night, and retained, as we have seen, by reason of the flickering torch being an accepted symbol of the uncertainties of life. Following this humble procession was the funeral of a child of wealthy parents, the deep notes of the bassoon accompanying the singing of a hymn. The body was followed by a long train of white-robed priests and their assistants, and the usual complement of torchbearers and mourners; by the side of the bier " four little boys were walking, wearing helmets decked with gaudy plumes, and each had a pair of immense wings flapping at his back." [1]

In this we see the old idea expressed of the angels taking charge of the little soul to conduct it into the spirit world, as the ancestors, represented by the masked mimes, were supposed to materialize for the same purpose. " The coffin was covered by a rich pall of green and gold, and upon it were wreaths of artificial flowers."

Originally the pall was the pallium or cloak with which the corpse was covered on its way to burial. When the use of coffins became general the pall ceased to be necessary for the original purpose, and it was then used for draping the coffin. This was probably an excuse to retain the services of the pall-bearer, for pall-bearing had come to be looked upon as a duty of honour and a mark of rank and esteem.

In earlier times the pall, and sometimes the bier, was carried by those of the same rank as the deceased; as at Wellington's funeral, when the pall was borne by officers who had shared the hardships of many campaigns by his side. In the case of a man who was of no particular estate, if married the bearers would be his married friends,

[1] Lady Dorothy Nevill, " My Own Times."

or if single his bachelor friends performed the task; nor was the matter always left to any chance arrangement, for a dying person frequently decided who should officiate at his funeral—who should carry his bier, pall and torches.

In the case of Royalty the pall is generally supported by princes or the nobility.

In Scotland the pall was called a "mort-cloth," and in the year 1598 it was decreed at the Kirk Session of Glasgow, that a "black cloth was to be laid on the corpse of the poor," a custom continued for two hundred years after, the "mort-cloth" being taken to the house where the body awaited burial and laid over it. The general assembly of Scotland decreed in the year 1563 "that a bier should be made in every country parish to carry the *dead corpse* of the poor to the burial place, and that those of the villages or houses next adjacent to the house where the *dead corpse* lieth, or a certain number out of every house shall convey the *dead corpse* to the burial place and bury it six feet under the earth."[1]

In country funerals, it is customary for the tenants or servants to undertake the office of bearers, as a mark of special esteem.

The bier or "bear" was originally a very simple affair, of the nature of a stretcher, on which the uncoffined body was carried to the grave; at a later period it bore the coffin also. To-day, the bier is seldom used, something much more ornate being considered necessary to the dignity of the proceedings.

The origin of a word is often helpful in tracing the origin of a custom, so we shall find that "herse" is a French word signifying a harrow. The form of the French harrow was triangular—an iron

---

[1] Wm. Andrews, "Bygone Church Life in Scotland."

FEASTS AND PROCESSIONS

framework to which the spikes were attached. The hearse of the fifteenth century was a simple iron stand on the lines of the French harrow, with the spikes or prickets adapted as candle holders (the original candle-*stick* was a spiked stick, on which the candle was impaled). A contrivance of this sort was used, partly as a means of obtaining a considerable light, and partly for ceremonial purposes, particularly at funerals.

In course of time, the funeral hearse became a very magnificent affair, and a great deal of fine craftsmanship was expended on its construction. It was sometimes made of brass and a blaze of wax candles flickered on the prickets. From each extremity of the triangle, supports were raised, meeting at the top, thus forming a framework, over which black cloth was draped. Fringes and various ornaments were added, and often wax images and garlands served as further decoration, whilst verses and glowing epitaphs were pinned to the material by the mourners.

Starkie Gardner describes the hearse-light at Osnabrück as a structure seven feet high, its massive tripod foot and moulded stem supports two spandrel-shaped brackets, fitted with tracery. On two sides of the triangle is a step-like arrangement of scrolls and spikes for fifteen candles, and on the foot are rings by which it can be moved. The hearse-light was planned to carry very large quantities of tapers to enhance the grandeur of great religious ceremonials, when the number of lights were so vast as to be compared with the stars descended from the firmament.[1]

Eventually the funeral hearse was made in such a form as to permit of the coffin being placed on the summit.

[1] J. Starkie Gardner, F.S.A., "Ironwork from Earliest Times to the End of the Mediæval Period."

In the case of the burial of a person of quality, it also carried the arms or hatchment of the deceased; the whole structure was surrounded by a rail. After interment the hearse remained for a considerable time in the choir of the church, votive candles being burned in memory of the dead, and it became in this form a cenotaph or memorial to one buried elsewhere.

The modern catafalque on which the coffin reposes during the service in the church was originally a temporary erection over the tomb, and was not intended to take the place of the hearse proper, as it does now.

In Roman Catholic churches to-day a metal framework is commonly found, often of a triangular form, on which votive candles are lighted, and this is a remnant of the earlier structure described; it is still called a hearse.

As has been stated, the hearse was by no means a *funeral* property only. The term was originally used to describe any kind of barbed grille or protection, such, for instance, as the portcullis—a strong framing of timber, *resembling a harrow*, which was suspended above the gateway of the mediæval castle, to bar the entrance in case of a surprise attack. In this sense the word here is still used in heraldry. As a screen of highly ornamental ironwork with a formidable row of spikes or prickets, it surmounted the tombs of the great in the Middle Ages, and on the anniversary of the death would be ablaze with candles. One of the finest examples is the Eleanor grille or hearse in Westminster Abbey, which was made in the year 1294. Cases are on record of these hearses being removed from the tomb over which they were originally erected, and resold at a considerable profit to furnish later requirements.

FEASTS AND PROCESSIONS

A pall or hanging of rich tapestry was used to deck the tomb on anniversary and feast days, of which the altar frontal, commonly used at festivals in Protestant and Catholic churches, is a survival, for it should be remembered that Mass was originally said at the tomb, which thus became the altar. Dr. Gasquet quotes the following from the will of Thomas Wood of Hull, draper, sheriff and mayor, who bequeathed to Trinity Church at his death, "one of my best beds of arrys work, upon condition that after my decease I will that the said bed shall yearly cover my grave at my 'dirge' and masse." [1]

When the public health became a matter of serious inquiry and new burial grounds were laid out at some distance from the more thickly populated districts, the old method of carrying the body, "chested" or otherwise on a hand bier, became much more difficult, and some sort of horse-drawn vehicle was found to be necessary. In country places a farm wagon was used for the purpose, draped in some simple manner, in order to add dignity to the procession.

In the rural villages of Brittany, a pretty custom once prevailed. The body was carried to the grave on a wagon, used in the ordinary way to carry corn or farm produce. Tied to the uprights supporting the sides of the vehicle, branches cut from the willow tree (symbolizing resurrection) were bent into arches over the body, thus making a framework across which a white sheet was placed, forming a canopy. The wagon was drawn by a team of oxen and the priest followed the cortège on horseback.[2]

In like manner the body of the poet-craftsman,

[1] Dr. Gasquet, "Parish Life in Mediæval England."
[2] De Braz, "La Légende de la Mort."

William Morris, was carried from Kelmscott one autumn day in 1896 to burial. The farm wagon, which bore the unpolished coffin, resplendent with red wheels and yellow body, was drawn by a sleek roan mare, led by a Kelmscott carter. Wreathed by vines and strewn with the traditional willow boughs, this " hearse " must have been a shock to many narrow minds, and the despair of the local undertaker.[1]

In the " good old days " when the roads (where roads existed) were so bad as to be almost impassable for the greater part of the year, four, or more generally six horses were found necessary to draw the wagon on which the body would be placed, in conveying it to more or less remote places for interment. As, for instance, when a country gentleman called on business, or for reasons of state, to the capital, may have died there, his relatives insisting—as was customary in such circumstances—that his body should be removed for burial to the ancestral vault in his own parish.

Collier, describing travelling in England in the time of the Stuarts, says, " the roads were so bad, that travelling was very difficult. In bad weather, there was generally only a slight ridge in the centre of the road between two channels of deep mud. Instead of sloping gradually, the roads went right up and down the hills—rich men travelled in their own coaches, but they were obliged to have six horses to pull them through the mud." [2]

Conditions were so bad, that the experience described by the poet Gay was by no means uncommon.

[1] " The Life of William Morris."
[2] Collier's " British Empire."

FEASTS AND PROCESSIONS 121

" In the wide gulf the shattered coach o'erthrown,
Sinks with the snorting steeds; the reins are broke
And from the crackling axle flies the spoke."

In the seventeenth century when the King went to Parliament, faggots were thrown into the ruts in the streets, so that it was possible for the State coach to drive over the uneven surface.

Evelyn gives an account of such a journey. " I caused her corpse to be embalmed, wrapped in lead and a brass plate soldered on, with an inscription and other circumstances due to her worth." The body was thus taken to Cornwall. " She was accordingly carried to Godolphin in Cornwall in a hearse with six horses, attended by two coaches of as many, with about thirty of her relations and servants. The corpse was ordered to be taken out of the hearse every night and decently placed in the house, with tapers about it, and her servants attending to Cornwall." [1]

We are hardly surprised to learn that the funeral of this lady cost not much less than £1,000.

Evelyn also tells us that he " went to Mr. Cowley's funeral, where the corpse lay at Wallingford House, and was thence conveyed to Westminster Abbey, in a hearse with six horses, and all funeral decency, near a hundred coaches of noblemen and persons of quality following, etc." [2]

The roads of Sussex were notoriously bad, and in winter often impassable. It was no uncommon thing for provision to be made in a will, by a clause, that the body was to be buried at a certain place " if the state of the roads permitted," otherwise at a more convenient place, the selection of which would be left to the discretion of the executors.

[1] Evelyn's Diary.
[2] *Ibid*.

FUNERAL CUSTOMS

Costly as the conveyance of the dead by road must have been, in the old days the funeral procession was allowed certain privileges which the ordinary travellers could not claim. The "toll," for instance, frequently demanded on the road, was not allowed to be imposed on the mourners, and on a long journey, this was a concession of some importance. On the other hand, the clerk and sexton of a parish through which the cortège passed were wont to demand a fee, which they would otherwise have earned, had the corpse been buried there, instead of passing on to some more distant burial ground; this imposition, it may be added, was wholly illegal, though no doubt in an age when the majority of people were quite illiterate, they would easily be frightened into paying a demand, apparently backed by the authority of the Church, for the clerk was a comparatively important person. In Scotland he was even allowed to conduct the burial service. Yet another illegal practice was "arresting" the corpse of a debtor and withholding it from proper burial, till the debt was satisfied.

Some extraordinary notions exist to-day in parts of Yorkshire concerning the legal rights of mourners in carrying a body to burial, and it is still believed that no trespass is committed, in passing through a private estate, if in so doing they are taking the coffin by the most direct route to the burial place appointed. Very possibly such a practice existed long enough to constitute a "right" as a relic of the days when the roads were impassable. The practice must have presented serious difficulties to the landowner, for it was also the belief that if once a funeral procession was allowed to make use of a private road, it was for ever after open for the general use of the public.

FEASTS AND PROCESSIONS

Howlett, writing on the matter, tells us that it was customary for the undertakers to stick pins in each gate as the corpse was carried through, as payment of a toll to the landowner, thus preserving his rights.[1]

As it has already been stated, the ancient Roman law allowed no one who might purchase land to exclude from it access to such burial places as it might contain. In the Hebrides the peasants prevented by force any attempts to close the short cuts from the burial grounds to the sea, which the dead were supposed to use *when they went to bathe*. In Brittany in the old days, rough tracks were made from the outlying farms to the villages, so that the people might go on Sunday to the church or to visit their dead in the graveyard. In the course of time, proper roads were constructed, and the old tracks were only used for funeral processions. It was indeed considered sacrilege to conduct the dead by any other way than that by which their ancestors had gone before them. Unhappy the landlord who attempted to prevent a funeral passing by the sacred route.

Many other curious beliefs have existed at one time or another affecting the conveyance of the body to the grave. It was considered a very dangerous thing to take the corpse twice across a bridge from the house where the death had taken place—to the church and back again to the burial place, for instance. If this rule should be transgressed, it was thought that the bridge would break, so in order to avoid such a catastrophe, chapels were frequently built on the bridge itself. The origin of this superstition is not very clear,

---

[1] England Howlett, F.S.A., " Burial Customs " (Curious Church Customs and Cognate Subjects). Edited by Wm. Andrews.

though the crossing of water has been held as a prevention against the return of the wandering spirit.

One is also reminded of the fact that when troops are crossing a bridge the order is given to "break step" to obviate a supposed danger to the structure, caused by the rhythm of their tread; the band ceases to play to discourage a unison of movement. So also in the case of the funeral procession (often followed by a multitude of people) custom forbade singing or the playing of musical instruments whilst on the bridge.

"Bumping" the coffin is another remarkable practice, considered to be necessary at the pedestal of every wayside cross passed on the journey, and also on the walls of the church, when the corpse was removed after the funeral service. This ceremony was performed by the bearers, anticipating the desire of the departed to bid a farewell in this inarticulate manner, and also to serve as a reminder to Saint Peter to open the gates of Heaven in order to receive the soul of the deceased.

In Ireland, should the cortège pass a church on its way to the cemetery, it was thought necessary for the "socraid" to proceed three times round the building with their burden before continuing its way to the grave.

Traditional usages are worth conserving only in so far as they are beautiful from an artistic standpoint, or of value as symbols of some greater truth to which we subscribe. Consideration of these old customs will enable us to see in our modern funeral procession only a number of dilapidated survivals—and much that is reminiscent of the travelling circus.

The modern hearse retains in a meaningless and degraded form certain features of the earlier

FEASTS AND PROCESSIONS

shrine for burning "votive candles"—for it was little else in its original purpose. The roof still exhibits something of the canopy form—fringes and trimmings are much in evidence, whilst a cresting of cast iron spikes or prickets on the roof and a rail running on either side of the coffin are quite unmistakable in their origin.

The elaborate funeral car which bore the body of the Duke of Wellington to Saint Paul's is a good example of the transitional stage between the hearse erected in the church and the sort of travelling shop window to display the handiwork of the undertaker, which we meet in the streets to-day. The addition of glass sides, often embossed with crude floral patterns (the passion flower predominating) in the manner of the public house door, is a further modern vulgarity.

According to what you are prepared, or can be induced, to spend, so you will get more or less of the "Dismal Trader's" sable horrors, plumes, palls, pinkings and furnishings, with anything from two to six of his flat flanked Belgian apologies for horse flesh, whose crimpy manes and swaying tails are so dear to his ghoul-like heart. The origin of the over-horsed vehicle we have traced to a necessity when travelling was difficult, having become an excuse for mere stupid display.

With many painful memories of traffic held up for a funeral procession crawling along a crowded street at ceremonial pace, we are reminded that the traditional rate of progress is dictated by the one-time invariable practice of heading the procession by a cross-bearer; the pace was thus restricted by his stride, and that of the bearers who *carried* the bier. On the other hand, it is rather a vigorous swing of the pendulum to hear of a (motor) hearse travelling at the rate of thirty-three miles an hour

—for which offence a Glasgow undertaker was fined the sum of £3. For the defence it was urged that being delayed in Glasgow he feared that the cemetery would not be reached before the gates were closed.

Of course the motor hearse was bound to come; it is now more frequently to be seen, but is mostly used for long distance journeys.

Too deep-rooted is the love of the old " Charon-of-the-road " for his nightmare paraphernalia to readily adjust his mind to anything so obvious and decent.

The first motor hearse the writer met with, some twenty years ago, was (symbolically enough) standing outside a public-house in a northern country town. There, sure enough, as might be expected, was modern mechanism tricked up with the traditional emblems dragged forward in a debased form, into yet another century.

Let it be said here and now, that justice may be done, that conveyances, some more or less, and others *entirely* freed from the shackles of convention, are occasionally to be met with in the streets to-day.

Well designed on a consideration of first principles of fitness and utility, there is an increasing demand for the motor carriage as a conveyance for the dead—that it is profitable to the " live " undertaker goes without saying.

The stuffy funeral " coach," in whose grief-laden atmosphere we are still invited to ride, dates back with little alteration in design to the days when the family coach was requisitioned for the purpose. In the days of the Stuarts black coaches were used, not only on the occasion of the funeral but for a year or more after death. It was considered impossible to travel in any other vehicle.

FEASTS AND PROCESSIONS 127

Many of our customs of "Court mourning" dated from this period, when even riding saddles were covered with black cloth. The conservative mind still continues the practice of clothing liveried servants in mourning and placing black rosettes on the horses' bridles.

To send a coach for the funeral procession was a recognized mark of respect in the days when there was nothing between the stage coach and the private conveyance. Thus it became a test as to the number and quality of your friends if the cortège contained few or many such vehicles. The hired mourners' coach, so prominent a feature in the undertaker's outfit, is still considered in some orders of society as indicative of the social position of the bereaved family, whilst in country places the doctor's carriage (with or without the doctor) is lent by custom in order to swell the procession.

Describing the burial of his daughter, Evelyn, that sturdy old champion of the funeral "decencies," writes: "She was interred in the vault, east end of the church at Deptford." "Divers noble persons honoured her funeral in person, others sending their coaches, of which there were six or seven with six horses."[1]

The velvet trappings of the funeral horse are similar to, and doubtless derived from the equipment of the pageant horse in the days of chivalry. The saddle cloth bears the crest or monogram of a personage of importance, as that of the officer's charger is embroidered with the regimental crest. Even horse cloths and carriage rugs are decorated in this manner.

The subject of the hearse must not be left without some mention of the funeral plumes. In

[1] Evelyn's Diary.

those districts where this "luxury" can least be afforded, and where its appearance is, if only for this reason, the more incongruous, the sable plumes of death are sometimes seen.

The roof of the hearse is covered with a forest of these forbidding ornaments and a sort of sweep's brush nods from the horses' heads—white in the case of the burial of a child. Thus do the uninformed love to do honour to their dead.

As a symbol of estate the use of plumes is a very old one, whether carried in the helm of the knight, or on the dainty head of the débutante. Its use at obsequies is intended to denote the rank and social position of the deceased.

On the plea that the use of plumes on horses' heads caused "unnecessary suffering" to the animals, the British Undertakers' Association urged "the trade" to discontinue the practice as from January 1st, 1914. This decision was arrived at after "protracted inquiries," surely a hopeful sign of "salvation coming from within." We earnestly recommend that further "protracted inquiries" into other funeral customs should be made by the same august body assembled.

Yet another matter we may note before leaving the funeral procession is the ceremonial staff or "baton" used by the Roman Master of Ceremonies, and still carried by the undertaker. It is in the nature of the Field-Marshal's baton, which was originally a box, in which his authority was sealed.

Wands are sometimes carried, as borne in royal processions by the dignitary known as "White Wand" who still breaks his symbol of office over the grave of the departed sovereign, to signify that his duty of attendance on his royal master is ended by death.

CHAPTER VII

EARLY BURIAL-PLACES

THE earth is one vast burial ground. Even the chalk deposits favoured by the early cave dwellers are composed of countless millions of primitive forms of life deposited in the dark morning of creation. These caves made by the natural course of water percolating through the cracks and crannies, provided shelter for the living and a sepulture for the dead. Here flint was found in abundance, from which rude tools were shaped. A number of such caves are known to exist—some of which are even inhabited to-day.

The excellent state of preservation in which so many of the remains are found, is due not only to the fact that subterranean work generally is less liable to disturbance than surface work, but the even temperature is also a great factor in the preservation of deposits.

Baring-Gould describes a custom at once practical and ingenious, which was adopted by the ancient Gauls and Britons for the disposal of refuse of various kinds.

Bottle-shaped shafts were cut in the chalk and everything that was not required was shot down the aperture, till the receptacle was full, when a tree was planted on the top, and another hole opened up in like manner. These shafts were used as common graves for slaves, and are found in France and also in the chalk downs of England. Several such pits were discovered in Nottingham —one containing a rusty slave-chain.[1]

Little wonder that we find in the caves and catacombs an endless field for the investigation of burial customs, for not only do they contain remnants of the period at which they were first occupied, but of successive periods and peoples.

When one of these primitive homes ceased to be used by the living, it was at once appropriated for the dead. The old fear of ghosts caused the living to seek shelter elsewhere: to this day Kaffirs burn down the hut in which a death has taken place.

The alternative was to find some new abode for the corpse, and so reserve the caves for a more useful purpose.

This led to the construction of the Dolmen (Dol = a table, men = a stone, Celtic) which gives an adequate idea of the forms adopted—a rude imitation of the cave which had been deserted, built up of cairns or heaps of stones.

Later, earth burial became general, and the barrows or cumuli were commonly used. These were placed conveniently near to the villages or settlements, but sufficiently remote to avoid a dreaded proximity to the dead. Thus we trace both the origin of the tomb and the cemetery.

From the earliest times the barrow was regarded as sacred ground, and near it the pagan temple was erected. When we look at our country churches, surrounded by rows of grass-covered mounds, we see a type of the olden practice very little altered, indeed, for the Christian Church was often built on the actual foundations of the pagan

[1] S. Baring-Gould, "Cliff Castles and Cave Dwellings of Europe."

EARLY BURIAL-PLACES

temple standing guardian over the dead. The present custom of piling turf over the grave, though it may have some reason in allowing the disturbed ground to "settle," owes quite as much to the barrow formation.

The earliest burying grounds may be recognized by an irregular formation of grass-covered mounds, but must be distinguished from somewhat similar earthworks, which are of military origin.

Johnson mentions the well-known tumulus at Taplow in Buckinghamshire. The remains of a church were cleared away in 1833, when it was found in removing the masonry that its foundation passed through an ancient ditch, for it had been erected at the eastern end of an enclosed barrow. Further, it occupied high ground known as "bury fields." Fragments of pottery, British, Roman and Saxon, and well worked flints, had been collected near or from the graveyards. It was evident that the tumulus had been intentionally enclosed when the boundary of the churchyard was first fixed.

The same writer mentions the graveyard of a very early church at St. John's Point, Co. Down, Ireland, where numerous pagan graves were discovered, arranged in a semi-circle, within which was another ring of smaller graves, the common centre being marked by a stone pillar.[1] This admirable arrangement modern cemeteries might do well to copy.

By arrangement with the owner of some property at Aston Upthorpe, members of the Reading University College recently made excavations and discovered Saxon interments in close connection with signs of the Roman occupation. Here they unearthed seventy-two coins, a bronze

[1] Walter Johnson, F.G.S., "Byways in British Archæology."

signet ring, an iron dagger and some spear-heads, together with numerous fragments of bronze and iron of uncertain era. There were also found several pieces of plain and decorated Samian ware, and coarse pottery. But the most important find was an undisturbed Saxon interment. The skeleton lay on its back, with its head to the south; on the right of the remains lay fragments of a bronze bowl and a bone comb. In a leather covered wooden case an iron sword, three feet and one inch in length, lay on the breast with the point towards the feet. A little above the head was an iron ring. A tinned-bronze stud was found beneath the left knee, which had probably decorated the shaft of the sword. There were also a pair of iron shears, and the remains of an iron buckle.[1]

Very many such finds could be mentioned which are interesting as intimately connected with the study of the early practice of interments, but fascinating as they are, they lead too far from our subject, forming a separate study, on which a great deal has been written.

Much also has been written about the greatest of all earth's burial-places—the Pyramids of Egypt, in which the Pharaohs were laid. Yet no sketch, however slight, on the subject of funeral practices would be complete without a glance at these stupendous monuments of the dead. They still hold secrets which have foiled the patient and exhaustive labours of many archæologists of various nationalities who have sought to unravel their mysteries.

Three large pyramids were constructed by the Egyptian kings of the Fourth Dynasty for the preservation of their royal remains.

The great Pyramid of Cheops which took

[1] *Reading University College Review*, 1913.

EARLY BURIAL-PLACES

twenty years to complete was the work of many thousand slaves, who toiled ceaselessly on its construction. It is supposed that the stones of which it is composed were dragged from the Nile to the site on a track prepared for the purpose, and that they were placed in position by means of inclined planes of sand.

Donnelly gives the measurements of the great Pyramid as 450 ft. in height and 746 ft. square. Some idea of its magnitude can be gathered from the fact that it covers between 13 and 14 acres of ground.

Most careful measurements have been taken of the passages and chambers in the interior, the proportions of which are held to have a symbolic significance.

A passage 49 ft. long and 11 ft. high leads to the sepulchre chamber. It is connected with other ways leading to various parts of the Pyramid.

It is supposed that the Pyramids in their original state were covered by slabs of a smooth shining white cement, and the apex probably gilded.

The Pyramids stand with their sides to the cardinal points, and are considered by the ancients as marking the centre of the earth.

Believing that the soul remains in the mummified body, early Egyptians took elaborate precautions to ensure the preservation of the remains of the dead, and the Pyramids were built to protect the kings from the much dreaded despoliation of the tomb. Several less important Pyramids near the ancient city of Memphis contained the bodies of other important Egyptians of rank. Here also the priests made sacrifices and held various rites in the interests of the dead.

Donnelly says, " There can be no doubt that

the Pyramid was a developed and perfected mound, and that the present form of their common structure is to be found in Silsbury Hill (Avebury), and in the mounds of earth of Central America and the Mississippi Valley." The Silsbury Hill referred to is an artificial mound 170 ft. high, connected with ramparts, avenues, circular ditches and stone circles almost identical with those found in the Mississippi.[1]

In the early days of Christianity when persecution was the lot of those who embraced the new faith, the Roman catacombs were used by the Christian community for the purposes of sanctuary and burial, for they well knew that the superstitious dread which the Romans had in common with the Jews for places of burial, rendered the labyrinths comparatively secure, where they might even meet to worship with a minimum risk of disaster.

That this was not always a safe harbour of refuge we know by the number of Christians who were actually martyred in the catacombs themselves.

Here in these underground vaults they buried their dead during the first four centuries of the Christian era.

It must not be supposed that this form of sepulture was used by the Christians only. The Jews who shared the Oriental custom of interment in subterranean chambers instead of earth burial, also used the catacombs.

The Jewish tombs are easily discovered by the symbols of the old dispensation, the Ark and the branched candlestick with which they are marked.

The tombs of the Martyrs were the first altars upon which the Christians solemnized the rites of

[1] Ignatius Donnelly, " The Antediluvian World."

EARLY BURIAL-PLACES

their faith. So it was that when the bodies of those who had been put to death were removed from the impending plundering of the Saracens and Lombards in the eighth and ninth centuries, their relics were placed *within* the walls of the city (a privilege previously forbidden by Roman law), and churches were built over them. In this manner the tomb became the temple.

The practice of placing several altars in a Christian church, which some have supposed a pagan survival of the "Many altars to many Deities," is in reality a continuance of the primitive custom of celebrating Mass on the actual tombs of the Apostles and Martyrs.

When with the growth of the Faith, churches became scattered all over the world, the "sepulchrum" was adopted—a receptacle cut into the altar stone in which relics of the martyrs were deposited—a practice still continued in Roman Catholic churches throughout the world.

The more wealthy Christians held title to certain plots of land for burial purposes, which later they shared with those of their faith. Thus, till such time as the Church could establish her claim to consideration, the common burial-places were extensions of these private properties.

These burial grounds were much like our own, they were surrounded by hedges or stone walls, cypress trees were planted and memorial chapels or sarcophagi were built on the spot. The dead were from quite early periods interred in graves dug from the surface of the ground, and as many as ten bodies laid one above the other, each separated only from the next by a slab of stone.[1] Such a method would not be tolerated by the Jews who

[1] Chas. N. Read, "Early Christian and Byzantine Antiquities."

are forbidden to place one body above another, either on shelves, in the sepulchre, or in the ground.

From this period the catacombs were guarded and preserved, and many of the mural paintings were executed, which are still in a wonderful state of preservation, and throw some valuable light upon many of the rites and ceremonies of the early Christians.

Frothingham says, "A considerable amount of the subterranean art was produced, the catacombs still being used for the burial of the dead as well as the veneration of the relics of the martyrs."

The fourth century brought forth the public use of Christian art during an age of mutual toleration under Constantine.

In order to give some idea of the length and many ramifications of the catacombs, he adds that " if they were continued in a line, it is computed that they would stretch the entire length of the Italian Peninsula, but they do not extend farther than the third milestone from the city of Rome. In these labyrinths the graves are placed one above the other like bunks in a cabin, and in each reposed one or more bodies. Here and there the sequence is broken by a cross passage that leads to a small chamber, the sides of which are perforated with graves. These were originally closed by slabs of marble or tiles." He continues:

" This is about the only distinction between the graves of the rich and those of the poor, of the slave from his master. Those who desired to distinguish it from those around, either had the name engraved upon the slab or rudely scratched with the sharp end of a trowel in the mortar by which the slab was secured, or else a bit of ornamental

EARLY BURIAL-PLACES

glass or a ring or coin was impressed in the mortar whilst it was still wet."[1]

It is not generally realized that a great number of catacombs exist other than those of Rome.

Burials in catacombs took place generally where disused quarries or excavations presented the opportunity, or where the soil was of a nature to render mining easy.

Those of Paris are of considerable interest. They were formerly quarries which largely undermined the city.

As the capital extended its boundaries many of the once outlying cemeteries were surrounded, and in such cases the bodies they contained were exhumed and reburied in the catacombs, which it is estimated contain the remains of at least three million people.

In the year 1784 the old burial-place of the "Innocents" was cleared by order of the Council of State, and the quarries which undermined the city and from which much of the early building material had been obtained, were cleared to receive the bones disturbed from the city cemeteries. A shaft was sunk in the neighbourhood of a house known as "La Tombe Issiore" from a famous robber, who with a dangerous gang once infested the district.

The cavities were propped up and enlarged and recesses provided to receive the remains of the dead. These catacombs were consecrated by the Archbishop of Paris in 1786. The work of transferring the bones was done at night. They were reverently removed in funeral cars covered with a pall, and followed by priests chanting the service of the dead.

In contrast with this respectful treatment it is

[1] A. L. Frothingham, "The Monuments of Christian Rome."

somewhat amusing to learn that at the end of their journey the bones were shot unceremoniously down the shaft into the depths below.

The old tombstones were arranged in some sort of order in an adjoining field.

During these removals, the lead coffin containing the remains of the notorious Madame Pompadour was brought to light, but it was destroyed three years later during the Revolution of 1789.

The catacombs of Paris contain the bodies of those who perished in the various revolutions and massacres, for which the "Gay City" has been notorious.

A certain Monsieur Hericast de Thury, an architect, arranged the relics in a systematic way. He also provided proper access to the catacombs by means of steps, and further helped matters by drawing off the considerable volume of water that had accumulated there.

In the spirit of the Grotto the skulls and larger bones were set out in geometrical and patterned effect.

Chapels were later arranged in memory of those who had fallen victims in the various social upheavals, which received such names as "Tombeaux des Victime," "Tombeau de la Revolution," etc.

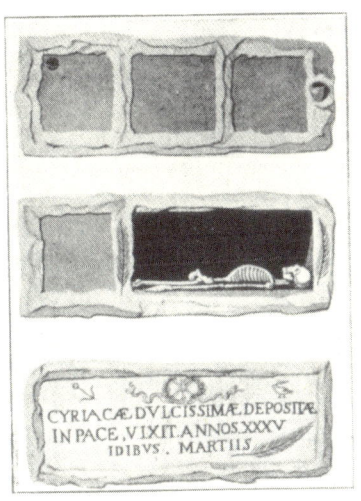

(Reproduced by kind permission of the Trustees of the British Museum).
LOCULI (HORIZONTAL RECTANGULAR NICHES) IN THE ROMAN CATACOMBS.

VAULT IN CATACOMBS OF ROME.
(decorated by a craftsman in human remains).

CHAPTER VIII

CHURCHYARDS, CEMETERIES, ORIENTATION AND OTHER BURIAL CUSTOMS

WE have already seen that the pagan burial-places were considered as something sacred and set apart, and how the early Christians inherited the guardianship of the dead, and erected their first places of worship on the actual site of the pagan temple. In course of time the substantial buildings we know as parish churches took the place of the poor edifices of wattle and mud.

Cemeteries and churchyards were under the immediate control of the Church, and the clergy were largely dependent upon the fees charged for interment, in return for which they exercised a general control, and took the responsibility of seeing that burials were conducted with reverence and decency, and that the bodies left in their charge remained inviolate. More than this, it was their duty to satisfy themselves that the body brought for burial was not the victim of foul play, no light responsibility in days when the guilt of blood was deemed of small consequence.

Even to-day, when civil law assumes all responsibilities, the Church has at least a nominal authority over our dead, for she it is who receives the body at the entrance to the burial-place, demanding an assurance that the cause of death has been investigated before conducting the remains to the grave prepared for its reception and safe-keeping till the day of Resurrection.

If we consider the vicissitudes through which the ages have passed, the fierce contentions for every yard of land, waves of unbelief, rebellion, wars and factions, we must admit that on the whole she has remained faithful to her charge.

In this she has undoubtedly been aided by the superstitious fear of disturbing the dead, which, in lawless times has made even the most callous hesitate to take liberties with the burial-places for fear of incurring the wrath of supernatural powers, not the least terrible because they were undefined.

In reopened pagan barrows the early Christians buried their dead, and we shall understand this practice better if we realize that the Christian was not necessarily an importation, but for the most part a pagan, converted to a new teaching, largely because it amplified his spiritual aspirations—such as they were—and in no instance more so than in the special reverence for the dead. It would be very natural then, that the pagan should wish to be buried with his forefathers, and especially so, since he had accepted the primary Christian doctrine of a general Resurrection. It was not till the ninth century that the consecration of cemeteries became customary.

In ancient times, burial always took place in the fields outside the walls of the cities and towns, for before the advent of Christianity, it was not lawful to bury the dead within the city. In the year 752, Saint Cuthbert obtained leave of the Pope to have churchyards added to the church, as places suitable for the burial of the dead.

Consecration necessitated a definite boundary being fixed for the enclosure of the graves, and we find many instances where it was insisted that consecrated ground should be isolated by walls or

BURIAL CUSTOMS

other means, and that special care should be taken that the ground so enclosed should not become neglected.

At the consecration of a burial ground, the bishop walks in solemn procession round its boundaries, expelling by special prayers, all evil influences which might disturb the dead. Even in times of national crisis, such as the plague, this was carried out in the case where new ground was required for the burial of the dead. It is interesting to note what the modern " psychic " has to say on this ancient practice.

" To the bishop also is restricted the power of consecrating a church or a churchyard, and the occult side of this is a really pretty sight. It is very interesting to watch the growth of the sort of fortification which the officiant builds up as he marches round, uttering the prescribed prayers and verses to note the expulsion of any ordinary thought forms which may happen to have been there, and the substitution for them, of the ordinary and devotional forms." [1]

In the year 1267, Bishop Quevil ordered that all cemeteries in his diocese should be securely enclosed, and that no animal should be allowed to graze on the grass which grew there. Even the clergy were warned of the impropriety of allowing their cattle to graze " in the holy places, which both civil and canon law ordered to be respected," for this reason the Bishop continues, " All churches and cemeteries must be guarded from all defilement, both because they are holy (in themselves), and because they are made holy by the relics of the Saints." [2]

In 1348, Bishop Edyndon wrote " that the

[1] C. W. Leadbeater, *The Theosophist*, June, 1911.
[2] Dr. Gasquet, " Parish Life in Mediæval England."

Catholic Church believes in the resurrection of the body of the dead. Sanctified by the reception of the Sacraments, it is consequently not buried in pagan places, but in specially consecrated cemeteries, or in churches, where with due reverence they are kept like the relics of the Saints, till the day of resurrection."

The custom of churchyard burial seems to have been suggested by the practice of the monastic orders, who desired to have the bodies of those of their community as near to them as possible, for they were considered in an exceptional sense, as very closely united to the living of their order. Once started, it very quickly spread. The most honoured of the flock received the special privilege of sepulture in the immediate proximity of the church, but this, like most concessions, presently became a general rule. It was a nice question as to where to draw the line between those who were worthy, and the lesser kind.

This wider tolerance had its sequel, for the saints were in course of time so elbowed by the sinners, that they sought seclusion in the sacred edifice itself. The pressure must have been great, for it was entirely against the spirit of the Early Church to enshrine a body under its roof unless that of a saint or martyr, for the corpse was considered as an unclean thing. Even as late as 1682, the practice gave offence to the orthodox mind. Evelyn writing in that year of the death of his father-in-law says, " By a special clause in his will, he ordered that his body should be buried in the churchyard under the south-east window of the chancel adjoining to the burying places of his ancestors, since they came out of Essex into Sayes Court, he being much offended by the novel custom of burying everyone within the body of the church

BURIAL CUSTOMS

and chancel, that being a favour heretofore granted to the martyrs and great persons, this excess of making churches charnel-houses being of ill and irreverent example and prejudicial to the health of the living, besides the continual disturbance of the pavement and seats, and several other indecencies. Dr. Hall, the pious Bishop of Norwich, would also be so interred, as may be read in his testament. Dr. Compton, Bishop of London, had also said, ' The churchyard for the dead—the church for the living.' " [1]

In 1566, the " Assembly of Scotland " had prohibited burials within the church, and those who contravened the ordinance, were suspended from the privileges of the church. Such burials continued, however, despite the edict, with families of rank, who demanded to be buried apart from the common herd.

Even to her own children, the Church has in special circumstances refused burial in the churchyard, not only to unbaptized children, suicides and lunatics (the latter being possibly possessed by a devil), but in particular to those, who, for one reason or another had been excommunicated; a whole parish was liable to excommunication for various periods for disregarding ecclesiastical law, during which time burials in consecrated ground were forbidden. In such circumstances it often happened that the body would be secretly buried in the night within the coveted spot, which if discovered, brought further penalties on the offender.

So great a horror have the Jews for the burial of the dead anywhere except in the earth, that the Chief Rabbi of England absented himself from the occasion of a State National Thanksgiving, at

[1] Evelyn's Diary.

which his official position entitled him to be present, not because it was held in St. Paul's Cathedral, but because the Cathedral was a place of sepulture for the dead.

At the entrance to most churchyards will be found a roofed timber erection known as a lichgate. The term is derived from the German "leiche," a corpse, for here it was that the corpse rested whilst the first part of the burial service was read in the days when it was not thought to be a fitting thing for the church to be used for the purpose. A lichgate is often added without reason to the modern burying ground, probably for its decorative qualities, and it may be met with even in domestic architecture. On an exaggerated scale this now meaningless structure often forms the entrance to the "Limited Liability Cemetery" with its mock Gothic cast-iron palisade and other atrocities.

In the days when the parish church was the centre of village life, to which all would repair as a matter of course on festivals and holidays, the churchyard was looked upon as the meeting place or playground of the village. Here, after the miracle plays were ejected from the church itself, they were performed till such time as the extra licence which their new surroundings afforded them caused them to be moved off again, this time into the market-place, where they still further degenerated, and finally ceased to be.

We can readily understand how the graveyard was liable to desecration by the boisterous churls, who played their rough games, dancing, fighting and drinking on the hallowed spot. How rough their games could be we are reminded by the frequent entries in the parish registers of deaths resulting from the participation in such rude

BURIAL CUSTOMS

pastimes. That the services in the church were often disturbed, and serious damage done to the graves by the erection of booths and the like, we can well believe, but before we condemn this coarse conduct as necessarily irreverent, we must remember that the bond between the living and the dead was in those days something quite different to what we conceive it to be in our country at the present time.

The untutored mind very often exhibits a depth of faith which is disconcerting in its simplicity and refreshingly contrasts with the pious veneer with which modern Christianity overlays its doubts. The following true story illustrates the point. An English priest travelling in Italy was invited to say Mass in a country church. Being very much disturbed by the noisy behaviour of some members of the congregation who were apparently discussing their private affairs very audibly, he spoke to the offenders, who were much astonished that he should be annoyed, " For are we not," they said simply, " in our Father's house."

We may suppose that it was in some such spirit as that the people of the Middle Ages thought of their dead as very near to them, and probably glad to hear the noise of their merry makings. Very different indeed was familiarity with the departed of these honest boors, to the disgraceful neglect of the burial grounds, which was such a scandal in the eighteenth century. Several instances could be quoted to show that the belief still exists that the corpse is interested to know what is going on in the world.

In Norway a space is sometimes enclosed over the grave, about three yards square, surrounded by a low iron railing, in the centre of which a seat is placed to hold two or three people. Here, at

Christmas and on other special occasions, the relatives meet and discuss family affairs and matters of local interest for some hours, in order that the dead may be kept posted with what is going on in the world in which they once played their part.

In other countries this principle has the widest recognition. At the time of the war between Russia and Japan, the Mikado sent a special functionary with a retinue to the tomb of his illustrious ancestors to inform them of his victories.

At the Reformation, when certain doctrines were abandoned which had served in a special way to link the living with the dead, some changes are readily marked which had far reaching effects. The Post-Reformation inscription on the headstone ceased to supplicate your prayers, and the old-time "Pray for the soul of John Bull," or the even simpler "Jesu Mercy," became a panegyric, setting forth the titles and virtues of the deceased as a trusty friend, loving husband and devoted father and the like, till it is little wonder that the infant, taken for the first time to the cemetery, wanted to know "where the bad people were buried."

In the reign of the Stuarts, the social status of the clergy in this country had sunk to a very low ebb, and both church and churchyard suffered in consequence. Collier says that "even if they got a parish, they lived and worked like peasants, their sons were ploughmen, and their daughters in service."[1] Of the churchyard, Evelyn writes, "I observed that most of the churchyards (though some were large enough) were filled up with earth, or rather the congestion of dead bodies one above the other, to the very top of the walls, and some above the walls, so that the churches seemed to be

[1] Collier, "History of the British Empire."

BURIAL CUSTOMS

built in pits.[1] The fabric of the churches was allowed to go to ruin, and they were commonly used as barns or for other irregular purposes. If this was true of the church, the state of the churchyard may be imagined. But it was in Georgian days that things ecclesiastical touched bottom—the days of the hunting parson. Epitaphs of this period are often extremely coarse and profane. Ditchfield says, in showing the general state of neglect into which things had gradually sunk, " Services in county churches were not very frequent, and in London during the early part of the eighteenth century, when people did attend, they behaved badly. The poor Vicar of Codrington, in 1862, found people playing cards on the communion table, and when they chose the churchwardens, they used to sit in the sanctuary smoking and drinking, the clerk gravely saying—with a pipe in his mouth —that such had been the custom for the last sixty years. He calls attention to the fact that the churchyard in Gray's Elegy is described as " This neglected spot," and also quotes from Webb's Collection of Epitaphs, published in 1775.

> " Here nauseous weeds each pile surround,
> And things obscene bestrew the ground;
> Sculls, bones, in moulding fragments lie,
> All dreadful emblems of mortality." [2]

This was the period when in order to protect the grave from the ravages of man and beast, those who could afford it erected heavy iron palisades round their tombs, which were sealed with huge slabs of stone often devoid of any Christian symbol. What would our forefathers—so jealous of the guardianship of the dead—think of such neglect where " bodies are buried within a few inches of the

---
[1] Evelyn's Diary.
[2] P. H. Ditchfield, " The Old-time Parson."

surface, and the dogs eat human remains, and bones are everywhere?"

Lovers of that critic of social abuses—Charles Dickens—will remember that haunting pen-picture of a neglected graveyard such as he had no doubt himself witnessed, which may serve to sum up anything further which need be said on the subject of neglected burial grounds. "By many devious ways, reeking with offence of many kinds, they came to the tunnel of a court and to the gas-lamp (now lighted) and to the iron gate. 'He was put there,' says Joe, holding to the bars and looking in. 'Where?' Oh, what a scene of horror! 'There!' says Joe, panting, 'over yinder, among them piles of bones, and close to the kitchen winder, they put them werry nigh the top. They were obliged to stamp upon it to get it in. I could unkiver it for you with my broom if the gate was open; that's why they *locks* it, I s'pose,' giving it a shake. 'It's always locked. Look at the rat,' he cries, excited. 'Hi, look! There he goes. Ho! into the ground.'"[1]

The observant will have noticed two peculiar things in connection with the dispositions of graves in the churchyards. The first of which is that they are arranged in such a manner that the bodies may lie with their heads to the West and their feet to the East, or "oriented" as we should say.

Occasionally, limitations of space may override this general principle, but only as an exception to a very old custom.

Johnson mentions a cemetery at Charvaise belonging to the earliest iron age, and containing more than seventy graves. "All but two or three were so oriented that the head lay at the west end."[2]

[1] Charles Dickens, "Bleak House."
[2] Walter Johnson, F.G.S., "Byways in British Archæology."

(Reproduced by kind permission of Messrs. Joseph Lyons and Co., Ltd.).

OLD LONDON BURIAL GROUND
(St. Olaves, Hart Street).

This graveyard is typical of many of the old London burial-places—protected by heavy iron gates and railings as a very necessary precaution against the activities of the " Body Snatchers." In most cases the earth is heaped up to the top of the surrounding walls, with the remains of the many thousand victims of the Plague. The continued use, and abuse, of these graveyards was a crying scandal during the eighteenth and early nineteenth centuries.

BURIAL CUSTOMS

It would seem that orientation is not primely of Christian origin, but a relic of the rites of the early sun-worshippers. We shall see the same practice in the orientation of Christian churches that governed the erection also of their pagan temples, the altar in each case arranged in relation to the rising sun. We may connect the matter even more closely than this, for many of our churches are built, not only in the eastward direction, but towards that point in the east from which the sun would rise on the feast day of the Saint to which the particular church is dedicated. In the sense that " Christ came not to destroy, but to fulfil the law of the Prophets " we shall find this and many other pagan beliefs carried forward as a Christian practice which probably contained the germ of some far-reaching truth. " Infinitely older than the Church everywhere," as St. Thomas à Kempis says of the Cross.

To the Christian the burial of bodies with their faces to the East is the outcome of the belief not only of the resurrection of the body, but also that from the East shall come the final summons to Judgment. Hence in Wales the east wind is known as the " wind of the dead man's feet."

We shall find other funerary customs dictated by this doctrine, such as the burial in an upright or in a kneeling position, even upside down in view of the supposed upheaval at the last day.

The second interesting point to note in the churchyard is, that whilst south, east and west of the church the gravestones are packed as closely as space will allow, on the *north* very often no headstones are to be seen. In some cases we may find that additions to the structure of the church have been made on this side only, for the simple reason that there were no graves to disturb, thus leaving the ground free for building operations. Why is this? If you look carefully on the north side, you may solve the problem, for one or two stone labels overgrown with rank grass and moss may have escaped your notice, and the village gossip will gladly tell you who lies buried there, isolated from the rest of the little community, a half-forgotten tale of blood and crime or maybe of suicide. Here, then, they bury their outcasts, the murderer on the north, his victim in a place of honour, east, west or south.

In order to understand the matter we must know that the north or left-hand side of the altar which is, of course, in the chancel at the east end of the church, is known as the Gospel side, whilst the right or south side of the altar is called the Epistle side. In the Roman Catholic church the Epistle is read on the south or Epistle side of the altar, and the Gospel at the north or Gospel side.

Before the Reformation, this country necessarily conformed to this Catholic practice. The underlying idea of this is that the Gospel was preached to "call not the righteous, but sinners to repentance." Hence the side from which the Gospel is read was delegated to those who, having committed crimes, were in greater need of salvation, and those so buried were said to be "out of sanctuary."

If it is thought that this treatment of the social outcast was too severe, what will be said of the earlier custom which denied him even so favoured a position? The body of the suicide has in all times been subject to some sort of penal measures.

The Romans, who held cremation as the honourable means of the disposal of the body, *buried* the suicide and murderer, whilst the parricide, held in especial horror by a nation of

BURIAL CUSTOMS

ancestor worshippers, had the further indignity of having a cock—the emblem of impiety—sewn up in the sack in which the body was interred.[1] Apart from the orientation of the body, there have been other superstitions in relation to the position in which the body is buried.

To place the corpse face downwards has a special significance. An old superstition has it that an infant buried in this manner—if a first-born child—will prevent any further additions to the family.

This mode of burial was also held to be a means of preventing trouble from a witch after death.

On the occasion of a serious epidemic of cholera which raged in a village in Hungary, it was supposed that the visitation was due to the maledictions of a certain witch. Her body was therefore exhumed in haste and buried again *face downwards*, in order that the plague might be stayed.

Astonished that this time-honoured remedy was of no avail, the villagers dug the body up again and after having turned the grave clothes inside-out, buried it once more. Even this did not have the desired effect, so once again the offending corpse was dragged to the surface, this time for the removal of the heart, which after being cut into four pieces, the quarters were burnt at each corner of of the village.[2]

The separate burial of the heart from the body was once a common practice, particularly in relation to the funeral of kings and warriors.

In this country it was the custom for many generations to bury the blood-guilty at the cross-roads, a practice which was not abolished till the

---

[1] Leopold Wagner, " Manners, Customs and Observances."
[2] Rev. W. Henry Jones and Lewis L. Kropf, " Folk-tales of the Magyars."

year 1823, when an act was passed insisting that such should be buried in unconsecrated ground which was provided by law in all burial-places, the hours for such burial being specified as between nine and twelve at night.

So great was the horror of the suicide that even the passing of the body on its way to burial was a matter for special legislation.

In 1582 the Kirk Sessions of Perth refused to allow the corpse of a man who had committed suicide by drowning to be " brought through the town in daylight, neither yet to be buried among the Faithful "—" but in the little inch (island) within the water." To trace the matter still further, we find it laid down by the canons under Egbert, of A.D. 740, that Christian burial was to be denied to those who laid violent hands upon themselves, and who thus *act by any fault*, so excluding those who may commit the deed in a state of frenzy. Not unfrequently the suicide was buried in the spirit of charity, without ceremony in the unconsecrated ground in the churchyard as we have seen, but the earlier practice was to take the body away from human habitation and bury it where four roads met.

Various reasons for this strange custom have been given; knowing as we do, that one of the prominent features of the treatment of the dead is the terror which all ages and all peoples have shown at the possibility of the return of a revengeful spirit, we are justified in thinking that the real object was to confuse the mind of the departed as to the direction of his former home, and the fact that it was a common practice to anchor the body down by driving a wooden stake through the heart tends to support this theory. We see the same attempt to " maze " the dead in a sense of direction

BURIAL CUSTOMS

in another custom, for it was once considered necessary for the funeral procession to return from the graveside a different way to that by which the corpse had been carried, in order to render it more difficult for the departed shade to return if it had any intention of haunting the relatives.

Some have supposed that the fact that a preaching cross was often erected at the meeting of ways, and used by itinerant clergy when the churches were few and far between, hallowed the ground to some extent, and in the shadow of the cross kindly hands might lay the poor outcast when the Church herself had refused him sanctuary.

Wagner denies this in saying that "the true reason is that Teutonic nations always set up their altars at such places, and as criminals were sacrificed to their gods, the place of execution was there also, and it was for this reason that in Christian times the felon was buried at the cross-roads *at night*,[1] a Roman custom intended to give the impression of a heathen burial.

Many of these unhallowed places once removed from populated districts, spots avoided by the traveller—especially after dark—have now been embraced by the ever-widening boundaries of the towns. Who, for instance, gives a passing thought as he rattles through prosaic St. John's Wood on a bus, by the little triangle of green opposite St. John's Chapel and Lord's Cricket Ground, where lies buried at the cross-roads, with a stake through his heart, John Mortland, who in 1823 murdered Sir Warwick Bampfylde in Montague Square, and afterwards died by his own hand.[2] This was probably the last case of cross-road burial, as the Act prohibiting the practice

---

[1] Leopold Wagner, "Manners, Customs and Observances."
[2] A. Montgomery Eyre, "St. John's Wood."

was passed the same year. Not only were murderers and suicides buried " out of sanctuary," but others, who for one reason or another were not considered fit to lie with the elect, were buried apart.

To-day if an actor achieves a place of honour in his art, he stands a reasonable chance of sepulture in Westminster Abbey, though his fame may scarce survive the generation which so honours him; yet in France it was not till the Revolution that stage players were even allowed the common right of burial in consecrated ground. The graveyards were divided into various parts; suicides, strangers, the unbaptized, and women who died in childbirth all had their separate allotments.

In Tyrone there is a male burial ground which women are not even allowed to enter, for it is supposed that the dead are very jealous about the company they keep, and would rise from their graves, if necessary, to eject a stranger.[1]

In Brittany in the Cemetery of Lanrevoare, 7,727 " Saints " are said to be buried; into this holy place you may not enter without first removing your boots, or it is feared that you may share the horrible fate of the stranger, who disregarding the injunction, " fell backwards so that his entrails came out and spread around him."

We have been inclined to suppose that whatever disadvantage death may bring, it would have certain advantages, not the least of these being a final freedom from all kinds of social obligations and class distinctions, and we may be surprised to find that this commonplace thought has by no means been generally accepted.

The following advertisement appeared in *The Times* (1914). " A family vault for sale (under

---

[1] Lady Wilde, " Ancient Legends of Ireland."

BURIAL CUSTOMS 155

cost) in the *best part* of Highgate Cemetery."[1] And we have seen with what indecent haste privileged places of burial have been sought by those who insisted even in the face of the law, to separate their dust from that of the common herd. Closed in their walled domain, subdivided into distinctions of consecrated and unconsecrated ground, these communities of the dead have to the superstitious mind been associated with the functions of the living, and all sorts of queer beliefs have at various times been accepted.

It was, for instance, a tradition in many countries that the last person buried had to act as a watchman over the graveyard till relieved of his office by a newcomer, and in certain parts of Ireland, the gravedigger would leave a pipe and tobacco for the solace of the ghost during his hours of vigil, a special box being kept on the grave for the purpose.

In Brittany also, the latest arrival is commanded by the old guard to get up and take over his duties.[2]

Naturally the post was unpopular and one to be avoided if possible, thus when two bodies arrived for interment at the same time, a rush was made by the friends of the deceased in order to avoid the corpse they carried being "last man in." This led to words, and words to blows, the corpse being left while the mourners fought the matter to a finish.

That those who are newly dead suffer from thirst has been very generally accepted, as shown by the old custom of placing a basin of water after the funeral in the room where the body had lain. The duty of quenching the thirst of the dead was added in Ireland to the functions of the watchman.

---

[1] *The Times*, November 6th, 1914.
[2] De Braz, "La Légende de la Mort chez les Bretons."

At Kilmurry the last person to be buried has to moisten the lips of the souls in purgatory, and in the cemetery at Kilranelach a well is provided to supply the water, with wooden bowls for the purpose, which for some reason not very clear, are presented to the cemetery by those who bury children under five years of age; here the soul of the last person buried must offer a bowl of water to each of his predecessors till he is relieved of his office by a newcomer.[1]

We meet with a variation of this belief in Brittany, where the last man to die in the year in each parish becomes the " Ankow " of that parish for the year that follows. The " Ankow " is Death personified, who summons in various ways the souls of those who are about to die.[2]

Various means have been adopted to dispose of the dead other than those of burial or incineration in the generally accepted form; of such, perhaps, the best known is practised by the Parsees, who place the corpse on a tower or on the tree-tops, there to be devoured by the vultures. At first sight this might seem a callous and inhuman practice, but the motive underlying it is not without beauty. It arises from the belief that the *elements* are sacred, therefore to bury the body is to defile the *earth*; to burn it would defile the *fire*, and to cast it adrift on the *river*, as some people have done in order that it might float out to sea, is held as defiling the *water*.

This, then, is the reason why the bodies are exposed on the walls of the tower, where the vultures having removed the flesh, the sun-bleached bones are swept into the depths of the structure by an attendant, in order to make room for others to be treated in a like manner.

---

[1] K. L. Pyne, " Burial Superstitions in County Cork."
[2] Arthur Ransome, *The English Review*, October, 1914.

BURIAL CUSTOMS

Holding such religious views, we may surely admit that the process—however little it may commend itself to us—is at least a reasonably sanitary manner of overcoming a difficult problem, and we may well acquit the Parsees of any wilful irreverence towards their dead. There is even a side to the matter which should appeal to a liberal Christian view, and that is in the thought that whatever the social position of the deceased, no difference is made in the final disposal of the body. Whatever barriers of wealth or birth may have separated individuals during life, naked and side by side they face the last ordeal in the spirit of common brotherhood.

The celebrated Towers of Silence on the Hill of Malabar are objects of great curiosity to visitors, as from the beautiful gardens which surround the buildings, they view with morbid interest the great birds of prey which hover over the spot.

The Parsees are not alone in leaving the dead to be devoured by birds or beasts.

Certain of the Kaffir tribes purposely abandon the body to the tender consideration of the jackals, so do the nomads of the plains of Central Asia, who first cut the body into small pieces, and leave it in the open for the wild beasts to devour. Packs of dogs were once kept for the purpose in the villages, the rich having the privilege of owning their own "undertakers." In Asiatic Siberia, the flesh was given to the dogs, the bones being preserved and religiously treasured.

The Persians have a great horror of all burial grounds, the poetical trend of their minds leading them to look upon the light of the sun and the purity of the air as a birthright from which, even in death, they refuse to be separated. The thought of walling up the body, or placing it in the dark depths of the earth, holds a special terror to their minds. They believe that the sun demands from each individual when death takes place, a return of those life-giving elements with which it has endowed the body during its physical existence. What is decomposition, the Persian argues, but the natural process by which the material elements are given back to the sun, the author of all forms of life? For this reason, the corpse with its feet to the East, is placed on a slab of jasper, which is then deposited on the top of a high column, in order that it may be secure from the attention of unclean beasts. For several days the remains are thus left undisturbed, during which time the heat of the sun, attracted by the polished surface of the marble slab, dries up the fluids. When this state has been reached, the birds of prey—which have been wheeling round the body—now settle to consume the dried flesh, a sign to the mourners who are watching, that the debt due to the sun has been satisfied, and that the birds have come to bear away the soul to the place of spiritual bliss which awaits it on the summit of the sacred mountains.

It is from the pages of the ancient Sagas that we learn how the dead Norseman was sent out to sea in his Viking ship, wrapped in a pall of flames, as befits a chief—with all his personal belongings about him. This practice of sending the body to sea (a symbol of the source of life) is to be met with in many parts of the world. The natives of Borneo have a similar custom, whilst the placing of the dead in the sacred river Ganges has been held to account in a large measure for the spread of cholera in India. Drying and preserving the corpse, and keeping it uncoffined, is another method of which we have many examples. Sometimes the remains are smoke-cured or partially burnt. In the Hayti Islands, the body so treated is dressed in its best

BURIAL CUSTOMS

apparel, when it is either suspended from or lodged against the walls of the house of its relatives.

At the Monastery of Krewzberg at Bonn, and also in that of the Capucine at Palermo, the mummified bodies of the defunct brethren, dressed in habit of their order, are arranged in rows, in various life-like attitudes in the vaults; forming a horribly fascinating exhibition which never fails to interest the privileged tourist.

Burials other than in the churchyard or cemetery have been common in all ages, when excommunication or other causes rendered it necessary.

The body of the victim of an accident is often buried by the roadside where the death took place, the spot being marked by a cross. Reference has already been made to burial at cross-roads, when for one reason or another, the Church has refused burial in consecrated ground—or in those cases where churchyard burial was not desired, bodies were frequently laid to rest in gardens or orchards. This method of disposal was at one time quite common; Wagner, it will be remembered, prepared a grave during his lifetime in his own garden, and loved to introduce the subject of death to his guests at the dinner-table, taking them into the garden to see his last resting-place, and back again to finish their meal with what appetite they might have left.

Sometimes consecrated ground is not available, as in the scattered hamlets in the mountainous regions of Norway, where the body has to be removed to the valley for burial, it is impossible, owing to the narrow and slippery mountain tracks, to carry it in a coffin. In these circumstances the corpse is strapped on a pack saddle as the body of the Corsican chief is tied to his horse, and the procession with its strange load winds its way down the zigzag paths to the plains below. It may happen that the body has the further advantage of crossing the fiords in a canoe to where the church is situated.

There are occasions, however, where burial in consecrated ground is out of the question owing to the widely scattered habitations, and in such cases the body is reverently laid to rest without any ceremony—except, maybe, the singing of a hymn—at some spot selected in the fields. A piece of wood is placed over the grave, to mark the place of interment. Sooner or later, perhaps after the lapse of several weeks, the Pastor will find this simple monument; he knows quite well what it means, and dismounting from his sturdy pony, he reads the liturgical prayers which circumstances denied to the dead when the grave was opened.[1]

Like all people who live very near to nature in its wilder moods, the Scandinavians have very little fear of death. Many centuries ago, they had a horrible custom, which was probably the outcome of their frank acceptance of death as a physical fact of no great importance. In those days, when it so happened that a serf or dependent had a greater number of children than his labours enabled him to support, his feudal lord had them all placed in an open grave, where they were heartlessly left to perish.

Naturally the stronger and more vigorous of the unhappy children would survive the ordeal longer than those who were weaker, and therefore of less value to their master. By this crude test, the strongest child was selected, being dragged from the grave in which brother and sister had succumbed from want and exposure.

Perpendicular burial, common in the East, is

[1] Paul Bureau, Norwegian Social Science (trans.).

BURIAL CUSTOMS

not unknown in this country. Ben Johnson was buried in this manner in Westminster Abbey. The reason in this instance would seem to have been an economy of space. It was at one time supposed that the small stone covering his remains had led to this tradition. In order to settle the matter, a faculty was granted for the opening of the tomb, when it was found that the body was upstanding, as it had been supposed.

An eccentric person named Richard Hull is buried beneath the curious stone tower which stands as a landmark on Leith Hill. Hull was buried on horseback upside down, in order that he might have the advantage of position on the Day of Judgment, when according to a once popular notion, the world would be reversed.

Thomas Cooke, who died in 1752, "stands" in Morden College, Blackheath, and one Clement Spelman of Nottingham is immured in a pillar of Nasburgh Church.

Burial at sea, for such reasons of sentiment as Kipling relates in "The Voyage of the Mary Gloucester,"[1] or the scattering of the ashes at sea, are methods of disposal which have always appealed to certain types of mind.

Such practices—except in the case of necessity—are strongly discouraged by law, for apart from the possibility of the body being eventually washed up on the shore it might very well aid criminal purposes.

The Jews have their own ideas on the subject of the burial-places which they call by the beautiful name of "House of Life." To them the family vault is forbidden, for it is against their doctrines to rest a body on a shelf; nor do they permit that one coffin should be placed above another in the earth.

[1] Rudyard Kipling.

FUNERAL CUSTOMS

Sanctuary was extended from the church to the churchyard, a privilege which one of the Articles of the Constitution of Claredon sought to repeal as far as goods were concerned.[1] The actual soil of the burial-place has always been held to be sacred in a special sense, as consisting of, or containing the remains of the dead. It was used for various purposes of magic and sorcery, and many curious beliefs were connected with it.

In Brittany it was believed that the dead were obliged to eat as much of it as they had wasted bread during their lifetime, whilst in Ireland a handful of earth taken from under your right foot and thrown on the funeral procession was accounted as a certain cure for warts.

An old Irish custom also directed that the priest should bless and sprinkle a handful of earth on the corpse before burial, as it was believed that should this ceremony be omitted, in the case of a suicide, trouble might be expected from the other occupants of the churchyard.[2]

The otherwise non-Catholic usage of sprinkling earth on the coffin, as observed by Protestants generally, is reminiscent of the Roman custom of thus covering a body found unburied with " at least three handfuls of earth " whilst saying the prescribed ceremonious farewell. It was instituted in this country by a rubric in the year 1542 as part of the duty of the officiating clergy, and later it was allowed to be done by " one standing by." The Jews placed a bag of earth in the coffin, each mourner present at the interment helping to fill in the grave.

---

[1] J. R. Green, " A Short History of the English People."
[2] Lady Wilde, " Customs of Ireland."

CHAPTER IX

TREES, FLOWERS, BODY-SNATCHING

INSEPARABLE from the picture which the mind presents at the thought of an old grave, is the yew tree. Often of great size and antiquity, it stands as a land-mark, overhanging with extended arms the tombstone it shelters. Here we shall probably find the weeping willow dear to the heart of the sentimental poet, perhaps also box and cypress trees.

The question arises, are they planted in these places for any particular reason? which seems to be answered by the fact that even in the newest cemeteries the custom is continued.

To seek the origin, we must go back to very early times, and consider ancient rites, which have, like so many of our modern funerary practices, long ceased to hold any special significance.

Abraham, it will be remembered, bought a field on the death of Sarah for a burial ground, but he was not satisfied till "the cave that was therein and all the *trees* that were in the fields and in all the borders round about were *made sure*."[1]

Trees, we know, were at one time objects of extreme veneration and worship.

To the primitive mind, movement was inseparable from the idea of life, thus the ripple of the stream or the whisper of the wind, or the creaking of the branches lashed by the storm, left

[1] Genesis xxiii. 17.

the impression of some subtle animation dwelling in natural objects, very powerful for good or evil: and as such necessary to be propitiated, thus, from the earliest times, we find trees worshipped in one form or another.

The early Christian missionaries had struggle enough to shake this deep-rooted notion out of the minds of our tree-worshipping forefathers, and in the end, it would seem that they were not altogether successful, and that their contentions ended up by something of a compromise, for we find holly still taking the honoured place at Christmas-tide that it held in the days when the Druids distributed it amongst the people at the great December festival, and if box and evergreen, banned by the Church, have crept into the sacred edifice, mistletoe is still out of sanctuary.

Even the Greek philosophers gave souls to the trees, and the gods of the ancients had special trees allotted to them; Phyllis weeping for Demophon, is turned by the gods into an almond tree. To the oak supreme honours were paid, and the ash was but little less esteemed.

> " Pat as a sum in division goes,
> Every planet had a star bespoke.
> Who but Venus should govern the rose,
> Who but Jupiter owned the oak? " [1]

The oak and the ash are trees particularly English, about which a number of superstitions and customs cling.

The rowan tree or mountain ash was believed to possess special powers against evil spirits, and bundles of its twigs were hung over the farmhouse and cottage doors to avert the dreaded powers of witchcraft.

Canon Mahé of Morbihan, writing of the year

[1] Rudyard Kipling, " Our Fathers of Old."

1825, mentions " Our Lady of the Oak " in Anjon and " Our Lady of the Oak " near Orthe in Maine, as the seats of famous pilgrimages.

The " clipping " festival at which the yew in the churchyard was trimmed, is still observed at Painswick, Cradly and other places.

The subject of tree worship is a large one, and we must not be tempted to consider it farther than is necessary, in order to trace its connection with the almost universal custom of planting certain trees in the churchyard and cemetery.

Various other theories have been put forward by those who do not like to admit pagan practices in Christian ages—but surely evidence is against them.

Some believe, for instance, that the presence of the yew tree on hallowed ground served the purpose of providing the wood for the bows of the archers, and that by making the churchyard an arsenal as it were, this valuable and slow growing wood might the better be preserved from destructive or indiscriminate " clipping "; that the " clipping " festival, indeed, might have been a day set apart for the public distribution of branches suitable for the purpose.

It is of course possible that the tree was so used, but it does not necessarily prove that it was planted for that purpose.

In the days when the bow was the general weapon of protection and the chase, the local yew would have been hard put to it to provide anything like enough wood of a suitable growth for the archers.

Others held that the great size of the tree protected the fabric of the church from the force of the tempest, and provided shelter for the worshippers.

Dr. Gasquet, writing on the subject, tells us that in the thirteenth century the guardianship of the churchyard was in the hands of the clergy, and that the trees growing there might be used for the repairs of the church, otherwise " as they had been planted to protect the church from gales, they were to be left for this purpose."

The duty of keeping the churchyard in order was the parishioners', but that which grew on holy ground *was* holy, and the clergy had the right to the trees, grass or anything which grew there; further, the clergy were reminded that the trees served to ornament and *protect* God's house, and must not be cut without due reason.[1]

Anyway, there were times when the matter seems to have been a fruitful source of dispute between the priest and his flock.

Sometimes an old custom when examined in the light of modern experience will be found to contain the germ of a scientific fact, and one is left wondering if the truth thus disclosed, was happened on by chance, or born of a knowledge with which we should hesitate to credit our forefathers.

The architect who plans our modern garden cities knows well enough the value of trees as purifiers of air contaminated by the decay of organic matter, for the mission of the leaves is to turn harmful gasses into pure, life-giving oxygen.

" Then from their breathing souls the sweets repair,
To scent the skies and purge the unwholesome air."

Was this common scientific fact known and made use of in the ancient days? Was this at least one of the reasons why these trees were planted in the crowded burial grounds, to cleanse the air from the poison arising from the ground?

Whatever the origin, no doubt the continuance

[1] Dr. Gasquet, " Parish Life in Mediæval England."

of the custom of planting certain kinds of trees in graveyards has been due to their appearance, suggesting by the force of associated ideas their use as symbols of grief immutable, and the like.

By some it was believed that the roots of the yew tree found their way to the mouths of the dead.

The weeping willow, by reason of its form trailing and bowed in grief, as its name suggests, caused it to be frequently planted in such a position where it might overhang a favoured tomb, like some perpetual mourner.

> " All round my hat I wear a weeping willow,
>   All round my hat for a fortnight and a day.
>   If any of you ask me the reason why I do it,
>   Tell them that my true love is far, far away." [1]

But the willow has yet another claim to a place in the burial ground, for it properly derives its source of life from the stream, and is generally to be found on the banks of the river, or in damp and marshy places. For this reason it is the accepted symbol of resurrection, and its branches are borne by mourners at a masonic funeral.

The value of a thirsty tree, in places where the gravedigger is troubled by water, as is frequently the case, will be obvious.

Myrtle, besides its sombre appearance, is a symbol of resurrection by the fact that it is evergreen.

> " The myrtle, laurel and bay stand for Victory.
>   The maple for Authority."

Various kinds of fir trees are also planted as recognized symbols of death; for unlike other trees, the life goes out of them directly they are cut.

[1] Old Song.

The cypress has held the place of honour throughout the ages, in connection with death. The Romans placed its branches in the vestibule as long as the body was there, to signify that it was a house of mourning, and it was also carried in the funeral procession.

"Rosemary," says Ophelia, "that's for remembrance," and in comparatively recent times, the mourners held sprigs of box and rosemary at the burial, and deposited them on the coffin before leaving. Medicinally, rosemary was held to be good for improving the sight and the memory.

The sprigs were arranged in a bowl on a table in the entrance hall of the house where the friends and relatives were assembled, to whom they were distributed.

In Japan, branches of sakaki are carried and used in part of the final ceremony—flowers also in abundance.[1]

We must not forget the palm, the symbol of victory over death, which the Christian festival of Palm Sunday reminds us was used at the "entry into Jerusalem," and which is associated by the Church with her martyrs. It is often to be found engraved on the Roman tombs.

A very curious superstition is worth noting in connection with the mandrake, a plant similar to belladonna, and credited with having a personality, or if growing in a graveyard, attached to the spirit of the dead. There seems to be no better foundation for this belief than that it roughly resembled the human form, having two taproots of equal length which suggested the lower limbs. When pulled from the ground, the small fibres breaking, a sound is produced which was readily translated by the imaginative into a "shriek."

[1] Mrs. Hugh Fraser, "A Diplomatist's Wife in Japan."

The Germans made the mandrake into dolls, dressing them with care and respect, and keeping them in caskets.

Midnight was the correct time to dig them up, when all kinds of absurd rites were practised, a "black dog" being employed to drag them from the earth.

Amongst other magical properties, they were supposed to be efficacious in the case of a barren woman, and are mentioned in the Bible in this connection.[1]

If trees have a close association with death, so too have flowers, and never more so than at the present time.

The writer recently attended a funeral at which the value of the floral "offerings" could not have been less than seventy or eighty pounds, and this is not anything very exceptional.

The fact that white flowers are almost exclusively used for the purpose reminds us that they are a special token of purity.

It was the practice of the Primitive Church to crown the heads of virgins with flowers.

In Corsica, when a young girl dies, the body is dressed in her best clothes, the feet tied with a white silk ribbon (to prevent the spirit from wandering on earth) and her head crowned with a chaplet of flowers by her friends, who thus address her, "We your companions, in bringing you lilies and roses, bring you your wedding garland."[2]

Besant mentions as a recent custom in Yorkshire, the hanging of a garland of flowers in the chancel of the church when a girl dies unmarried. The fact that the wreath was placed in the chancel, and that it was considered unlucky to carry away a piece of the ribbon with which the

[1] Bible, Genesis xxx. 14.
[2] J. E. Rossi, "Les Corses"

blossoms were tied, and the still more significant fact, that as the wreath decayed, the pieces were reverently buried in the churchyard, indicates that it was looked upon as an offering to the dead, rather than a sign of condolence with the living.[1]

Sometimes a white glove was attached to the wreath on which the name and age of the maiden would be inscribed.[2] The white glove, like the white veil with which the Greek Church bury their dead women, has generally been used as a token of innocence. The white glove signifies a "clean hand," and it is still the custom to present a pair to the Judge when there are no criminal charges to come before him, or, as at an earlier period, it was hoisted in the market-place on high days and holidays, a truce to those who were "wanted" for various crimes, who might venture forth from their hiding places to join in the festivities only as long as they were so protected.

From what we have seen of the matter, it would seem that the funeral wreath of white flowers signifies virginal purity, and if this is so, we must admit that it is singularly out of place for general distribution.

Were we to ask the "mourner" why he purchased those wire-tortured exotics almost identical with a dozen others, which would arrive at the house of mourning at the same time, his first surprise overcome that anyone should question so universal a custom, he would probably say that he did it as a "mark of respect." Pressed a little further if his patience stood the strain (for people who are asked why they do things which they have never thought about, often seek refuge in

[1] Sir Walter Besant, "London in the Time of the Stuarts."
[2] England Howlett, F.S.A., "Burial Customs" (Curious Church Customs and Cognate Subjects). Edited by Wm. Andrews.

BODY-SNATCHING

righteous anger), he might admit that he was not sure if he had intended to please the living or honour the dead; on the whole—since you question it—he would be inclined to think that his intention had been to show sympathy with the relatives, since the black-bordered card supplied by the florist contained an expression of his "deep sympathy and condolences." If quite candid, he would be forced to admit that it was nothing more to him than the fulfilment of a social obligation, and that the half sovereign he paid for it saved him from the mental exercise of composing a suitable letter of condolence, which would have presented many problems, ranging from a struggle with the unaccustomed use of the third person singular, to the scratching up of suitable scriptural quotations from a rusted mind.

The fact is that the funeral wreath is a survival of the belief that it is necessary to provide comforts for the use or delectation of the departed spirit; more than this, we may see it in at least an implied sense of sacrifice, for flowers were strewn to be crushed by the feet of the victor, as they are to-day thrown by children before sacramental processions, or used to line the grave. In the Highlands the grave is lined with heather.

A story is told of a soldier visiting the spot where a fallen comrade was buried in a foreign country for the purpose of placing flowers on his grave. On his way he met a native carrying a food offering to the ancestral tomb. Amused by this superstitious absurdity, he asked him when his ancestor would come up from the tomb, as he would like to see him enjoy his meal. "About the same time as your friend comes up to smell your flowers," was the unexpected rejoinder.

To-day, if we are spared the task of admiring

the tranquillity of the corpse (a treat which no one in the lower orders of society would miss) we are, at least, called upon to express a rapturous surprise at the beauty of the floral offerings sent by friends. "Aren't they *lovely*," you say, in hushed whispers (for even to-day you are afraid of waking the sleeping corpse).

Had we the courage of our opinions, or if we gauged the matter by the same standard of taste we use in testing any other beautiful things, we should find the funeral wreath neither necessary nor beautiful, but a foolish custom kept alive, and sedulously fostered for profit.

White flowers, which as individual blossoms are charming enough, if one can disassociate their waxy perfection and sickly odour from morbid thought, gain nothing but monotony in quantity.

Strung into the forms of harps, anchors, broken columns, etc., they are frankly vulgarized; and if this much may be said of natural flowers, how can we describe the "immortelle" in its glass case, with the added horrors of sugary doves and clasped hands—the despair of those whose duties it is to regulate the decencies of the churchyard. And how we long for the day when it will no longer be necessary to advertise "No flowers by request."

"May the grave of your ancestors be defiled!" Of the endless variety of Oriental curses this is the most dreaded. Life, which the Eastern mind values cheaply, and looks upon philosophically as a fleeting and uncertain thing, holds no terrors half as fearsome as the thought of the spirit wandering as an outcast from the rifled tomb.

To laugh at the childish precautions taken by people of all times and countries to prevent the dead from wandering from the place of sepulture, is to underestimate the terror which haunted them of being disturbed after death; and the certainty of retaliation, swift and terrible, which would assuredly overtake those who were rash enough to dishonour their remains.

Nor was it necessary to remove the bones to incur the full force of supernatural wrath—a ceremony forgotten, an honour due, unpaid, neglect of any kind was certain to bring disaster upon a careless relative.

Fear of the dead is the origin of almost every funeral custom which has come down to us to-day; from the pomp of the procession to the laudatory epitaph on the tombstone, to propitiate the acute sensibility of the departed.

So sacred was the grave to the Roman mind that even when it was necessary by force of some extraordinary circumstances to sell the land on which a tomb was placed, the law forbade that the sacred spot should even be considered as part of the contract, nor might anything be done which had the effect of excluding the relatives in perpetuity from the right of access to their dead.

It would indeed be an endless task to chronicle the special precautions taken by all nations and peoples to preserve the dead from any form of disrespect; that the tomb itself should be rifled and the bones scattered was an unpardonable crime.

The well-known injunction sheltering the remains of the immortal Shakespeare is a type of many to be found in this country.

> " Good friend, for Jesu's sake forbear,
> To dig the dust incloséd here.
> Blest be the man that spares these stones,
> And curst be he that moves my bones."

Whether the gravedigger bears a charmed life,

or the maledictions of the departed shade are really less potent than was supposed, it would be difficult to determine, but the fact remains that this humble and necessary official has constantly been called upon to disturb the resting-place of the dead, and to remove the bones in order to accommodate the bodies of a later generation.

As hamlets became villages, and villages grew into towns, many old burial-places had to be rearranged and provision made against overcrowding. In order to meet this necessity it became a common practice to provide a charnel house or "ossuary" in connection with the cemetery to which the bones of the dead might be removed after a reasonable number of years had elapsed to allow for complete decomposition. This was done for the most part reverently enough, and was often accompanied by some form of religious ceremony.

In some cases this custom, dictated by necessity, has even come to be looked upon as a *virtue*.

In the Breton churchyards the "ossuary" is considered of great importance, frequently with sculptured figures, and surmounted by a "Calvary."

Murray says in his handbook, " To allow the rude forefathers of the village to repose in the grave is *opposed* to the ideas of purity and affection in these rude people; after a certain number of years the survivors are required to show their remembrance and respect for their parents and relatives by removing the skull and bones from the coffin and placing them in the "ossuary," where the former are arranged on shelves open to the view of all, each with the name or initial in black painted across the fleshless brow."

The removal of the bones is done by the priest, and a municipal official has also to be present in

BODY-SNATCHING

order to certify that the matter has been carried out in due order; as in our country, an official sanction has to be obtained before exhumation can take place.

The wealthy Bretons enclose the skull in a small box made in the form of a miniature church, the roof of which is surmounted by a cross. Through the open door the skull may be seen. The door or peephole is made, as a rule, in the shape of a heart, over which is an inscription asking for prayers for the departed soul. These curious skull boxes which are carried in procession on the feasts of the dead, at other times repose in niches, or are in some cases nailed to the walls of the church.

With the exception of those rare occasions when it is necessary in the interests of justice to exhume a body in a case where foul play is suspected, we have considered all the circumstances in which we are justified in disturbing a body after burial; unfortunately there are many records of wilful pillage from motives of plunder, ransom or revenge.

The foolish custom of burying jewellery or money with the body has undoubtedly been the cause of desecration in the majority of such cases, and the practice is by no means uncommon to-day.

Apart from motives of personal vanity which induces the courtesan or the professional beauty to be sumptuously arrayed and decked with the costly toys from which, even in death, she would not be parted, it is the custom even now for the symbol of office to be buried with those who have held positions of state, signet rings and official badges of all sorts, which offer a tempting bait to the rifler of tombs.

Sometimes a sentimental attachment is held as

sufficient reason for the interment of valuables with the body.

The following is an extract from a will which was proved in 1916: "I wish to be buried in my wedding ring, and two medals taken from those I always wear put on a piece of white or blue ribbon and tied round my neck."

Evelyn, writing in 1685, says: "The King showed me a golden cross and chain taken out of the coffin of St. Edward the Confessor at Westminster by one of the singing-men, who as the scaffolds were taken down after his Majesty's Coronation, espying a hole in the tomb and something glisten, put his hand in and brought it to the Dean, and he to the King." "It was of gold, about three inches long, having on one side a crucifix enamelled and embossed, the rest was graven and garnished with goldsmith's work, and two pretty broad table amethysts (as I perceived), and at the bottom a pendant pearl; within was enclosed a little fragment, as it was thought, of the true cross, and a Latin inscription in gold and Roman letters." [1]

Even richer spoil than this was discovered in the time of Pope Paul III, when the marble tomb of the Empress Mary, wife of Honosius, was opened, where over and above the gold, forty pounds in weight, were curious vessels of crystal and agate, and many jewels.

How far it is justifiable to rifle the tomb for purposes of archæological interest may be an open question, but even the most hardened delver must have had some doubts on the subject, as he gazed on the newly opened grave where the peaceful form of some long forgotten mortal lay, surrounded by toys or tools which, centuries ago, ministered to his needs.

[1] Evelyn's Diary.

BODY-SNATCHING

That the fastnesses of the Pyramids should be broken after thousands of years' security, and the bodies of kings, to whom countless peoples had bowed the knee, removed from the place they had prepared with so much thought for security seems sacrilege enough, but that these royal bodies should be exhibited and ticketed for the idle curiosity of the British Cockney, opens up a question which happily it is not within our province to decide. If the opening of tombs for purposes of scientific research is questionable, what shall be said when it is done to satisfy the lowest motives of greed or revenge?

There have been times of social upheaval when the public conscience was so blunted that the value of the lead from the coffins was thought sufficient excuse to justify the crime. At the time of the French Revolution the republicans ordered that lead coffins should be despoiled and melted down for bullets.

In one of these orgies a workman tried to save the body of Marguerite of Lorraine, whose holy life and work amongst the poor had caused her to be venerated. He offered to make a new coffin of wood by his own labour, but was not allowed to do so, and with the rest, the remains held in such esteem were shot out of the broken end into the city ditch.[1] Unfortunately the history of our own country will furnish instances of this kind where even the value set on the lead coffins could not be put forward as a cloak to malice.

The body of Oliver Cromwell, with those of Bradshaw and Ireton, were torn from their resting-place in Westminster Abbey to be hung on the gibbet at Tyburn; a fate shared by the Puritan, Steven Marshall.

[1] Percy Dearmer, "Highways and Byways in Normandy."

M

In 1642 the soldiers under Sir William Waller pillaged the tombs of the Saxon kings at Winchester. Breaking open the coffins, they threw the bones at the painted windows which were mostly destroyed. The tomb of William of Wykeham was saved, it is said, by one Cuff, a rebel officer, who having been educated at the college, risked his life in order to protect the remains of the munificent founder from the plunderers.

If we may well turn our thoughts with disgust from such scenes as these, the acts of a frenzied mob, how shall we excuse the cold and calculating brutality of Leopold of Vienna, who in 1670 extorted from the Jews a sum of four thousand florins under threat of a vindictive desecration of their burial-places.

In the early years of the nineteenth century, when religious life in this country was at its lowest ebb, and scientific research in the ascendant, a great scandal presented itself.

The body-snatchers, or resurrection men as they were called, finding that good prices were paid by the anatomists for the bodies of those recently dead, opened up a nefarious traffic with the schools, which assumed the most disgraceful proportions before any severe measures were adopted to stamp out the evil. At this time the demand for bodies far exceeded the supply.

The grant of four felons each year to the Barber Surgeon's Company had been supplemented by the bodies of all criminals whose offences brought them to the gallows; good prices were paid for additional "subjects," and no awkward questions asked, a fact which so encouraged despoilers of the dead, that it became necessary to set a guard to protect the newly interred whose remains were much coveted

(*Reproduced by kind permission of Odhams Press, Ltd.*).

BURKE AND HARE.

Two notorious "Resurrection Men." They flourished in Scotland, their speciality being murder for the sake of the bodies, for which they found a ready and apparently unquestioning market at the Anatomical Schools. Sixteen murders were proved against this enterprising pair before they were brought to justice. They were convicted at Edinburgh in the year 1828.

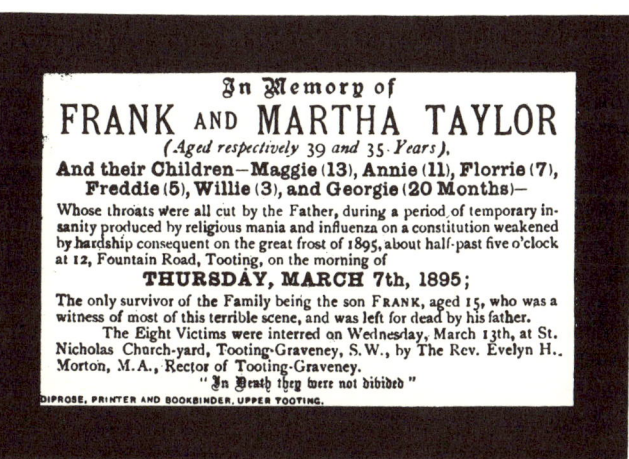

EXAMPLE OF A BALLAD-CARD

Sold by streetvendors to commemorate a sensational crime.

BODY-SNATCHING

for the purpose mentioned. Foiled by these means of doing business in the churchyards, it became a common practice for these ruffians to waylay and murder in the dimly lighted streets, any poor wanderer they encountered, with the sole object of making profit not by his purse, but by his person. After allowing this sort of thing to go on for a long time, at last the law rose to a sense of its responsibilities, and a system of licence was devised which did much to check the abuse; but the problem of supplying the schools remained unsolved, and remains so to the present day.

There is no doubt about it that the pauper was exploited when his need brought him to accept the charity of the nation, and even to-day, we find amongst the poor a horror of institutions generally, born of such malpractices which were regulated by the Poor Law Amendment Act of 1844.

Perhaps even more profitable than the sale of a corpse to the anatomical schools, if not so common, was the practice of stealing and holding the body of a wealthy person as hostage for the payment of ransom.

A celebrated case of this kind was that of Charles Souter, sentenced in 1882 to five years penal servitude, whose romantic career was recently recalled by his death.[1] He was found guilty of complicity in the theft of the body of the twenty-fifth Earl of Crawford from the family vault at Dunecht (near Aberdeen). The mystery was never completely solved. The family tomb of the Balcarres' family was of massive granite, built under the private chapel adjoining Dunecht House. The last Earl died in Florence in 1881; his body was embalmed and taken to Scotland, where it was interred: three coffins were used—a leaden shell,

[1] *Daily Express*, January 6th, 1914.

an inner case of wood, and the outer coffin of carved wood, richly mounted in silver. Some time after the funeral, a visitor to the chapel noticed that the slab sealing the entrance to the vault had been tampered with, but no importance was attached to this at the time. Later, an anonymous letter was received, stating that the vault had been entered and the body removed. This letter was also treated as a hoax. Some months later, part of the railing surrounding the tomb was found removed, and the entrance slab now lifted away and placed against the wall. The police were then summoned and the vault entered.

They found that the coffin had been removed from the shelf on which it had rested, the outer case unscrewed, the inner coffin forced open and the lead shell had the end cut away, from which the body had been pulled out by the feet. The fact that the valuable silver fittings remained intact showed that this was not the work of a common thief, and it was decided that the object of the outrage was to obtain a sum of money as ransom. Any hopes of this sort that the despoilers may have cherished were dispelled by a public announcement made by the family, that in no circumstances would they offer a reward for the recovery of the body.

Meanwhile, many clues were followed by the police without success; even "psychic" means were tried. Some spiritualists from London visited the place and declared that they had "*seen*" the body carried from the vault to a house on the estate, from whence it was afterwards removed to a "field that slopes towards a wood." Less vague was the light thrown upon the matter four months later by the man Souter, who in a drunken confidence offered to show his companions where the body of the Earl was concealed; when sober, he appeared to be frightened by his indiscretion, and on his arrest he made a statement to which he stoutly adhered. He swore that whilst poaching on the estate at night, he was detected by a gang of men engaged in burying some object, and that he only escaped with his life on swearing that he would keep their secret.

He was presently taken to the spot he indicated, where the body was found wrapped in a blanket, five hundred yards from the mansion, and covered with a few inches of soil. If he had accomplices, he never divulged their names and he died protesting his innocence.

CHAPTER X

PLAGUE

It is to be hoped, that with all that modern science has done towards the better ordering of our sanitary arrangements and the scientific treatment of the refuse of the cities, we, in this country, may never again experience such a devastating scourge as the plague which swept over this land in earlier centuries.

Even now in India, China and other countries the mortalities from these awful visitations exceed anything we can imagine in our comparative security.

There, despite organized relief, the death roll from plague and its fearsome companion famine, wiped out in the affected districts hundreds of thousands of human lives, and we cannot pretend to have dealt with the subject of death without consideration of the provisions made in such calamities to dispose of great numbers of bodies mown down like corn under the sickle.

The Indian famine commission of 1898 reported that in the year 1877 no less than five million of the natives perished, and that during the forty years between 1860 and 1900, no less then ten widespread famines devastated India.[1]

In the progress of the human race, as scattered

---

[1] R. C. Dutt, "Indian Famine."

PLAGUE

tribes became nations herding together in communities, for one reason or another, they became subject to periodical ravages of plague in various forms, fostered by uncleanliness, which claims a full measure of the natural increase of the population.

Far exceeding all visitations of the kind in Europe, stands out the Black Death of the fourteenth century and the Great Plague of the seventeenth century.

The Black Death which appeared in London in 1348, started in China and rapidly spread from country to country, leaving an appalling devastation in its wake.

Green says, "Of the three or four millions who then formed the population of England, more than one half were swept away in its repeated visitations."[1]

The Black Death left its mark on all phases of national life for a hundred and fifty years.

Whilst no accurate estimate could be expected, the total death-roll is probably not over-estimated as having claimed twenty millions of victims.

In attempting to relieve the most urgent necessities of the sick, the great religious institutions, which in the Middle Ages represented sanctuary, shelter and such medical care as they could offer to the people, were quickly overwhelmed and rendered powerless by the losses which they themselves sustained by infection, when tending the bodily and spiritual needs of the sick and dying.

The reader who may wish to learn more of this matter will study the great authority on the subject, Dr. Gasquet.[2]

The outstanding feature of the Black Death

---

[1] J. R. Green, "A Short History of the English People."
[2] Dr. Gasquet, "The Black Death."

was the great rapidity with which it spread, proving fatal to every kind of life that it touched.

It was brought to this country by traders at the ports of the eastern shores of the Black Sea. It spread along the trade routes from Bagdad to the southern ports of Asiatic Turkey. So sudden and violent was its attack, that the victims unhesitatingly abandoned all hopes of recovery at the first symptoms of the disease, thus rendering themselves unfitted to fight against the sickness.

There is an old story which so well illustrates the effects of the terror it caused, that it is worth recalling.

A pilgrim making his way to Bagdad was overtaken on his journey by a grisly figure. "Who are you?" asked the pilgrim. "I am the Plague," was the response, "and I am going to Bagdad to kill a thousand people." On his return journey the pilgrim overtook the spectre and stopping him said: "Why did you tell me that you were only going to kill a thousand people in Bagdad, whereas I found ten thousand of your victims in the city?" "I spoke truly," said the Plague, "I killed but one thousand, the remainder died from fright."

However, our present interest is not in the slaying, but in slain. Dr. Gasquet, speaking of the ravages of the Black Death, says, "There was no time for Christian burial. The corpse was hurried to the nearest church, where it was consigned to the tomb without the least attempt at ceremony."

Consecrated ground was quickly filled to overflowing, and it became necessary to dig trenches into which the bodies were placed in hundreds, layer upon layer, with but a little earth sprinkled in between till the pit was full to the top. Where the Charter House now stands in London more than fifty thousand corpses are said to have been buried. The same wholesale interments were found all that it was possible to give in other countries also.

" Help us! " they cry in Pisa, " to bear the body to the pit so that we in our turn may deserve to find someone to carry us."

Di Tura at Sienna, a contemporary chronicler, writes : " And I, Agniolo di Tura, carried with my own hands my five little sons to the pit, and what I did many others did likewise." So great was the labour of burying the dead, little wonder that fear seized the stoutest hearts, and the people dreading infection ran into the houses as the corpses were carried past. No outside help could be had for love or money.

The " passing bell " tolled continuously that the clerk and the sexton might gain their fees, rather than to urge the living to pray for the dead, and perhaps they might be excused, with food at famine prices and all sources of supply cut off.[1]

As the churchyards were filled new cemeteries were hastily consecrated. In all this stress of circumstances it should be noted that no thought was given to the cremation of bodies; surely proof enough that the practice was repugnant to the people, who even in such circumstances as these refused to adopt the pagan practice as being against the usage of the Christian Church.

The historian Stowe gives the following picture of London in these dark times.

" The pestilence increased so sore that from want of room in churchyards to bury the dead of the city and suburbs, one John Corey, clerk, purchased of Nicholas Prior of The Holy Trinity,

---

[1] Dr. Gasquet, " The Black Death."

Aldgage, one 'loft' of ground near unto East Smithfield for the burial of those that died, with condition that it might be called the 'Churchyard of The Holy Trinity,' which ground he caused by the aid of divers devout citizens to be enclosed by a wall of stone. Robert Elsing, son of William Elsing, gave £5 thereunto, and the same was dedicated by Ralph Stratford, Bishop of London, where innumerable bodies of the dead were afterwards buried, and a chapel built in the same place to the honour of God."

From the same source we gather that the said Bishop of London "bought a piece of land called 'No-man's-land,' which be enclosed by a wall of brick and dedicated to the burial of the dead, building thereon a proper chapel which is now (1598) enlarged and made a dwelling-house, and the burying plot is become a fair garden retaining the old name of Pardon Churchyard."

After this, in the year 1349, Walter Mannering, "in respect of a plague and infection, purchased thirteen acres and a rood of adjoining the said 'No-man's-land,' and lying in a place called 'Spittle Croft' because it belonged to St. Bartholomew's Hospital." "Since then," he continued, "in this plot of ground (also consecrated by the Bishop of London) there were (in that year) more than fifty thousand persons buried, as I have read in the Charters of Edward III."

It will be noted that the good bishop at least played *his* part in the great drama; and how careful he was even in such difficult times to see the cemeteries enclosed with "walls of brick or stone" (no light matter), and duly consecrated in accordance with Christian custom.

Little attempt seems to have been made to stay the course of the Black Death, and it may well

PLAGUE

be supposed that to bury its victims was as much as could be coped with, but Collier mentions the following curious incident.

"A set of enthusiasts called Flagellants came from Hungary and passed through the country, lashing themselves till the blood ran down their shoulders that the plague might be stayed." As to what effect this self-imposed penance had he leaves us uninstructed.[1]

Between the visitation of the Black Plague in the fourteenth century, and the "Great Plague" of the seventeenth century, a "sweating sickness" ravished England in the year 1551. It was peculiar inasmuch as it seemed to select its victims exclusively from the natives of these Isles.

Froude, writing of that visitation, remarks: "If it broke out in a foreign town it picked out the English residents with undeviating accuracy. The sufferers were generally men between thirty and forty years of age, and the stouter and healthier they were the more readily they caught the infection.

"The symptoms were a sudden perspiration accompanied by faintness and drowsiness. Those who were taken with full stomachs died immediately, and those who caught cold 'shivered into dissolution in a few hours.'

"The disease produced on the victim an intense desire to sleep, which, if yielded to, quickly proved fatal. So rapid was the disorder that of seven householders who supped together in the City of London, six before morning were corpses."

The cure advocated for this strange malady seems rather at variance with the necessity of keeping awake. The sufferer was advised " to

[1] Collier's "British Empire."

keep close in a moderate air," and to drink " posset ale and such-like " for *thirty hours*, when the patient was supposed to be out of danger.[1]

"It was a terrible time," says Stowe; "men lost their friends by the sweat." In London alone, eight hundred men died in one week in July.

In the seventeenth century no less than four plagues swept over the country. When we realize the comparatively spare population compared with our own times, the following death toll is simply appalling:

1603	...	30,578
1625	...	35,417
1636	...	10,400
1665	...	68,596

or a total sacrifice of 144,991 lives.

As these figures will show, the mortality of the "Great Plague," as it was called, far exceeded them all.

The authorities seem to have learned little from these repeated experiences.

By a remarkable dispensation of Providence, a year later, the fire of London burnt out the foulness which had so long accumulated. Every sort of filthiness had soaked into the very foundations of the houses, which, together with the churchyards into which bodies had been hastily packed away in thousands, were cleansed and purified by the intensity of the heat. That goods placed for safe storage by the merchants in the crypts of the churches should have been destroyed indicates the thorough way in which the great conflagration did its work.

At the first alarm of the plague the rich merchants of London fled to the country districts

---

[1] James Anthony Froude, "The Reign of Edward VI."

to avoid infection, leaving their poorer brethren to face the coming storm.

Some sort of organization seems to have existed with a view to stamping out the epidemic, for the city was divided into districts each with nurses, watchers and gravediggers.

The women who tended the sick carried a red staff in their hands that those whom they met might avoid them. The infected houses were marked with a cross and a prayer—a cry to Heaven when nothing more could be expected of material assistance. The warning cry "bring out your dead" and the rumble of the "dead-carts" disturbed the stillness of the night, all too short for the collection of the bodies from the streets and houses.

Besant also quotes the following regulations, drawn up by the City Fathers in their hopeless efforts to stay the ravages of the plague.

"That burial of the dead by this visitation be at most convenient hours always, either before sunrise or before sunsetting, with the privity of the churchwardens or constable, and not otherwise, and that no neighbours or friends be suffered to accompany the corpse to church, or to enter the house visited, upon pain of having his house shut up or be imprisoned, and that no corpse dying of infection shall be buried, or remain in any church in time of common prayer, sermon, or lecture; and that no children be suffered at time of burial of any corpse in any church, churchyard, or burying place, to come near the corpse, coffin or grave, and that all the graves be at least six feet deep; and further, all public assemblies at other burials are to be forborne during the continuance of the visitation." The regulations further enjoined that the houses which the plague had visited were to be marked with a red cross on the middle of the door one foot in length, and the words " Lord have mercy on us " to be also inscribed.[1]

> " Yes, when the crosses were chalked on the door,
>   (Yes, when the terrible ' death-cart ' rolled),
> Excellent courage our Fathers bore,
>   Excellent hearts had our Fathers of old." [2]

In view of the regulation that none might follow to the grave, the corpse was hurried out of the house at night, wrapped in any sort of an improvised shroud, to be committed to the pits, with, or more likely without, a muttered prayer from the labourer already accustomed to the sickening sight of wholesale slaughter.

Liberal libations of beer and tobacco and good pay were the only consolations of a sorely tried official, who, from force of circumstances, or some sense of duty, was pressed into this service.

Whatever the efforts made it was certainly not science that finally overcame a national calamity which, nurtured in a hot-bed of filth, would, once it had started, have sorely taxed our most earnest efforts to-day.

All that we have to remind us of this last of a series of plagues is the old burial grounds, over the entrance to which may be seen the sculptured representation of skull and cross-bones distinguishing the sites of the plague cemeteries.

In the Brompton Road, once far removed from habitation, a row of empty houses stood for many years, which none would occupy. They were built on the spot where many thousands of victims of the plague lay buried.

---

[1] Sir Walter Besant, " London in the Time of the Stuarts."
[2] Rudyard Kipling, " Our Fathers of Old."

CHAPTER XI

STATE AND PUBLIC FUNERALS

A DEAD lion may be a more impressive sight than a dead mouse, yet with the hand of death heavy upon them there is little to be said for any difference between the two, and even less when Nature has finished her task. As to the value of popular esteem and hero-worship even our own history shows us countries stifling their yawns at the death-bed of kings when the inevitable moment of dissolution seemed unreasonably delayed, and thinking only of their chances of ingratiating themselves in the favour of the successor to the throne. Deserted, save by such, and perhaps a few staunch and simple souls, the last moments of many a monarch has little enough to recommend it.

Few sovereigns have received a larger measure of popular devotion than Queen Elizabeth, yet the closing scene of her life was sad enough.

Of all our kings and queens the death of William the Conqueror was perhaps the most dramatic. Feared rather than honoured the fierce old king died in Rouen. Long before the body was cold his followers deserted him, leaving his corpse to the care of his servants, who, after stealing everything that was of value from his person and from the house where he lay, followed the example of their betters. Alone and dishonoured the clergy found him when they came to offer the last consolation of religion. The body was taken by water to Caen in the charge of the monks of St. Benedict, and with them walked Anselm, the Abbot of Bec, who had risen from a bed of sickness in order to hear the last confession of the Conqueror—but too late.

"In the midst of the solemn pomp there arose a cry of terror, flames burst from a house by which the procession was passing; it was unsafe to proceed as the whole quarter was threatened with destruction. Once more the body of the unloved Duke was deserted, only the monks followed it to the convent."

Even the actual burial at St. Etienne was attended by dramatic events. As the Bishop of Evreux ascended the pulpit to pronounce a funeral discourse, a rich burgher of Caen, who was present with a formidable body of sympathizers, demanded a hearing. "I forbid you to cover the body of the robber with my soil or to bury it in my heritage," he shouted—the ground on which the chapel stood, having been wrested from him by force. The commotion that ensued may well be imagined; peace was only restored when the Bishop handed sixty sous as an instalment of his claim and promised that the remainder of the price he demanded for the rights of interment should be made good to him. This episode was surely dramatic enough, but the final scene was full of horror. "The coffin was not large enough, or strong enough, and all the strength of incense smoke could not prevent the congregation from hurrying out of the church, leaving the terror-struck monks to finish the service as best they could, and then retire all trembling to their cells."

Many years later the Calvinistic mob broke

into the tomb and took all the bones of the king. These, with the exception of the thigh-bone, were given to a monk, but were lost when the Abbey was a little later sacked. The thigh-bone, which passed into private hands, was brought back and is now all that remains of William the Conqueror.[1]

A somewhat similar incident to that which scattered the mourners at the Conqueror's funeral occurred at the burial of Mademoiselle de Montpensier (first cousin to Louis XIV). In accordance with an old custom the heart had been removed for separate burial. Owing to imperfect sealing of the casket containing the relic, which was placed on the credence table, it burst in the middle of the service with a loud report. The intolerable odours sent priests and many eminent mourners flying from the church (of St. Denis).

The Bourbons were buried in the vaults of St. Denis, and it was customary for their bodies to be opened and the more perishable parts removed and embalmed.

Many instances are on record of this once common practice of burying the heart apart from the corpse. The tradition is still carried out by the Saxon royal family. Directly death is assured the body is opened and the heart and entrails removed. The heart is enclosed in a casket and placed on a white satin cushion on one side of the coffin, and the entrails in a white satin-covered jar on the other side. When the coffin is deposited in the vault these unpleasant objects repose on a bracket beside it.[2]

The heart as the legendary seat of the emotions has often been buried in some favoured spot to

---
[1] Percy Dearmer, " Highways and Byways in Normandy."
[2] " My Own Story," Louisa of Tuscany (Ex-Crown Princess of Saxony).

which it has been impossible to remove the body. The usage is also connected with the desire that premature burial would thus be avoided.

In the year 1838 the heart of Richard I, "The Lion-hearted," was discovered in Rouen, enclosed in a case of lead, in which it had been placed at his death in 1199. His body was buried at Fontevand.

Other royal hearts were thus disposed of: that of Henry III in Normandy; Eleanor, Queen of Edward I, in Lincoln; Louis IX, XIII and XIV in Paris. An interesting story is told of the heart of Robert Bruce, which he desired should be buried in the Church of the Holy Sepulchre in Jerusalem.

It was entrusted to Douglas, who carried it enclosed in a silver casket, which was suspended from his neck. On his journey he became involved in a fight with the Spaniards against the Moors, in which he was killed. The treasure was recovered and brought to Scotland, where it found a resting-place in Melrose Abbey.

Another "wandering heart" was that of James, the Marquis of Montrose, who was executed in the year 1650. Enclosed in a steel box it was sent to the exiled Duke of Montrose. The casket was stolen on the journey and was eventually discovered in an obscure shop in Flanders. Later it was taken to India by one of the family, where it was stolen by a native; finally it reached Europe once more, only to disappear at the time of the French Revolution.

The separate burial of the heart was forbidden by Pope Boniface VIII in 1294, but Benedict XI withdrew the prohibition.

The practice was common from the twelfth to the eighteenth century. The heart of the poet Shelley, it will be remembered, was snatched from

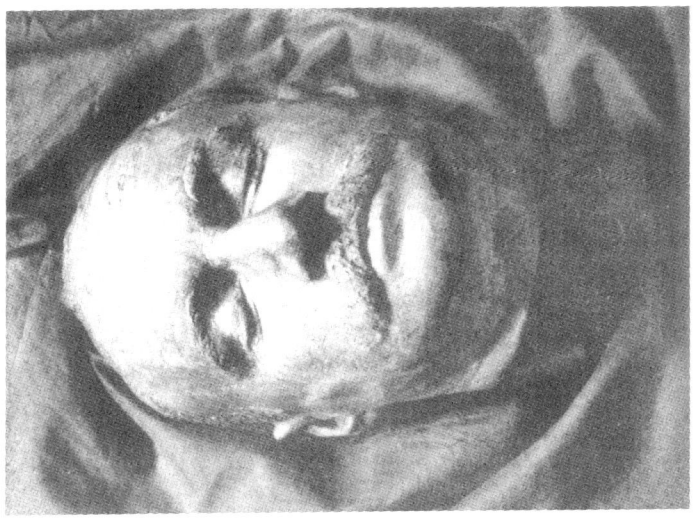

DEATH MASK
Captain Webb, the celebrated swimmer.
(*Reproduced by kind permission of John Tussaud, Esq.*)

THIS HEART CASKET, NOW IN THE BRITISH MUSEUM, ONCE CONTAINED THE HEART OF SIR HENRY SIDNEY.

STATE AND PUBLIC FUNERALS 195

the funeral pyre by his friend, Trelawney, and sent to England.

An account of the funeral of Henry VII will give some idea of the scale of magnificence considered appropriate to royal obsequies during the Tudor period.

The body of the King was brought from Richmond and was met at St. George's Bar, Southwark, by the Mayor and Aldermen, accompanied by a body of commoners on horseback, appropriately dressed in black. The streets were lined by members of the various " companies " carrying torches, the lower crafts occupying the first place. After the Freemen of the City came the " Strangers," Easterlings, Frenchmen, Spaniards, Venetians, Genoese, Florentines and Lukeneres on horseback and on foot, also carrying torches. In Cornhill the lower crafts were so marshalled that the " most worshipful crafts stood next to St. Paul's."

On the day following the shrouded but uncoffined body of the King was taken from St. Paul's to Westminster. " The lowest craft " was placed nearest to the Cathedral and the " Most Worshipful " next to Temple Bar, where the civic escort terminated. The Mayor and Aldermen proceeded to Westminster by water to attend " Masse and offering." The Mayor with his mace in his hand made his offering next after the Lord Chamberlain, those Aldermen who had passed the chain offered next after Knights of the Garter.[1] It must have been a well ordered and imposing spectacle at which the crafts were honoured, an element strangely lacking in these days when royal processions are for the most part confined to a military display.

[1] Sir Walter Besant, " London in the Time of the Tudors."

FUNERAL CUSTOMS

The chapel of Henry VII, containing his beautiful tomb by the Florentine artist Torrigiano, also enshrines the body of his consort, Elizabeth of York. Here, too, we are reminded of a much less pompous ceremony. For reasons of state the body of Charles II, which lies in a vault beneath the chapel, was buried with only the barest formalities " and soon forgotten after all this vanity," Evelyn tells us.[1] Here, too, lies the great Duke of Marlborough, the magnificent pall which covered his remains—rightly the perquisite of the Dean of Westminster—being stolen after the funeral.

The city guilds of craftsmen loved to honour their dead with imposing processions.

Describing a civic funeral, Machyn says, " First the company to which the deceased belonged appeared in their livery. The company of clerks attended the funeral of the better class and sang over the graves; black gowns were given to as many poor men and women as the condition of the deceased permitted." When a great citizen died like Master Husee Squire and Gutt Marchand Vintorer, of Muskovia, and haberdasher, he was followed by a hundred mourners, he had five pennons of arms and a " cotte armur," and two heralds of arms, etc.

" He was attended by the choir of St. Paul's and by the company of clerks. He was buried at St. Martin's, Ludgate Hill, the church hung with black and with escutcheons of arms; the Reader of St. Paul's preached both days."[2]

The funeral oration or " funeral " as it was at one time called—denoted the obsequies generally, but more particularly the sermon.

Webster, in his dictionary, gives examples of

---

[1] Evelyn's Diary.
[2] Sir Walter Besant, " London in the Time of the Tudors."

STATE AND PUBLIC FUNERALS 197

the word used in both senses. "King James's 'funerals' were performed very solemnly in the Collegiate Church at Westminster"—also "Mr. Giles Lawrence preached his 'funerals.'"

The ancient Greeks and Romans employed their finest orators for this purpose, the procession generally stopping on its way to the pyre in some important public place to listen to a lengthy panegyric on the virtues of the dead.[1]

In this country it was a common practice to leave by will a specified sum of money to defray the cost of a funeral sermon. In later days the "mortuary"—a charge levied on the estate of a deceased person by the Church—became associated with the post-mortem oration.

Master Flammock, who died in 1560, was apparently a Puritan; many gowns were bestowed by his executors. He was taken to the church without singing or clerks, and was buried with a Psalm "After Genevay," and a sermon.

Master Hulson Scrivener was one of the masters in Bridewell, so the masters of Bridewell attended his funeral with green staves in their hands, and all their children, "and there was great syngyng as ever was heard."[2]

Such elaborate functions nearly always finished with a repast, "and all dune, to the place fir there was a great diner."

With much pomp and civic honours the City Fathers loved to bury their dead, especially the members of their own Guilds. The bearing of torches on these occasions reminds us that burial by night—a custom which added very considerably to the dramatic effect of the proceeding—was con-

---
[1] See as example "Pericles Funeral Oration," translated by Richard Crawley. "Thucydidis Peloponnesian War," published in the Temple Classics.
[2] Sir Walter Besant, "London in the Time of the Tudors."

sidered as a special honour to persons of rank or distinction. Those of the Aldermen of London who had passed the chair were thus interred. The practice gradually fell into disuse, partly because of the opportunity it afforded for riotous behaviour on the part of the sightseers; it was prohibited in the time of Charles I. The prohibition was, however, frequently disregarded, the tradition being retained by some families and in certain districts. The last English king to be buried by torchlight was George I.

Something of the cost of great public funerals may be gathered from the following extract from Evelyn's Diary (1695). He says, "I saw the Queen (Mary) lie in state—the Marquis of Normanby told me King Charles had a design to buy all King Street and build it nobly, it being the street leading to Westminster." "This," he adds, "might have been done but for the expense of the Queen's funeral, which was fifty thousand pounds—against her desire."

After the burial a paper was found expressing a wish that her body might not be opened, and that no expense might be incurred at her funeral.

Macaulay gives a picturesque account of this funeral:

"While the Queen's remains lay in state at Whitehall the neighbouring streets were filled every day from sunrise to sunset by crowds, which made all traffic impossible; the two Houses with their Maces followed the hearse—the Lords robed in scarlet and ermine, the Commons in long black mantles. No preceding sovereign had ever been attended to the grave by a Parliament, for till then, the Parliament had always expired with the sovereign. The banners of England and France,

STATE AND PUBLIC FUNERALS

Scotland and Ireland were carried by great nobles before the Courts. The pall was borne by the chiefs of the illustrious houses of Howard, Seymour, Grey and Stanley. On the gorgeous coffin of purple and gold were laid the crown and sceptre of the realm. The sky was dark and troubled, and a few ghostly flakes of snow fell on the black plumes of the funeral car. Within the Abbey, nave, transept and choir were ablaze with innumerable wax lights. The body was deposited under a sumptuous canopy in the body of the church, while the Primate (Tenison) preached. Through the whole ceremony the distant booming of canon was heard every minute from the batteries of the Tower. It was rumoured at the time that a robin which had taken refuge from the cold in the same building was observed to perch incessantly, and, as it were, affectionately and sadly upon the Queen's hearse, a touching incident greatly appreciated by the spectators."

As in the case of Queen Mary elaborate obsequies are often given in honour of a person who has previously expressed a desire to be buried in a simple and decent manner, and much of the vulgar ostentation of the modern survivals is for the aggrandizement of relatives rather than the honour of the departed.

Such was the fate of the great Italian composer, Verdi, who gave the most strict and definite instructions to his friends that his body was to be laid to rest without any sort of public display whatever. Despite this, he was buried in Milan in 1901, in an ornate marble tomb, and it was computed that no less than a hundred thousand people lined the streets to witness the procession.

We can hardly conceive that the elaborate

funeral ceremonies afforded to Oliver Cromwell were such as would have been desired by a man of such simple and unostentatious habits.

Whilst his body was being embalmed his effigy was exhibited to the public, decked with royal robes, crown and regalia. His remains were afterwards removed from Somerset House on a state bed of velvet, drawn by six horses, the pall being borne by various noblemen. Knights and heralds, guards of honour, and a noble procession of notable persons accompanied him to Westminster Abbey. Evelyn describes the event as "the joyfullest funeral I ever saw, for there were none that cried but dogs, which the soldiers hooted away with a barbarous noise, drinking and taking tobacco in the street as they went"—a description which, if it gives something in the way of local colour, is clearly prejudiced.

The same chronicler, who never missed any public occasion of interest, particularly a funeral, in describing the obsequies of Ireton under date March 6th, 1652, writes: "Saw the magnificent funeral of that arch rebel Ireton carried in pomp from Somerset House to Westminster, with divers regiments of soldiers, horse and foot, then marched the mourners, General Cromwell (his father-in-law), his mock Parliament men, officers and forty-four men in gowns; three led horses in housings of black cloth, two led in black velvet and his charging horse all covered over with embroidery and gold on crimson velvet: then the Guidons, ensigns, four heralds carrying the arms of state (as they called it), namely the red cross, and Ireland with the casque wreath, sword and spurs, etc., next a chariot canopied of black velvet and six horses, in which was the corpse. The pall held up by mourners on foot, the mace and sword, with other

STATE AND PUBLIC FUNERALS

marks of his charge in Ireland (where he died of the plague), carried before it in black scarves.

"Thus in a grave pace—drum covered with cloth, soldiers reversing arms—they proceeded through the streets in a very solemn manner."

Attempts were made at various times to curtail by law extravagance at public funerals, but with very little result.

In the year 1681 the Scottish Parliament restricted the number of persons who might attend the funeral of a person of rank to one hundred, prohibiting at the same time the using or carrying of branches, banners and other honours at church except "the eight branches to be upon the pall or upon the coffin where there is no pall." The funeral sermon was also condemned.

Despite this Act the funeral of Sir William Hamilton, who died in 1707, was so costly that it dissipated the sum equal to two years of his salary as a judge.

Whilst, especially in modern times, it has been customary to accompany the funerals of kings and those of exalted rank with a display of military, rather than civic honours, this has been more reasonably done in the case of famous military leaders. The burial of Napoleon occurs at once as an example. The Warrior-Emperor died at St. Helena on May 5th, 1821. He had previously selected a beautiful spot on the island, where he desired that his body should be interred in the event of permission being refused to take it to France. Here, in the presence of a few faithful friends who had cheered his exile, and the military authorities on the island, his body was carried by British Grenadiers on May 8th. He was clothed in the dress he had worn during his many campaigns —his head covered by his historical three-cornered hat—volleys were fired over his grave, and a huge stone was afterwards placed to mark the deserted spot where the remains of the great soldier lay.

It was not till the year 1840 that the British administration restored the relics of Napoleon to the French. Before being placed in the frigate *Belle Poule*, the coffin was opened, when it was found that the body was not decayed and the features were still recognizable. All that remained of the great Napoleon was thus conveyed to the scene of his former triumphs, to be interred in the company of other illustrious warriors in the church of the Invalides. Though it was winter time, and bitterly cold (December 15th, 1840), some six hundred thousand persons assembled in the streets of Paris to do honour to Napoleon. Louis Philippe was present at the service, which was the occasion of much pomp and magnificence; a touching tribute to the memory of a great leader, and one which was not witnessed without the deepest emotion, was the appearance of a guard of honour composed of war-scarred veterans, who had fought by his side in many a famous battle. Napoleon's favourite charger also followed the body to its final resting-place.

The funeral of Wellington was hardly less magnificent than that of the vanquished Emperor. It took place on November 18th, 1852. The body was interred by the side of Nelson in St. Paul's Cathedral.

During the procession the streets presented a remarkable sight; enormous crowds were assembled many hours before the ceremony, and every possible point of vantage had been occupied where even a distant glimpse of the cortège might be expected. Both rich and poor were dressed in deep mourning. Whatever the popular feeling might have

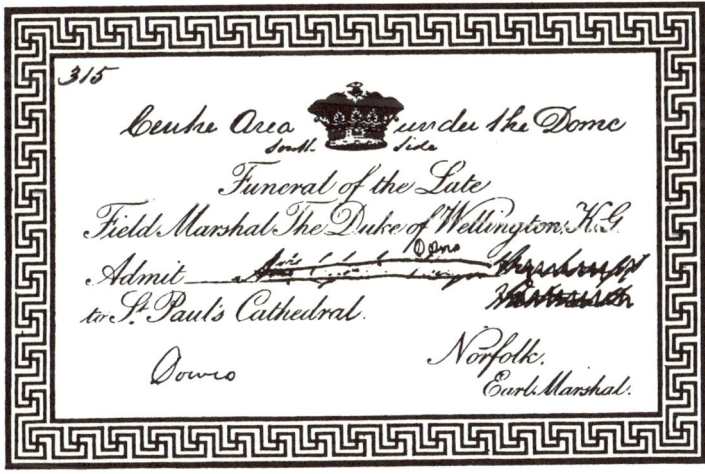

INVITATION TO THE FUNERAL OF THE DUKE OF WELLINGTON AT ST. PAUL'S CATHEDRAL.

LORD NELSON'S FUNERAL CAR.
This pageant-car was designed on the lines of his historic ship, the *Victory*.

been at some periods of the life of Wellington, there can be no doubt that at his death a generous and heartfelt sorrow was displayed. With great military ceremony, arms reversed and drums muffled, the enormous structure on which the body was carried rumbled through the streets to the sound of the " Dead March."

This funeral car is interesting as it resembled the later examples of the hearse proper. Mounted on a substantial wagon, the enormous superstructure, decorated with banners and weapons, bore an altar-like erection covered by a magnificent velvet pall. On the top rested the coffin, on which the Duke's celebrated " cheese-cutter " hat reposed with the other insignia of his rank. Over the whole car a canopy was erected, supported by four ornamented poles. A large team of horses was required to drag the heavy structure, all of which wore nodding plumes on their heads whilst velvet saddle-cloths covered their flanks in the orthodox manner.

Large bodies of troops representing all the picked regiments in the British army lined the route or followed in the procession.

Not only in this country, but abroad, on the day of his funeral honour was accorded to the " Saviour of Europe," as Wellington was called.

In Austria a grand parade of the whole army was ordered, at which the Emperor was present in person to direct the salute of artillery.

In all the ceremonies which accompany the soldier to his grave, whether he be a general of renown or a trooper of humble rank, we see much the same forms resorted to, which we shall find presuppose that he has been slain and is to be buried on the field of battle.

Even in modern warfare, where conditions are so widely changed from the old order of things, the earliest practices are still in vogue. The identity disc may take the place of the tattoo mark, but the purpose is the same.

The art of tattooing—if it be art—was used, if not originated, for the purpose of identification of the dead and the wounded on the battlefield. By this means did Edith the Swan Neck discover the body of Harold on the field of Hastings.

William of Malmesbury (1066) says, " The English adorned themselves with punctured designs." Kingsley says, "May not our sailors and soldiers fashion of tattooing the arms and chest with strange devices be a remnant of the very fashion kept up if not originated by the desire that the corpse be recognized after death." [1]

The forms prescribed for the burial of soldiers are set down with military punctiliousness and regard for detail. The uniformity of the proceedings and such enforced simplicity as burial on the field of battle dictates, adds a dignity to all things based on essential principles which never fails to awaken the sympathetic interest of the observer.

The regulations provide for different escorts according to the rank of the deceased, but otherwise the same honours are paid irrespective of degree.

The " firing party " consists of a sergeant, corporal and twelve privates. To those selected as pall-bearers falls the duty of seeing that the flag which covers the body, and the headdress and accoutrements are tied on the coffin in such a manner as will prevent their falling off when the coffin is " shouldered." The arms of the escort are reversed, that is to say, the muzzle of the rifle is directed to the rear under the soldier's left arm, the right hand holding it in position behind his body.

---

[1] Chas. Kingsley, " Hereward the Wake " (Preface).

STATE AND PUBLIC FUNERALS 205

The coffin is placed on a gun-carriage prepared for the purpose (that used on the occasion of Queen Victoria's funeral may be seen in the London Museum). The procession moves off at the slow march, followed by the riderless charger in appropriate circumstances, with his master's boots reversed in the stirrups. The firing party leads the cortège, followed by the band and drummers. After the gun-carriage march the bearers in attendance, the mourners following. The band plays the " Dead March," and when it ceases the pace is quickened till the burial ground is within sight, when the slow march is resorted to again. At the entrance to the cemetery the firing party leading, halt and open out, in order that the procession may pass between them as they stand with heads bent and arms reversed. The coffin is then lifted from the gun-carriage by the bearers and carried feet foremost to the grave, where the firing party follow, remaining with covered heads. The ceremony is concluded by the firing of three volleys, and the sounding of the bugle call known as the " Last Post." A lively march is played by the band on the way home.

Such a scene as this is a common enough incident in any garrison town, but it never becomes commonplace, for it has history behind it.

The use of the gun-carriage as an improvised hearse has an obvious origin in the time of war.

The reversed arms were once a recognized signal to the enemy that a truce was called whilst the dead were buried. The three volleys fired over the grave announce that the ceremony is over, and that the burial party is prepared to accept battle again.

The wailing notes of the " Last Post " is the sound that nightly lulls the camp to rest.

The use of the flag as a pall is an obvious

makeshift in circumstances where coffins are unobtainable.

As we have noted in a previous chapter, the custom of leading the warrior's horse to the grave is a remnant of the days when it was considered necessary to slaughter the animal there in order that its master might have a charger in the spirit world to carry him to fresh fields of victory.

The hoisting of a flag half-mast high, though a common usage, is essentially of military origin. It typifies the victory of death over life, the victor's flag being at one time flown over the flag of the vanquished, which was lowered for this purpose.

Of naval funerals there is little to tell. When they take place on land, they follow the military custom—at sea, the uncoffined body is commonly sewn in a hammock or in sailcloth, to which shot or a weight is attached, in order that it may sink in the deep waters to which it is committed.

We cannot claim to have dealt even briefly with the subject of public funerals without making some mention of the burial of the murderer or his victims. Morbid curiosity and an inherent and ghoulish love of tragedy renders such occasions dear to vulgar minds. Thousands will gaze with intense interest at the shabby ending to a squalid drama.

In comparatively modern times, when the public execution of criminals took place outside Newgate Prison, long hours before the condemned man was brought out in the chill morning air to be hanged, dense crowds of the lowest elements of society swarmed in thousands from the slums of the city to gloat over the horrid sight which the execution afforded.

Even in these enlightened days, when an execution takes place a crowd assembles outside the prison walls in order to enjoy—we can use no

STATE AND PUBLIC FUNERALS

other word—the sound of the tolling bell, and to see the black flag hoisted.

The prison officials who receive the unhappy victim of passion and take his life, are also responsible for the disposal of his body.

With a haunting suggestiveness Wilde tells the sordid story in the " Ballade of Reading Gaol."

> " Only a stretch of mud and sand
> By hideous prison wall,
> And a little heap of burning lime,
> That the man should have a pall."

Whilst at the present time there undoubtedly exists a growing strength of public opinion against the death-penalty, the cause of the murderer often on the slightest pretext has very generally been supported. " Release unto us Barabbas " is a cry not confined by any means to the ancient Jews.

A remarkable case of this kind occurred in the year 1815.

A girl named Eliza Fenning was accused of attempting to poison the family with whom she was employed as a servant. Her innocence was supported by one of those curious waves of intense popular feeling which arise in some such cases. Amongst the advocates of her cause were numbered many celebrated people of the day. The girl's character—if one may judge it from the evidence given at the trial—was anything but blameless.

Despite numerous petitions and the serious reconsideration of the facts at the last moment by the Lord Chancellor and other officials, she paid the full penalty of the crime which she was said to have committed. A public funeral was accorded to her, the body being handed over to her relatives for the purpose. The streets through which the procession passed were thronged with sightseers the whole day. A strong body of guards was on duty to keep the peace. The pall was borne by girls dressed in white, as a symbol of her innocence, the relatives walking behind the hearse. Difficulty was experienced in forcing a way for the procession to the cemetery through the dense crowds of people.

It is remarkable that the name of this woman of very humble origin appears, with detailed particulars of the event, in the Dictionary of National Biography.

Reference has been made to the custom of burying murderers at the cross-roads. Many curious beliefs have been held in this relation. Jewish law forbade the cutting down of a body which had been hanged, for at least a day after the execution, in order that the ground might not be rendered " unclean."

Hanging in this country was only substituted for burning alive as late as the year 1790.

At Portsmouth in 1784, Mary Bayley, who murdered her husband, was drawn to the place of execution on a hurdle and was then burnt alive.

If special precautions were considered necessary in order that the spirit of the dead might not annoy the living, certainly the dread of the ghost of a murderer or his victim presented special horrors to the superstitious mind.

For this reason, a stake was driven through the heart of the criminal, and other means adopted to prevent unpleasant reappearances.

Webb records the fact that during the Arran murder case in 1889, it transpired that the boots of the murdered man had been removed by the local constable, who according to tradition buried them on the sea-shore " between high and low water level " to prevent this ghost from walking.

CHAPTER XII

CREMATION, EMBALMING

WHATEVER may be said for or against cremation as a method of disposing of the bodies of the dead, frequent controversy on the subject in recent years has been the means of inducing people to give some thought to the whole matter of funeral reform.

Under a protecting cloud of sanctity, our funeral observances have been handed down unquestioned from generation to generation till the introduction of scientific cremation opened up a healthy discussion and forced the average mind to consider such things from the point of view of essentials.

We cannot give even a few moments of serious thought to cremation as opposed to earth-burial without being forced to define our *real* beliefs concerning an existence after death. Even orthodox minds may be surprised to discover how little assurance they have, when faced with the possibilities of a conscious sacrifice of their bodies to the flames.

Those who have but a tolerant smile for the orthodox beliefs in a spiritual existence are apt to hesitate when they contemplate the destruction of their physical bodies by a process of incineration, however scientifically it may be carried out.

"Why run any risks in so serious an experiment?" we may ask ourselves, when the grave, despite its obvious drawbacks, seems to offer, by contrast, some comparatively definite attractions.

In vain will the advocates of cremation argue the larger question of the welfare of the public health with those who have the smallest lingering doubts. A natural horror of fire is the first obstacle to be overcome if cremation is to become a general practice. Even "advanced" people dwelling in a certain garden suburb near London have been seen to cast uneasy glances at the tall chimney of the "grill room" as the crematorium is playfully called, which has been erected so conveniently at the entrance to their sylvan retreat.

The controversy between the advocates of the two methods of disposal is an old one.

At the death-bed of Gurca-Nanak, the founder of the Sikh's religion, the question arose as to whether his body should be buried—as was the custom of the Mussulmans—or cremated according to the practice of the Hindus.

Knowing their minds, Nanak ordered that flowers should be placed by the Hindus on the right of his body, and by their adversaries on the left. He promised that those offerings which remained fresh in the morning should have the disposal of his remains. After death had taken place the body was covered by a sheet. In the morning, when this was removed, *nothing* was found beneath it but the flowers, all of which were as fresh as when they were gathered.[1] It is a beautiful story, but it leaves matters pretty much where they are to-day.

Looking backwards over the ages we find the method of the disposal of the dead in the following order:

1. Burial.
2. A period of both burial and cremation or a partial burning of the body.

[1] Dorothy Field, "The Religion of the Sikhs."

CREMATION, EMBALMING 211

3. Cremation gradually becoming obsolete, and earth burial the general practice.[1]

The Greeks and Romans originally buried their dead, but later cremation became customary.

Incineration was the general practice of the ancient world, with the exception of Egypt, which embalmed. Judea, which learnt its embalming and other practices from the Egyptians, buried in the *sepulchre*, and China in the earth (in accordance with the doctrine of Feng-Shin).

The Romans had so great a respect for all burial-places that the Christians were allowed to inter their dead undisturbed, whilst otherwise persecuted.

The Greeks continued both methods with a decided bias towards cremation. What was the reason underlying these preferences?

Clodd tells us " the well-nigh common practice of burning the dead in the Bronze Age was probably resorted to, as a yet more effective way of getting rid of the ghost than by the burial of the body." [2]

Once again we shall note the primitive dread of being haunted, which plays so large a part in all our funeral customs.

Even the placing of weights on the body, and the construction of a ring-fence round it seems to have been considered as less efficacious, *for to burn was to annihilate.* Clodd adds " that it would be specially adopted by nomadic peoples, who, leaving their dead behind, would be unable to make provision for appeasing offerings at their graves. Hence the burning of the body to prevent the neglected ghost from following and harassing the living."

With the growth of Christianity cremation, which

[1] Walter Johnson, " Byways in British Archæology."
[2] Ed. Clodd, " The Story of Primitive Man."

was generally practised, received a check, for, from the earliest times, the Christian Church put all the weight of her increasing influence against cremation and strictly forbade it to her converts; nor has she ever altered her attitude towards this form of disposal.

"The Christians execrated funeral pyres and condemned the sepultures of flames," Minucius Felix wrote in the third century, a statement which he thus qualified, "Nor do we fear, as you may suppose, any harm from this mode of sepulture, but we adhere to the old and better custom."[1]

In considering cremation we must distinguish between the funeral pyre of the ancients and of primitive peoples, and the modern methods of scientific incineration.

The earliest pyre was merely a heap of wood upon which the body was placed, and in most cases only half destroyed, for it is no easy matter to reduce to ashes a body containing a large percentage of fluid matter. This altar-like erection must have been very nearly related to the pagan sacrifice of human and animal offerings to the gods, and may have had something to do with the Christian attitude.

Pine or other resinous wood was selected, and some light combustible materials added such as dried grass and twigs, in order to set the pyre alight. Oak and hard woods generally, that resist the flames, take twice as long in producing the same results. With these materials oil, pitch, etc., were in later use, adding much to the heat and effectiveness of the flames.

Christianity found the Romans building their pyres of pine logs constructed altar-wise. The interstices were stuffed with pitch and brushwood

[1] Minucius Felix, "Dialogues Octavius."

CREMATION, EMBALMING

to which sweet-smelling gums were added, the structure being decorated with the symbolic branches of cypress. When all was prepared the uncoffined body was placed in position, and the chief mourner, with head averted, set fire to the pyre with a torch. When the whole was reduced to ashes, wine was poured on the embers to cool them. The bones were then reverently collected, washed with milk and placed with perfume in a cinerary urn.[1]

The poor who were unable to do things on such a lavish scale had to rest contented with cheaper and less effective methods; as an alternative they could bury their dead in the catacombs, or cast them with the slaves into a common pit.

These cruder forms of destroying the body by fire are still to be met with in certain parts of the world.

In Siam the ceremony of cremating a king is, or was, conducted with an elaborate ritual.

The body was placed in a sitting posture in a special form of chair, beneath which reposed a golden vessel. A quantity of mercury having been poured down the throat to dry up the body, a golden mask was put over the face of the dead ruler. A grand procession of state visited the body each day and ceremoniously emptied the fluid from the jar into the river. When the body was sufficiently dried it was placed in a large urn, where it remained for about a year. Meanwhile preparations were made for the final ceremony.

Logs of the finest sandal wood were collected in the forests to form a catafalque some three hundred feet in height, to which the body was presently brought by a procession of great

[1] T. G. Tucker, "Life in the Roman World of Nero and St. Paul."

214　FUNERAL CUSTOMS

magnificence to be deposited on the summit of the pyre. For seven days public games took place in honour of the occasion, as the Romans honoured their dead by gladiator shows.

The final act was the ceremonial lighting of the pyre by the heir to the throne. After the flames had done their work the ashes were collected, mixed with clay and distributed as souvenirs amongst the people.

In the times of plague or war cremation has sometimes been excused by those who were otherwise opposed to the practice.

We have a curious instance of its use as a precautionary measure in the romantic circumstances attending the cremation of the body of the poet Shelley.

Many of those to whom the picture depicting the event is familiar (the original hangs in the Walker Art Gallery, Liverpool) might suppose that the method of disposal was chosen in this instance by the poet as a dramatic ending to a romantic career; or it might be thought that Byron, who was present, was responsible for the unusual arrangements. The facts are worth recalling. Shelley and his friend Williams were travelling in Italy when they were both drowned. A good deal of mystery surrounded the accident, it having been suggested that their boat was purposely capsized. The bodies were not recovered for some ten days after the catastrophe, when they were washed up in different parts of the shore at Via Reggio. Here they were temporarily buried in the sand whilst the authorities made the necessary arrangements for their cremation.

The fact is that there was no option in the matter, for, according to Italian law, anything washed up from the sea *must* be burnt on the

ROMAN FUNERAL PYRE.—*Livy*.

The illustration depicts the traditional "gladiator show," the lighting of the pyre with face averted, and the use of the toga as a veil indicating the heir or chief mourner.

PLAQUE REPRESENTING AN EARLY FORM OF HORSE-DRAWN BIER.

CREMATION, EMBALMING 215

shore where it is found. This is an old precautionary measure against the introduction of plague into a sea-girt country which has suffered so often from such visitations. A military guard was at once dispatched to the spot in order to see that the regulations in force were strictly adhered to. The soldiers collected driftwood from the beach and pine logs from an adjacent forest for the funeral pyre, and a grid of iron was provided in order to secure a proper combustion on which the wood was piled. These arrangements were carried out under the personal supervision of an officer from the Office of Health. The body of Williams was cremated first, and that of Shelley on the following day. Frankincense, salt, wine and oil were thrown on to the burning pyre, and in a few hours all that remained of the poet's body—except the heart, which was recovered from the flames—was gathered up to be interred in the Protestant cemetery of Rome, where Keats had been buried.

Leigh Hunt witnessed the proceedings with much emotion from Byron's carriage, whilst Byron, unable to bear the sickening odours, left before the body was consumed. " Don't repeat this with me," he said. " Let my carcase rot where it falls."

It is safe to say that if no better methods of incineration had been devised than those which have been described nothing would have been heard of the modern revival.

Before we follow the introduction and growth of scientific cremation let us see what inducement it offered as compared to burial.

In the year 1658 Sir Thomas Browne published a quaint book entitled " Hydriutaphia or Non-Burial," but it was Sir Henry Thompson who first seriously brought the matter to public notice in this country.

If we would discover in what spirit he approached the subject we cannot do better than examine the actual terms of the problem he had set himself to solve.

"Given a dead body to resolve it into carbonic acid, water and ammonia, rapidly, safely and not unpleasantly."

We may be amused to find the scientific mind throwing in as a last clause or sop to suit more delicate stomachs, "that the process should not be '*unpleasant.*'"

The early advocate of the scientific system drew the most encouraging pictures of the *commercial* value of their proposals. The actual number of tons of bone imported into this country for the purposes of manufacture and manure was most carefully computed, and the benefit to the community in pounds, shillings and pence to be derived from human remains, formed what they supposed would be one of their most convincing arguments. Yet another proposition which was seriously set forth in favour of cremation was the possibility of producing gas for lighting purposes by means of a retort or kind of "mortuary gasometer."

As a French writer observed, "If you want to prevent cremation in France—a country which has a deep veneration for her dead—you cannot do better than spread abroad such arguments as these."

But, after all, it is a point of view. If we are *quite* satisfied that a corpse is simply so much fat, so much water, ammonia, lime and so forth, and *nothing else*, what possible harm can there be in separating such parts from the whole as would be usefully employed for manufacture or agricultural purposes?

Many eminent scientists as well as others have

CREMATION, EMBALMING 217

bequeathed their remains to science. Jeremy Bentham, the famous philosopher, left his body to the University College Hospital, where it was preserved, fully dressed, and may be seen by the curious. Sir Victor Horsley bequeathed his skull and brain to the Neurological Society of London, but his untimely death in Mesopotamia prevented the fulfilment of the promise.

We have read of the methods alleged to have been adopted by the Germans in their " Kadavar Utilization Establishment," a commercial enterprise, about which full and gruesome stories were related. We were told that the corpses from the battlefields, neatly tied up in bundles, find their way to this establishment. Here they are passed on by a system of endless chains from one process to another, leaving behind them all sorts of valuable by-products, particularly those of which a shortage existed in the enemy countries. But why not? Whence the horror which was expressed, be the facts true or otherwise? Here we have a materialistically minded nation putting into practice in times of stress, those principles advocated by the pioneers of cremation in times of peace, namely the use of the bodies of the dead for utilitarian purposes.

The position is surely logical if we believe that a corpse is so much decaying flesh—and nothing more.

About the time that the advocates of cremation started their propaganda, science was in the main not only opposed to the spiritual aspects of death, but was considered by many as the appointed means by which a purely materialistic conception would be brought about. As we know, the unexpected happened, and some of our leading scientists to-day are not only taking us in the opposite direction, but leading us both farther and faster than many of us are inclined to be led. Let us remember that the utilization of human remains was not the *only* claim put forward in favour of the funeral reforms advocated. For instance, the pioneers insisted that the compulsory cremation of all persons dying of infectious diseases would do very much towards stamping out certain epidemics.

They further claimed that by doing away with the burial grounds, not only would the public health be safeguarded but that a vast acreage of land, instead of lying idle, could be put under cultivation and a considerable revenue gained thereby. These ideas were the main arguments put forward by the cremationists.

To many minds, they went a long way in establishing a reasonable case against earth burial. Leaving aside as a separate question the use of the bodies of the dead for utilitarian purposes (a doctrine which is certainly repugnant to a vast majority of people) we have two main claims to consider; first, the utilization of land which would otherwise be conserved as burial grounds for an indefinite period, with the consequent loss of revenue; and secondly, that cremation is a cleaner and a more expeditious method, and as such, a necessity in the interests of the public health.

It is the latter which appeals to the majority of those who prefer incineration to the thought of bodies rotting in a grave.

Before dealing with what we may term the "spiritual" side of the matter, let us see what reply the defenders of earth burial give to the challenge of the cremationists, "that the interment of bodies in the earth is necessarily dangerous to the living."

Dr. Brouardel, the eminent French authority,

CREMATION, EMBALMING

who had spent the greater part of his life in the study of various aspects of death, gives the following, based on the result of exhaustive experiments: "I believe that when coffins are placed from five to six and a half feet deep, and covered with earth, the hydrogen and hydrocarbons which are given off during decomposition are absorbed by the thickness of the earth," [1] a result which is consistent with general experience.

As a reply to the argument that a large and valuable area of ground is locked up and rendered profitless by its use as cemeteries and burial grounds, the critic Amédée Latour said, that "had cremation been the accepted form of disposal since the time of Socrates, humanity would have died out long since, as a result of cold brought about by the destruction of all the available combustible materials."

To this, Marini, the exponent of cremation, objects that whilst it might have been so had the old funeral pyre been used, modern methods render anything of the kind impossible.

Even from the strictly utilitarian point of view, there are very reasonable objections to be raised against the practice of cremation, when we consider how much of our knowledge of the past is derived from what we have discovered in the graves of the ancients—how great would have been our loss had the funeral fires swept everything before them, leaving us at the most a few urns full of unprofitable ashes.

But a still stronger argument against cremation is the very great incentive it affords to crime.

Sir Henry Thompson realized this, and he suggested an expedient as a means of overcoming the difficulty which is hardly convincing.

Dr. Brouardel and Benham, "Death and Sudden Death."

Two carboys were to be supplied, one in which the stomach would be preserved, and a second to be provided for the intestines in case the interests of justice necessitated a post-mortem examination being made for poison. The suggestion is ridiculous, and in practice open to fraud. As to the sanitary side of the question—the less said about it the better.

It was probably with a view to preventing crime that stringent laws were in force against cremation, till recently modified by the insistence of the pioneers of the modern movement.

In France it was illegal till the year 1889, when it was allowed under certain restrictions. The safeguard provided against foul play is absurd.

Two doctors have to view the corpse before incineration, and give a certificate of death to the authorities—a precaution which is ridiculed by Dr. Brouardel as hopelessly inadequate without an analysis which is not even suggested by French law, and certainly could not be insisted upon in general practice.

The first serious experiments in modern cremation were carried out by Brunetti in Italy in the year 1869. The apparatus bearing his name was exhibited in Vienna in 1873, the process being conducted in the open.

A later contrivance invented by Siemens was of the closed type.

We shall not be surprised to find that Germany was early in the field, having erected an apparatus in Gotha in the year 1878. Between the years 1887 and 1906 nearly every country in Europe had erected a crematorium.

The French installed the Gorini furnaces, a municipal venture first used for the destruction of anatomical parts from the hospitals and later for

(Reproduced by kind permission of the Trustees of the British Museum).
AN EGYPTIAN COFFIN. COVER OF COFFIN OF PENSENSEN-HERU FROM THEBES, XXVI DYNASTY, B.C. 500.

(Reproduced by kind permission of the Cremation Society of England).
A MODERN CREMATORIUM.
VIEW OF THE COLUMBARIUM AT ST. JOHN'S, WOKING.

CREMATION, EMBALMING

those who had died of smallpox. The first building erected disgusted the art-loving Parisian who likened it to a "dust destructor" or "sewage farm," for it certainly compared very unfavourably with the English efforts at Woking.

In the early forms of incineration, the body placed on the pyre was literally roasted by the flames, and reduced to a cinder.

The first scientific efforts were in the direction of the forming of a *wall* of flame, covering but not touching the body. In its perfected state, a light pine shell is provided in which the body reposes wrapped in a flannel shroud. The coffin is placed on a platform during the funeral service, at the conclusion of which, mechanism set in motion by a lever in the chapel, carries the coffin out of sight of those present on its way to the furnace, where coffin and body are soon reduced to ashes by the intensity of the heat.

To burn a special form of furnace-coke in a forced draught is a very different and much less costly matter than the old method of burning wood, as used by the ancients. If a sufficient demand existed to keep the modern type of furnace at the proper temperature, the cost of a cremation need not exceed half a crown.

The first cremation at Woking took place on March 26th, 1885, the "Gorini" furnace being used.

The first "subject" was a woman, a fact which appears to have been overlooked by the leaders of the "Woman's Movement," for purposes of propaganda, and to whom the writer respectfully commends it.

Three years later, nearly a hundred bodies had been dealt with, and the accommodation was improved by the erection of further buildings.

The necessary funds in the early days of the movement in England were subscribed by a few ardent reformers, amongst whom the Dukes of Bedford and Westminster took a large share of the financial responsibilities. The Duke of Bedford provided a private crematorium for the exclusive use of his family, which was first used at his own death in 1891.

In France, any person of age has the right to dispose of his or her body by will to be either buried or cremated as they may desire. These instructions are legally binding on the executors, who render themselves liable to a considerable fine in the event of non-compliance. This opens up an interesting point, for very strong views are commonly held on the matter.

In this country a person ceases to have any legal control of his body at the moment of death, so that one wishing to be cremated or buried as the case may be, whose relatives are likely to take an opposite view of the matter, must resort to a trick.

Property should be left in these circumstances to those responsible for the disposal of the body, *conditionally* upon the wishes expressed being faithfully fulfilled.

A good story illustrating the point was told by the late Sir Benjamin Richardson—one of the early advocates of cremation.

An old gentleman called on Sir Benjamin one day. He stated that he had been so much impressed by what he had read on the subject that he most earnestly desired that his body should be cremated at his death, but his family would not hear of such a thing. In these circumstances he begged Sir Benjamin to consent to act as executor in order that his wishes might be carried out. Sir Benjamin explained the legal position, and suggested his visitor should leave a large sum of money to the cremation society in the event of objections being raised by his daughter, who would otherwise receive his fortune.

Shortly after this interview the old gentleman died. Almost immediately Sir Benjamin received a visit from a clergyman, who said he had heard of his father-in-law's peculiar desire to be cremated, but he was sorry to say he could not allow this to take place as both he and his wife held very strong views on the subject. Sir Benjamin Richardson observed " that of course if it was really against the wishes of the family he could do nothing to prevent them disposing of the body by burial, but," he added, " as a matter of fact, I'm jolly glad, for in that case my society will benefit to the extent of something like ten thousand pounds." This unexpected announcement produced the desired effect.

On the following day Sir Benjamin received a letter from the clergyman, who wrote that after due consideration the family had decided that as it would be a greater sin to allow the money to go to the society they withdrew all opposition to the cremation of their relative's remains.[1]

It has been stated that from the earliest times to the present the voice of the Christian Church has ever been emphatically raised against any form of cremation. It is true that since its introduction into this country less than fifty years ago a number of the laity and even the clergy of the Established Church, as also those of various other Protestant bodies, have submitted to this form of disposal, but they have done so as a matter of individual preference and on the strength of a personal opinion. They have ignored, not

[1] *The Observer*, October 15th, 1916.

denied, what history makes so perfectly and indisputably clear, that since the inception of Christianity it has been not only a non-Christian practice but one that was strictly forbidden. In dealing with the Christian standpoint we must therefore differentiate, without making any invidious distinction, between those who without denying a tradition hold an individual opinion, and act as their private inclination dictates, and those who place the Christian tradition before their individual preferences. Generally speaking, however, the advocates and supporters of the modern crematorium are those who, for want of a better term, may be described as "free thinkers."

Superficially, the reason why the Early Church objected to the funeral pyre is that the body of its Founder was buried, but this in itself can hardly be called a logical reason. Traditionally, the body was not buried in the earth, as we bury, but walled up in a sepulchre, according to the manner of the Jews.

We have considered reasons given by early Christian writers for such common funeral practices as the ceremonious washing of the dead, "because this was done to the body of our Lord." In view of the fact that these were customs of Jewish origin we must trace them further back than the Christian era if we wish to know something more about them. The Jews notoriously acted in all matters affecting personal cleanliness and hygiene with an extraordinary discernment.

How great was the horror of cremation among the Jews is clear from the fact that the burning of the body was added to the death penalty as a final indignity, much in the same manner as a felon was condemned at one time by the laws of our

CREMATION, EMBALMING 225

own country, first to be hanged, then drawn and quartered.

The burning of the body of Saul might seem to be a remarkable exception to the rule, but the immediate circumstances must be taken into account. In the first place, Saul died by his own hand, and secondly, his mutilated remains were secured only by a dangerous expedient from the victorious Philistines.[1] In this case, if we follow the narrative, we shall find a strong supposition that the remains were thus destroyed by fire as the only means of saving them from greater indignities. The matter is still further elucidated by the fact that the burning of the body was held to account for the three years of famine in the time of David.

Modern orthodox Jews oppose cremation as "not in consonance with the spirit of Judaism." Dr. Herman Adler, the Chief Rabbi of Great Britain, pronounced it "a violation of Jewish laws."

More liberal minds have held that it is the duty of a Rabbi to officiate if asked to do so at the funeral of a co-religionist, rather than to refuse on the grounds that cremation is an anti-Jewish practice. Others would give their services as ministers of religion, but retire before the actual cremation. Such instances are, however, quite modern and notable as exceptions only.

The Jews, believing that the stages of decay in the grave were experienced as physical pain by the deceased as an atonement for sins, might very well hesitate to commit their remains to the flames.[2]

A Jew recently deceased, left a remarkably unorthodox provision in his will, insisting amongst

---
[1] I Samuel xxxi. 12.
[2] "Jewish Encyclopædia.

P

other things that he should be cremated and the ashes cast to the winds without any religious ceremony or memorial.

A representative of the *Daily News*, wishing to learn the attitude of the Jewish community on the matter, approached the Chevra Kadisha, one of the leading Jewish societies connected with the rites of the dead. Here he learned that "the Society has on several occasions deprecated cremation as opposed to the sentiment and spirit of Judaism."

It would seem, therefore, that whether the Christian merely adopted the Jewish custom *because* it was Jewish, and despised cremation because it was pagan—or if they disposed of the body of their Founder in the Jewish manner for some separate reason—the fact remains that neither Jews nor Christians can be cremated without violating the most ancient and sacred traditions of their respective beliefs.

That such reasons will not deter many professing either faith from so disposing of their bodies goes without saying.

The revival of psychic investigation came much into vogue about the same time as scientific cremation. The growth of this cult has been very remarkable, and it may be interesting to note what the modern occultist has to say about the matter. Amongst a lot of contradictory experiences we gather that it is generally held that the spiritual counterpart or personality does not leave the body for a considerable time after death, and that it is attached meanwhile to the seats of the emotions by a cord visible to those who are psychic. Any violent interruption of the slow processes of nature is therefore harmful. In this connection it is interesting to remember that the Jews did not seal the sepulchre after the dead had

CREMATION, EMBALMING 227

been deposited there till three days after death had taken place, during which time the relatives constantly visited the tomb hoping that signs of returning life might be manifested.

In the ancient world the Egyptians are credited with a very special knowledge of occult matters, and they performed very many most elaborate rites for the dead, with which the Israelites became familiar, having learnt embalming from them. To this nation incineration was utterly opposed to their traditional practices.

Without any attempt to dogmatize on a subject about which really very little is defined, even a superficial study of the question of cremation will show us that this method of disposal is certainly not a *necessity* from the sanitary point of view. That it introduced a certain element of danger in the hands of the criminal, and that it is directly opposed to western practice and tradition.

It may be said in favour of cremation that it is both quick and cleanly, and that it dispenses with the necessity of burial grounds. In its place we have the " columbary " or dove-cot, so called from the niches or pigeon holes it provides for the cinerary urns containing the ashes. These receptacles, which may be hired for a term of years, take up so little space that it would be difficult to spend any large sums of money on their adornment.

In this matter they certainly have an advantage over the grave. As a rule a marble lining and a bronze grille enclosing the aperture is the sum total of extravagance. Needless to add that in most cases the vulgarity and shoddy ugliness peculiar to the undertaker's works has left its impress on the urn and casket. The inscription is invariably lettered in the worst possible style, or perhaps more correctly in no style at all.

Here and there, as the eye wanders over row upon row of niches, an exception may be found, designed perhaps by an artist, and not selected from the catalogue of the trader.

With such exceptions, by far the best receptacles are those which are either actual replicas of, or designs based on the ancient Greek or Roman examples found in the catacombs and elsewhere.

Undoubtedly the revival of cremation has necessitated the reconsideration of many funeral practices, and it might be reasonably hoped that " grave goods " would have been abolished amongst other things.

This unfortunately is not the case, for it is quite common to find in the niches sentimental offerings for the solace of the departed spirit—if for any other purpose what is the object of placing it in or near the urn, photographs of relations, artificial flowers, favoured volumes of poetry and other personal trifles?

In view of the fact that the Dismal Trader has been responsible for conserving from one generation to another the rags and tatters of pagan survivals, it may be interesting to inquire what are the views of the modern undertaker on the subject of cremation, but let him speak for himself. The following is an extract from a letter written by an undertaker to the editor of the *Undertaker's Journal:*

" Has the undertaker considered the value of cremation from the commercial point of view? Looking it straight in the face, I think if it became more general the undertakers would not be required to supply much in the way of '*beautiful caskets,*'

CREMATION, EMBALMING

and possibly at times the crudest and cheapest form of coffin would be used to convey the body to the crematorium. If such is the case," he continues, "the undertakers are acting in a most noble and unselfish manner in advocating cremation, or they have failed to realize the importance from this point and possibly have never considered the value of embalming."

Here, then, we have a frank and unvarnished admission of a fact that cannot be too widely recognized, namely, that the undertaker is a tradesman, and as such we must expect him to "push" the line which brings in most grist to his mill, and as long as the public is foolish enough to be gulled by his "pinkings and prickets" he is going to provide them—naturally!

Before leaving the subject of cremation there is one little matter which seems worth attention.

When the dramatic moment arrives for the coffin to pass from the sight of the mourners on its way to destruction, and before it goes forward to its fiery ordeal, the undertaker "behind the scenes" is given an opportunity to remove the "beautiful furniture" with which the coffin is provided.

The writer was informed by an undertaker that it was "generally hired," a fact which no doubt is always made *quite* clear to the distressed relatives when the funeral arrangements are made. But there seems a possibility of this little matter being forgotten as a case reported recently in the daily press seems to indicate. A lady saw a coffin-plate bearing her husband's name exhibited as an advertisement in the window of an undertaker, whom she promptly and successfully sued. This leads one to wonder what happens to the coffin or casket in similar circumstances. Cannot one imagine as the great craftsman contemplates the labour and artistry of his craft about to be ruthlessly and even needlessly committed to the flames, that he may desire to "snatch" from the burning, so to speak, the child of his creation, not overlooking, of course, to deduct its second-hand value from the bill.

We have seen the ancient practice of embalming recommended to the trade as a more profitable matter than cremation.

If we know anything at all of the activities of the modern undertaker we must have noted that the study of scientific embalming is receiving at the present time the greatest attention from all progressive members of the trade.

Even Canada has its "Embalmers' Association," and we find their annual convention being "opened with prayer," for prayer is, of course, more or less connected with the business, and the undertaker generally, and particularly the embalmer is a great stickler for niceties, as the following quotations will show.

A gentleman described as a Professor,[1] in speaking on the subject of embalming, urges the necessity of a close attention to detail. For instance, he advises that "the body should be laid in a *comfortable* position in the casket." "Everything just exactly as you would like to have it done for one of your own family," he advises. In order to demonstrate the point he gives us an instance within his own experience of neglect in such matters. It appears that a young friend of the Professor had died unexpectedly "in the East," the body being embalmed and forwarded to him, presumably for burial. The embalming seems to

[1] *The Undertakers' Journal*, October 15th, 1913.

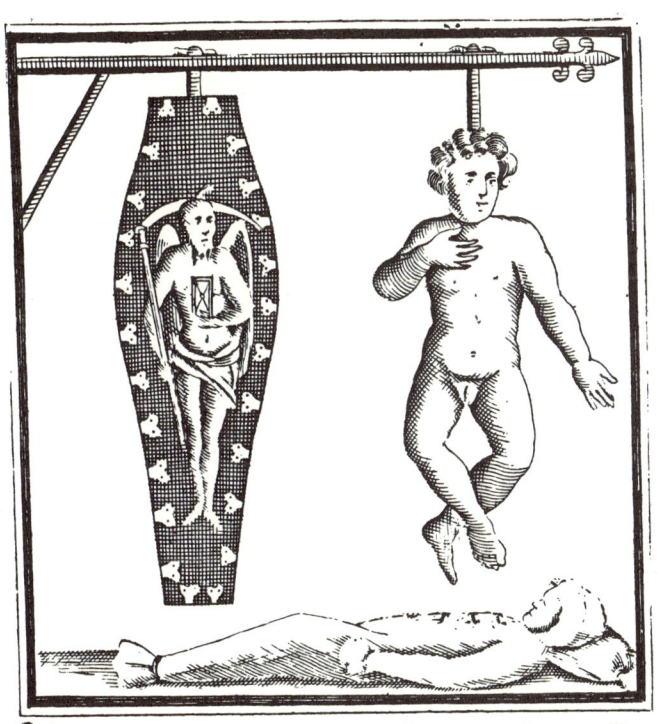

At ÿ lower Corner of Fleet lane at ÿ Signe of ÿ Naked Boy & Coffin you may be Accomodated wth all things for a Funeral as well ÿ meanest as those of greater Ability upon Reasonable Terms more particularly Coffins shrou^d Palls Cloaks Sconces Stans Hangings for Rooms Heraldry Hearse & Coaches Gloves nth all other things not here mentioned by W^m. Grinly Coffin Maker.

UNDERTAKER'S SIGN AND ADVERTISEMENT
(Eighteenth century).

have satisfied an expert examination, but other things were most irregular. "They had put a suit on him," we are told, "but the trousers were turned up"—evidently not the permanent turn up so often recommended by the tailor, "for straw and stuff" were disclosed in the folds. Moreover, the clothes had not been brushed, "Fortunately," says the Professor, "the body came to my establishment, but *suppose it had gone home first!*" There were other marks of carelessness exhibited in this particular instance, which were, no doubt, put right with a generous hand.

"I don't object to spraying the casket and lining with some nice perfume in order to get the odour of flowers instead of the odour of death," he continues, and one cannot help wondering if there must be an odour of some kind, if the honest and homely smell of carbolic or some other clean disinfectant would not be preferable to a choice blend of corpse and camellias recommended by the Professor.

What is there to be said for or against embalming? From the point of view of the trade it has no doubt very much to commend it, for you can sell your richest, most beautiful casket and obtain in addition a liberal fee for embalming.

In cases where a body is brought from a distance, certainly some such sanitary methods might be usefully employed, but we have still to be convinced that there is any circumstance or combination of circumstances where the removal of a body from the place where death occurs is either necessary or advisable.

CHAPTER XIII

IN MEMORIAM

" They shall not grow old, as we that are left grow old,
Age shall not weary them, nor the years condemn
At the going down of the sun, and in the morning
We will remember them."
—*Lawrence Binyon.*[1]

In dealing with the subject of this chapter, important as it is, to some extent it is outside the general purpose of this book, which properly ends with the consideration of burial. The writer claims and hopes to have demonstrated the fact that the funeral traditions to which we unreasonably and tenaciously cling are not dictated by our religious beliefs, and only approach them in those cases where obviously pagan or Jewish customs have been made use of by the churches, as a means of expressing a Christian sentiment.

From the earliest times, and by people widely divided in their mode of life and their beliefs in a future spiritual existence, the special care for the well-being of the soul after death has been a primary consideration.

What is generally referred to as the "worship of the dead" is one of the primitive instincts.

To speak of *worship* in this sense, is, however, misleading, for it is possible to correctly place a variety of widely different interpretations on the

---

[1] Lawrence Binyon, "For the Fallen."

word, which expresses anything from the "paying of *divine* honours" to "treating with *civil* reverence." What is the sense of the word in the marriage service, for instance, "with my body I thee *worship?*"

History offers many examples of the "worship of the dead" in either of these senses, and in various shades of intermediate reasoning.

The ancient cult of ancestor worship gave a special significance to the virtues of family life, for it placed a serious load of responsibility upon the children of the future generation, to carry forward not only the traditions of the family to which they belonged, but also to tend lovingly and faithfully in varying fortune the spiritual and even temporal necessities of those who had gone before them. Ancestor worship is, moreover, directly associated with the special privileges and responsibilities of the first-born son, who assumed with his inheritance certain definite duties, nor were these duties a pledge of sentiment only. Further, it alone explains many of our present-day notions concerning succession.

It was the duty of the first-born son to tend and protect the graves of his ancestors, supplying food and performing many elaborate ceremonies. In another chapter we have dealt with food offerings and sacrifices founded on the belief that the spiritual counterpart at least of the material substance offered was necessary in order to protect the soul from actual starvation.

The practice is still general in the East to-day, whilst the enlightened West continues the superstition as long as it is content to sacrifice "offerings" of costly exotic flowers to wither and perish with a few hours' exposure at the graveside.

What we have chiefly to consider now is the

offering of *prayers* for the welfare of the departed souls, and to trace the history of this very general usage.

The first thing that must strike an unprejudiced mind is the fact that like the Eastern food offerings, either prayers are—or they are not—absolutely necessary to the departed spirits. Was the welfare or the existence of the soul imperilled, whose children neglected to provide the food offering? Either it starved or it did not, there could be no half measures.

Does the soul whose relatives neglect or refuse prayers for its repose and spiritual welfare suffer in any way as a direct consequence of this neglect? Either it does or it does not—once again, there can be no half measures.

When we study the special festivals for the commemoration of the dead we shall find a strange counterpart of the feasts of "All Souls" and "All Saints," and moreover, timed in the same month, and frequently on the same day as the Christian festivals.

Haliburton tells us that the festival of the dead or feast of ancestors is now, or was formerly observed at or near the beginning of November by the Peruvians, the Hindus, the Pacific Islanders, the people of the Tonga Islands, the Australians, the ancient Persians, the ancient Egyptians and the northern nations of Europe, and continued for three days amongst the Japanese, the Hindus, the Australians, ancient Romans and the ancient Egyptians. The month of November was formerly called in Persia "the month of the Angel of Death."

With regard to the Peruvian festivities of the dead, he writes: "The month in which it occurs, says Rivers, is called Aya Marca, from Aya a corpse, and Marca 'carrying in arms,' because

IN MEMORIAM

they celebrated the solemn festival of the dead with tears and lugubrious songs and plaintive music, and it was customary to visit the tombs of relations and to leave food and drink, and this on the same day as the Christian festival (November 2nd). In Mexico the festival of the dead was held on November 17th, and a human victim was offered up to avert the dread calamity believed to be impending over the human race."[1]

The Corsicans slaughtered oxen at the grave, giving the meat to their neighbours in honour of the dead. Bread, wine and meat were thus distributed, whilst in modern times bread and wine are served to the poor in this manner on the anniversary of the death of those who can afford to do so, and *particularly on the feast of the dead, November 1st*.[2]

Garnier says that "in Rome the festival of the dead, or Feralia (called Dii Manes or 'The day of the spirits of the dead'), commenced on February 17th, corresponding also to the 17th day of the second month."[3] Many other instances could be quoted.

In some countries it is believed that on the special day set apart in honour of the dead, the spirits return for the occasion in order to be once more with their friends.

In Japan on this festival, little boats made of straw and paper are placed on the water in order that the souls may thus be conveyed to their relations.

In Brittany a plate of pancakes is provided for their entertainment, but the ghostly visitors must not linger too long over their meal, for they

---

[1] R. G. Haliburton, "The Year of the Pleiades."
[2] J. E. Rossi, "Les Corses."
[3] J. Garnier, "Worship of the Dead."

are bound to return to the spirit world before cockcrow.[1]

The Serbians give their dead a special entertainment on the occasion of the Feast of their Patron Saint George (May 6th, orthodox calendar). It is a time of much rejoicing, and is accompanied by a great slaughtering of animals, which are roasted on spits in the open air. The graves are decked with flowers in profusion, whilst the choicest dainties are also placed there for the delectation of the honoured dead.

This is an ancient pagan ceremony of ancestor worship which, since Christian times, has been respectably hidden beneath the cloak of St. George.

What is the fate, we may ask, of those unfortunate souls who by disaster or mischance have failed to secure a resting-place in the burial grounds, and are therefore likely to be left out in the cold in these annual rejoicings—the patriot, for instance, dying for his country on some foreign field of battle—how is he to be provided with material or spiritual refreshment?

Such a fate was more dreaded by the ancients than the most violent means of death. It was even used as a form of final insult and degradation after the worst that could be inflicted on the poor wretch's body had been done. It was a revenge more horrible than the "drawing and quartering" of the body which once expressed the last word in contempt and hatred in this country.

An Act passed as a result of the rising in Scotland in the year 1745, and not repealed till 1772, necessitated the taking of a very binding oath against the carrying of arms. It is interesting as showing the horror expressed at *that* time

[1] A. Mauricet, "L'isle aux moines ses mœurs et ses habetants."

of the thought of a non-Christian burial. "If I do so (carry arms, etc.), may I be cursed in my undertakings, family and property—may I never see my wife and children, father, mother or relations—may I be killed in battle as a coward, *and lie without Christian burial in a strange land, far from the graves of my forefathers and kindred* —may all this come across me if I break my oath."[1]

The cenotaph or empty tomb of which many of our memorials are a remnant, was erected when the body lay elsewhere, in order that due honours might be paid to the dead.

We are reminded how the vanquished Hector begged upon his knees—not for his life—but that his body might not be given to the dogs. "Take the gold my father will offer you," he supplicates, "that I may have *honour* at the funeral pyre." The thought that his body should be chopped and hewn by "The Seller-of-the-Dead" and weighed against its weight in gold held no terrors to his mind compared with a dishonoured sepulture.

First in the pagan mind was the apprehension of an endless torment, of neglect at the tomb, hunger, thirst and helplessness.

How touching, too, is the old story of the parents of the dead Athenian soldiers, who, dressed in mourning garments, clamoured before the Council—and not in vain—for the execution of the victorious general, despite the fact that he had returned a victor—had indeed saved Athens from the spoilers—in his haste to claim his laurels he had left the dead unburned on the field of battle. To appreciate the story we must remember that the Greeks committed the bodies of the slain to the flames of the funeral pyre *on* the battlefield, the bones being collected and brought back to

[1] Alfred Mark Webb, "The Heritage of Dress."

Athens with the utmost reverence, where with much solemnity, orations and processions they were provided with a fitting tomb.

Again we may ask what of the sailor who dies at sea?

The fisherfolk of Brittany have a picturesque custom to keep alive the memory of those poor fishermen of whom the sea yearly takes its heavy toll.

On receiving the news that a sailor had been drowned, the parents or nearest relatives constructed a cross of wood which they placed on the empty bed or on the family table; candles were lighted and placed round the cross, whilst the friends and relatives of the deceased were summoned to spend the night in the house, where prayers were said for his soul exactly as if the body were present. On the following day a procession was formed and the cross carried to where Mass was said. At an earlier period the cross which reposed on the altar during the ceremony was afterwards buried, but in more recent times it was deposited in an urn and left in the church till several other crosses were collected, when the whole were buried.

On All Saints' Day the womenfolk make a trip in the boats, and having sailed a certain distance from the shore they solemnly recite the "De Profundis" for their husbands, sons and brothers who have been drowned in earning a scanty livelihood, and whose bodies have not been recovered.

We cannot go very deeply into the custom of offering of prayers for the welfare of the dead without realizing that the practice presupposes some state other than the states of bliss, or of final condemnation. As far as the Christian standpoint is concerned it brings us to the highly controversial

IN MEMORIAM

question of the existence or non-existence of the intermediary realms of purgatory, where it is believed by the Greek and Roman Churches that the souls of the departed work out the results of their misdoings during their life upon earth, and here—and here only—can be helped by the intercession of their friends and relatives.

In the "Zuna" or holy book of the Moors (Mohammedan) we read that when a man dies two angels visit his grave, one bearing a rake and another a heavy iron weight. Presently a third angel appears and begins to question the dead man as to his mode of life. Did he give alms to the needy? Did he observe the various rites in connection with his religion? If these questions were answered to the satisfaction of the inquisitor then two attendants were summoned who were in robes of dazzling whiteness; one of these took the head of the corpse and the other the feet, and so lifting it from the grave they hold it in this manner till the Day of Judgment. If, on the other hand, the inquisitors were not satisfied with the replies to their questions, or had reason to suppose that the truth was being withheld, then he called to the angel who bore the iron weight with which the corpse was crushed back again into the grave "seven forearms deep." When this had been done the angel with the rake proceeded to drag the body up again, and so this unrestful process continues without cessation till the Judgment Day.

This crude conception of a purgatory necessitated a special form of tomb in which a tiled space was provided so that the corpse could kneel during its interrogation. It was further provided that the grave clothes were not fastened in such a manner as might restrict the movements of the body. Attached to the shroud was a letter written with saffron and salt water, by means of which an appeal was made to the Angel of Justice that the corpse might altogether escape or at least have a speedy release from the purgatorial pains.[1]

The ancient Egyptians preserved the body in the belief that in a space of three or four thousand years the soul would return to inhabit its earthly form once more. In the meantime it was thought to wander through a series of incarnations in the shape of the lower animals, which for this reason are not killed for food.

In view of the fact that the early Christians adopted such Jewish customs as the anointing of the body because this was done traditionally with the body of their Founder, it is interesting, before examining the Christian tradition, to ascertain if the Jews themselves believed that prayers for the dead were effective or necessary.

"As the well-known passage in the second book of Machabeus (2 Mach. xii. 44-46) abundantly proves," says Thurston, " the idea of a resurrection and the belief that the time of that resurrection might be accelerated by the intercession of the living was present to the minds of some at least of the Jews in the first or second century *before* the Christian era." The sacred writer states in unmistakable terms that, " If he (Judas Machabeus) had not hoped that they that were slain should rise again it would have seemed superfluous and vain to pray for the dead. . . . It is therefore a holy and wholesome thought to pray for the dead that they may be loosed from their sins."

" It may be said that the prayer known as the Kaddish is now commonly considered by the Jews to have the power of releasing the soul

[1] Guichard, " Funérailles."

IN MEMORIAM

of the deceased from punishment in the next world."

A curious case came before the Whitechapel County Court (1916). A Jew, whose aunt had lent the sum of £47 to a builder, sued him for the repayment of the loan on which a few instalments had been returned before the death of the lender. The defence was put forward that it had been agreed that in the event of death any balance of the loan then due was to be cancelled on the understanding that the borrower should say prayers for the repose of her soul. This unique agreement was said to have been made in the presence of witnesses, who " crossed hands " over the covenant. For the plaintiff it was claimed that prayers *purchased* were not considered as of value by the Jews, and that the builder in order to cover his debt, would have had to pray for nearly a year.

This incident, however, clearly shows that praying for the dead is still a Jewish custom.

Thurston gives some interesting particulars of early Christian practices. He says:

" The earliest unmistakable example of Christian prayers for the dead is probably that afforded by the famous Abercius monument, discovered some years ago at Hieropolos, in Upper Phrygia, by Sir William Ramsay. The significant part of the inscription which alludes allegorically to many of the most distinctive mysteries of the Christian faith, terminates with the line—' That the fellow-believer who understands these words, pray for Abercius.' " [1]

Here is another of the *third* century. The broken slab containing it is now in the Christian Museum of the Lateran.

[1] Herbert Thurston, S.J., " The Memory of our Dead."

" To sweet Lucifera, my wife all sweetness,
  To her husband nought remains but deepest grief,
  But she has surely merited to have an epitaph set up to her,
  That whoso of the Brotherhood who read it may pray to God
  That he take to Himself her holy and innocent soul." [1]

It should be remembered that whilst the early Christians made a special point of celebrating the anniversaries and the festivals of the Saints and the departed generally, they did not think it necessary to mark the actual year of the decease, so that it is often rendered very difficult to trace the period.

There seems to be abundant evidence that from the earliest days of Christianity prayers for the dead were a common practice, as they are to-day, in the Roman, Greek and other Churches throughout the world.

In our own country, the Established Church definitely repudiates the existence of the spiritual state of purgatory or place of purification, and therefore also the value of prayer as helpful to the dead.

The authoritative decrees of the various denominations merely denote the position of each.

The Catholic view was defined by the Council of Trent, viz., " That there is a purgatory and that the souls there detained are assisted by the suffrages of the Faithful, but ' especially by the most acceptable sacrifice at the altar ' " (i.e., the Mass).

In pre-Reformation days this doctrine was responsible for the erection of many churches, the foundations of many charities and the support of the chantry and the chantry priest. The chantry

---

[1] Herbert Thurston, S.J., " The Memory of our Dead."

chapels were built as a memorial of the founder, where the priest frequently said various offices for the dead and celebrated a special Mass on the anniversaries of the founder and his family, and distributed alms to the poor.

Ditchfield says, " There were in England about two thousand chantries, founded chiefly in the fourteenth and fifteenth centuries, which were all despoiled by Henry VIII and Edward VI at the Reformation, on the grounds that they were devoted to 'superstitious' purposes. Much of the wealth was the property of the poor left to them by pious benefactors."[1]

The Established Church holds that purgatory and therefore prayers for the dead cannot be supported by the Scriptures. This position is defined in the twenty-second Article of Faith, to which all her clergy subscribe, which reads, " The Romish doctrine concerning purgatory is a fond thing, vainly invented, and grounded upon no warranty of Scripture, but rather repugnant to the Word of God."

However, there appears to be a tendency amongst a certain section of the clergy of the Church of England to-day to fall into line with the rest of Christendom in the belief not only of the existence of purgatory, but in the practice of praying for the souls of the departed.

At the Westminster Assembly of Divines in the year 1647 the Presbyterians put on record their belief in this matter, which may be held to be that of the Free Churches generally. Dealing with " the state of man after death " they assent in the belief of heaven and hell, and conclude, " besides these two places for souls separated from their bodies, the Scriptures acknowledge none."

[1] P. H. Ditchfield, " The Old-time Parson."

FUNERAL CUSTOMS

In the year 1645 the " Directory for the Public Worship of God " decreed " concerning the burial of the dead, and because the custom of kneeling down and praying by or towards the dead corpse, and other such usages in the place where it lies, before it be carried to burial, are superstitions, and for that praying, reading and singing, both in going to and at the grave, have been grossly abused and are in no way beneficial to the living, therefore let all such things be laid aside."

At the time of the Reformation the " Directory " made the further unmistakable protest to the older custom, " when any person departs this life, let the body be decently attended from the house to the place appointed for public burial and there immediately interred without any ceremony."

Let us now look at the festivals of All Saints and All Souls, which, as we have noted, appear in the Christian calendar at much the same time as they are celebrated by non-Christian peoples in various parts of the world.

All Saints' Day, November 1st, known also as All-Hallows' Day, was instituted in the year 837 by Pope Gregory IV to take the place of the much earlier festival of the Peace of the Martyrs.

All Souls' Day is said to have been instituted in the year 1048 by St. Odilo of Cluny. It is celebrated on November 2nd in addition to the feast of All Saints by the Roman and Greek Churches, for the special memory of the souls in purgatory. All-Hallows' Eve is still observed in many families by games and superstitions which are a relic of pre-Reformation times, when the eve of the festival of All Souls was welcomed by a great burning of fires on the hills, to attract the wandering spirits, and the ringing of bells.

In some parts of England the occasion is kept

MEMORIAL CARDS.

IN MEMORIAM

in mind by the children who sing from house to house, as they sing the Christmas carols:

" Soul, soul for a souling cake,
 I pray you, good missus, for a souling cake,
 Go down in your cellars and see what you can find,
 Your apples or your pears or your good red wine;
 If you ain't got a penny, a ha'penny will do,
 If you ain't got a ha'penny, then God bless you."

This request is followed by the customary " bang " of the knocker, as a reminder that a gift of some kind is expected. Needless to say, the modern child is simply " out for spoil," but in the old days the poor seriously collected in this manner the wherewithal to celebrate the *feast* of All Souls which was kept on the following day in good earnest, with a great consumption of cakes and " wassail " (a concoction of apples, sugar and spiced ale). " Soul-cakes " were baked for this occasion similar to the " soul-cakes " of Belgium, which are distributed to-day at the funeral repast.

The connection between this feast and the eating of apples calls to mind an interesting ceremony which was at one time common in Brittany, where the cult of the dead has ever been rigorously observed. On All Souls' Day in every parish several houses would be opened for the purposes of the festival, which was celebrated in the following manner:

A cake of bread was baked and placed on the kitchen table, which was covered with a " fair white cloth." Planted in the centre of the bread was a little tree, from the end of whose branches red apples were suspended. The whole was covered by a serviette.

The neighbours being assembled round the tree, the master of the house proceeded to recite the special prayers for the repose of the souls of the dead, to which the people made the customary responses. At the conclusion of the prayers, the serviette was lifted and the bread was cut into as many pieces as there were persons present to receive it. Each, as he took his portion, was expected to make a small payment. Should anyone withhold his money, it was believed that he would shortly meet with the greatest misfortunes, brought about by the revengeful spirits of his parents. The money so collected was given to the church in order that Masses might be said for the repose of the souls in purgatory. At night, the tree which had graced the ceremony was carried away with great respect by the person selected to act as host on the next anniversary. The apples might be eaten, but the tree was a sacred trust, to be tended with care till the following year, when a fresh supply of apples was provided.[1]

In the West of England, cider making commenced on All Saints' Day and for the reason that it was connected with the pagan autumn or fruit festival, for which the Christian Church substitutes the feast of the dead.

Under the name of "La Mas Ubhal," or "Apple Mass," it was at one time recognized in Ireland.

We may also trace a connection in the custom, which is hardly extinct in this country, for the farmer to give a supper to his men on All Saints' Day to mark the end of the wheat sowing. Tusser thus refers to the practice:

" Wife, sometime this week if ye weather hold clere,
And end of wheate sowing we make for the yeare,
Remember ye therefore, though I do not,
The seed cake, the pastries, the furmety pot." [2]

---

[1] De Braz, "La Légende de la Mort chez les Bretons."
[2] Tusser, "All Saints."

Let us see what traces exist in modern times of the ancient cult of ancestor worship.

In France, to-day, we still find the light-hearted Parisian lunching at the cemetery each year, on the occasion of the feast of the dead, and decorating the graves of his ancestors. A Catholic country and a Catholic practice, it may be said, yet we find the Welsh—staunch Protestants as they are—decorating their graves with flowers at the great November festival.

The "memorial card" still holds its own in this country as a necessary part of the funeral observances, though its original function, as a reminder to pray for the soul of the departed, may have been forgotten.

It sometimes happens on the Continent at carnival time that the gorgeous procession of fantastic revellers is confronted by a procession of quite another character—a passing funeral. At once a respectful silence hushes the noisy laughter. Instantly a hundred silly headgears are doffed, whilst with bent heads a prayer is muttered for the repose of the soul of the departed.

In our own streets, the roughest wayfarer—more often than men of other classes—pulls off his cap—perhaps a little self-consciously—when he meets the dead. Ask him why he does so, and he cannot tell you—"out of respect" he may answer, after thinking the matter over, possibly for the first time, for he is all unconscious that he is merely obeying a traditional impulse which has its roots in pre-Reformation piety.

The writer witnessed the following incident in a crowded London street.

Four soldiers, one a Belgian and three Englishmen, were standing on the kerb when a funeral passed by. The English Tommies gazed at the commonplace sight disinterestedly and continued to smoke; directly the Belgian caught sight of the procession, he clicked his heels and came smartly to attention, raising his hand to the "salute," and keeping it so till the hearse had passed. The English soldiers watched the little Belgian for a moment and first one, then two, followed by a hesitating third, cigarette dropped half-finished into the gutter.

Perhaps no more remarkable example could be found of the deeply rooted belief in the service due from the living to the dead, than the custom of erecting "war shrines" in the streets—a practice which became very general throughout the country after the war. Not content with the "roll of honour" which might reasonably be disassociated from any charge of worship, these "shrines" as they are commonly called (Nuttall defines a shrine as "a case, a reliquary, a tomb, a sacred place") are to be found as a rule outside a place of Protestant worship, where they have been erected by loving hands. A Crucifix is generally placed over the shrine, which is decorated with floral offerings. Lest we should misjudge the intention, let us take an extract from the daily press, which is largely responsible for the movement.

In an article in the *Evening News*, we read:

"Even now, many people may have but a hazy idea of what a 'war shrine' is. A 'war shrine' is a roll of honour, on the tablets of which the names of those who have gone from the street in which the shrine stands into the navy and the army, and those who have died for their country, are written. The frame contains a form of prayer for the men. There is a canopy of flags, and the whole is ornamented by flowers, laid fresh upon

IN MEMORIAM

the shrine by the wives and children, sisters and sweethearts who stand in silent prayer for the heroes for a few moments every day." [1]

To suggest that these war shrines are a public rejection of the Protestant doctrine on the subject of prayer for the dead would be to overstate the case, nor is there necessarily any intention shown in this surely very beautiful innovation to return to Catholic and pre-Reformation practices, but that it points to a deeply inherent desire to bridge the gulf, which has in this country separated the living from the dead, is equally incontestable. The " war shrines " would certainly have shocked the narrow views held even one generation ago.

Every year adds to the number of those who for one reason or another prefer to remain outside the sphere of the generally recognized Christian denominations, but who by no means accept the views of the materialist. It is always interesting to follow the trend of their inquiries, and we shall do well to study their views where we find them definitely expressed. What, for instance, have they to say who are unbound by traditional doctrine on such a subject as the utility or otherwise of prayers for the dead?

From an article on the subject contributed to the *International Psychic Gazette*, we quote the following :

" Side by side with the enlarged views of life advanced by the new theology, we have ever multiplying instances of the ability of some gifted persons to act as mediums for communicating with the unseen world. Everything of this nature must

[1] *Evening News*, October 6th, 1916.

tend to raise the question—can we by our sympathy and prayers do anything to help departed souls along the path of progress we believe it is their destiny to tread? Will our prayers for them avail to bring them the help they need? I have not the slightest hesitation in answering these questions in the affirmative, for my own experiences leave me without a shadow of doubt."

The writer of the article then proceeds to relate personal experiences resulting from a mission he was called upon to undertake "from the Unseen," to help "unprogressed souls in the Unseen" who were *brought* to him for the purpose. He describes the state after death where he tells us all souls progressed, or unprogressed, make a stay according to their individual necessities, in which they learn the lessons they should have learned on earth before going on to a higher existence, and he adds " it is these unprogressed ones who want all the sympathy and help their friends on earth can give them." Further, he quotes a story said to have been related to him " by one of the clergy of St. Peter's, London Docks, of a woman who had recently passed away appearing to reproach a district visitor for a forgotten promise to pray for her soul, a fact afterwards verified by notes." [1]

Not only at the time of death, but on the anniversary of the event, and on special festivals and occasions of family importance, it has been the custom to honour the dead in various ways.

The anniversary has always been celebrated with certain formalities, a curious method being the "chime-barrel," the prototype of the barrel

[1] Thomas Atwood, " Prayers for the Departed," *International Psychic Gazette*, November, 1913.

organ, on which a dirge is played from street to street in order that the neighbours might not forget to offer their prayers for the repose of the soul of those whose memory was thus kept green.

In Brittany even the betrothal ceremony was blessed by the departed ancestral spirits, an instance of the intimate relations which tied the "quick and the dead."

It was the proper thing for the lover to send a message to plead the cause with the father of his beloved. This was done in verse, which after setting forth the qualifications of the suitor and the depths of his passionate devotion to the lady, ended thus: "the benediction of the dead of your family I cannot ask, because in so doing I should render sad the many loving hearts; better is it, therefore, to pray for their souls, and I beg of you to join me in saying a song for their repose." The song having been said, the "De Profundis" was recited, after which the parents would give or withhold their consent to the union as circumstances might dictate. It was believed that if this ceremony should be omitted the spirits of the slighted ancestors would surely avenge themselves on the bride.

Whilst on the subject of marriage we are reminded of a present-day custom. In the Roman Catholic church a coin, the symbol of worldly possession, with which the bridegroom promises to "thee endow," is afterwards treasured all her life by the bride in order that it may eventually be given back to the church for Masses to be said for whoever dies first, the husband or the wife.

To hold that the question of the value of prayers for the dead is merely one of personal opinion seems unreasonable, for the intercession of the living is either of vital importance or superstitious and useless. It is, however, a matter in which each must act according to his lights, and perhaps the brief outline which is all that it has been possible to give in considering the whole aspect of our funeral customs, may serve at least to remind those who have never given any thought to the matter of the importance of this controversial problem.

CHAPTER XIV

MEMORIALS, EPITAPHS, RINGS AND MOURNING CARDS

At a time when a lavish expenditure on "memorials" of various kinds has taken place, we shall do well if we consider the origin of a very old custom.

When we have stripped any one of our funeral observances of its crape and tinsel—those grave-clothes of convention in which they have been preserved and embalmed—we shall find very little that is worthy of continuance.

Any excessive manifestation of grief is the outcome of self-pity and disbelief in a spiritual existence. The wearing of "doole," the funeral procession and other such ceremonial observances, have their origin in a vulgar pride of estate and an inherited dread of revengeful spirits.

So, too, we shall find that a passion for erecting memorials to all and sundry has little more to commend it.

In the early days of commercial prosperity in this country we have seen how the successful trader hustled his spiritual or social superior in the graveyard to such an extent that he fled for sanctuary into the neighbouring churches; nor was he allowed to remain long in this favoured position before the wealthy merchant bought *his* way in also.

Pushed to extremity with the trader in full cry, a chase ensued round the walls of the church to the final place of privilege at the very steps of the altar, where saint and sinner could do no more than mingle their dust. Yet there was a further opportunity for self-aggrandizement, and we may be assured that it was not neglected. Competition started in the erection of elaborate memorials. Every degree of society went one better than its predecessors, whilst those who remained crowded out in the burying places, not to be outdone in their desire for a public recognition of the achievements of their dead, gradually left the simple green mounds which had sufficiently covered the more worthy remains of their ancestors, and on a rising tide of prosperity advanced step by step from wood to stone, and from stone to marble, building monuments larger and more vulgar and ostentatious each time that Nature provided them with the opportunity of exalting the family name.

To see this madness at its climax we have to go no farther than the nearest cemetery, packed with columns, pillars, crosses, urns and railings, as closely as the bristles on the back of a hedgehog.

For paucity of invention, vulgarity of conception and feeble craftsmanship—for lack of effect, collective or individual, for unsuitability and costliness—it cannot be outdone. Perhaps there is nothing which we shall hand down to future generations more utterly damning to our intelligence or artistic pretensions than the enduring monuments we have erected to our dead.

We find the early Christian Church building shrines in which to preserve the venerated remains of her saints and martyrs, and we may be sure that the saints and the martyrs would be the very last to make provision for any such memorial to their

MEMORIALS, EPITAPHS, RINGS

own honour. At the most they would have desired a small stone, asking for the prayers of the faithful.

The object that the Church had in view was to perpetuate the memory of those of her community whose life was recognized as full of virtues, and as such, worthy of emulation.

In like manner the Romans perpetuated the memory of their great warriors and citizens.

This was all very admirable as long as it was regulated by an authority competent to judge to whom posthumous honours should be paid.

The King inherits with his office the power to confer titles, and to raise the commoner to the ranks of nobility. We can well imagine if the right to confer such honours was common to all who considered that the dignity of their family justified the distinction, then, in a very short time, we should all be lords or dukes, and such titles would cease to have any special significance. The abuse of the once honourable title of esquire is an example.

In this manner the erection of a memorial for the perpetuation of a name without any authority, stands for nothing more than the personal and biased opinion of an individual who has enough money to gratify the pretensions of his family.

In pre-Reformation days we find large sums of money spent to keep green the memory of the dead, but in a spirit of humility rather than of self-advertisement.

Those, indeed, who had committed some outrage on society were often the first to lavish money on memorials of one sort or another, in order to gain the prayers of such as would benefit by their liberality.

" Pray for the soul of —— " is the perpetual

FUNERAL CUSTOMS

form of inscription in stone or brass on the tombstones in the Middle Ages. Munificence in the provision of mourning garments, jewellery, gifts of money, food and the foundation and endowment of churches, chapels and charitable institutions was at one time very common, for it claimed as a first consideration the assurance of a lasting memory, and a place in the prayers of future generations.

Such of these institutions as have escaped the greed of those who often used sectarian differences as an excuse for robbery, still celebrate their "founder's day." If this annual festival is not kept exactly in the spirit in which the patron would have desired, some thoughts of affection at least must go outwards if not upwards to those who made such good use of the riches with which they had been entrusted.

"A great man's memory may outlive his life by half a year, but by'r Lady he must build churches then," says Hamlet.

Three separate reasons have impelled the erection of monuments to the dead. First, a belief that the body dwells or *sleeps* in the place prepared for it. Secondly, to mark the spot where a person of some special attainments has been buried, in which case a suitable inscription is provided, setting forth the claims of the deceased to public recognition for the edification of future generations. Thirdly, the provision of a stone or tablet asking the prayers of co-religionists for a departed soul.

We have examples of all these methods in this country. Many of the ancient barrows offer ample evidence of the once common practice of making food offerings to the dead. The pagan (as well as the Christian) mode of honouring the great by a recital of their claims as pattern lives is well illustrated by various Roman remains which still exist in this country, notably at Colchester, where there is a finely sculptured stone bearing the effigy of a Roman centurion, clad in richly decorated armour, and holding a staff (the symbol of his authority) in his hand. Beneath this figure the following inscription is engraved:

"Marcus Favonius, the good natured (or courteous) son of Marcus of the Tribe of Pollia, a centurion of the twentieth legion. Verecundus and Novicas, his freedmen, placed this (memorial). He lies here." The work has been pronounced by Hubner to be probably of the age of Vespian.[1]

Despite the ruthless iconoclast many examples yet remain of the pre-Reformation memorial.

What of the modern graveyard on which we spend countless thousands of pounds yearly?

Surely it is optimistic to suppose that our present standard of moral excellence is so high that all these labyrinths of stone commemorate lives so noble and deeds so worthy, that for the public edification they should be thus immortalized. Were we to do so unusual a thing as to walk in a cemetery for the purpose of gathering lessons from the deeds of the dead, we might be deeply impressed by the recital of their sanctity—of indulgent husbands, loving fathers and saintly children buried there, apparently leaving behind them a world broken and desolated by the tragedy of their departure.

We are reminded of a certain pious individual, whose expression was likened to a hymn—so that people who saw it on week-days wondered what it looked like on Sunday. Conversely we may ruminate on the solid and unexpected virtues

[1] A. Clifton Kelway, "Memorials of Old Essex."

of our fellow citizens " as advertised," and wonder what they were like on a week-day, but it is hard to believe with so much yeast of perfection, the whole lump of humanity has not long since been leavened.

It will not surprise us to find the religious sentiments of a generation expressed by the inscriptions on their tombstones.

Several admirable books have been written on epitaphs, but only so far as they are useful as types shall we quote from the almost inexhaustible sources in our churches and burial-places, which anyone with a little interest in the matter may easily collect?

The following epitaph well illustrates the pre-Reformation idea of giving to charity or supplying the needs of the Church with a view to being remembered after death. It comes from Holm-next-the-Sea, Norfolk (early fourteenth century).

> " Henry Notyngham and hys wyffe lyne here
> Yat maden this chirche stepull and quere
> Two vestments and belles they made also
> Christ hem save therefore ffro wo
> Ande to bringe hem soules to Chris at heven
> Sayth Pater and ave with Mylde Steven."

The constant formula, "Pray for the soul of ———" or "Jesu Mercy" of the pre-Reformation inscription, was forsaken after that event in favour of a much more confident style, which remains more or less the pattern which we follow to-day.

The following, taken from an inscription in the parish church of Rye, Sussex, is only one of endless examples which might be quoted.

" Here lyeth the body of Thomas Proctor, who died November 27th, 1775, aged 73 years.

MEMORIALS, EPITAPHS, RINGS

> "Trust to his word, a friend sincere,
> From every vicious folly clear,
> In all his dealings what he gained
> Was truly honestly obtained.
> He ne'er through life the poor did grind,
> Nor any owing him confined;
> Peace he maintained with all his neighbours,
> And well paid all men for their labours.
> Do as he did, God will you save,
> And cause you happy from the grave."

These claims are far reaching, but perhaps not so inclusive as those expressed on another stone to be seen in the same place:

> "Sacred to the memory of Ann Maria Stonham,
> Who died September 20th, 1846, aged 63.
>
> Ye that would learn her worth who sleeps below,
>   Read Virtue's pages through from end to end,
> Leave not a word unmarked, and thou will know,
>   The virtues that adorned a valued friend."

Sometimes the virtues of the deceased are commemorated with rather curious frankness. The following appears on a tomb in Bunhill Fields:

> To
> DAME MARY PAGE,
> Wife of Sir Gregory Page, Bart.,
> died March 11th, 1728, in her 56th year.
>
> In 67 months she was tapped 66 times 240 gallons of water drawn without ever repining at her case or ever fearing the operation.

In the eighteenth century, when religion in this country had sunk to the lowest possible ebb, we shall naturally find the effect upon the tombstone. From the pompous recital of personal qualities and achievements we have epitaphs which vary from the jocular to the frankly obscene.

FUNERAL CUSTOMS

On the spot where the hideous statue of William IV now stands, facing London Bridge (which he opened), once stood a celebrated hostel known as The Boar's Head Tavern. Here it was that one John Preston served as a potman, and we select the inscription on his vine-covered tombstone in the churchyard of St. Magnus, the Martyr, as typical of the doggerel of that period (1730).

"ROBERT PRESTON
Late ' Drawer ' at The Boar's Head Tavern
Bacchus to give this toping world surprise
Produced one sober son and here he lies
Though nursed amongst full hogsheads, he defyd
The charms of wine and every vice besides
Oh, reader, if to justice thou'rt inclined
Keep honest Preston daily in thy mind.
He drew good wine, took care to fill his pots
Had sundry virtues that outweighed his faults
You who on Bacchus have the like dependence,
Pray copy Bob in measure and attendance."

A favourite form of epitaph about this time was one which played on the name of the deceased. An amusing example of this is contained in the story told of Jerrold the wit, who expressed an opinion that a good epitaph should contain no more than two words, including the name of the deceased. Charles Knight, who was present when the remark was made, at once handed Jerrold a pencil and a piece of paper, and asked him to write his (Knight's epitaph) with these limitations. Jerrold took the paper and wrote, "Good night."

Sometimes the humour is not intentional, as in the case of the widow, who after much thought and consultation with her friends, caused the following to be engraved on her husband's tomb:

" Rest in peace—until we meet again."

THE EPITAPH OF ROBERT PRESTON IN THE CHURCHYARD OF ST. MAGNUS THE MARTYR.

TOMBSTONE OF DANIEL DEFOE IN BUNHILL FIELDS, WHERE JOHN BUNYAN IS ALSO BURIED.

MEMORIALS, EPITAPHS, RINGS

It is not without significance that the eighteenth century tombstone very rarely bore any cross or other Christian symbol. The skull and cross-bones, urns and fat cherubs were the motives generally employed. On the other hand, the shape of the stone was often very admirable, and the carving, and especially the lettering, infinitely better than anything produced to-day.

We have been considering the epitaphs of the orthodox Christian types, but if it be true that the religious sentiments of any period are reflected by the inscriptions in the graveyard, it will also follow that the free-thinker, the materialist and the philosopher will express their particular views by the same means. Some of these are very beautiful, freed as they are from the shackles of convention. Perhaps the best known comes from Hull.

" Here lie I, Master Elginbrod,
Have mercy on my soul, O God."

So far it might be one of the ordinary pious expressions of pre-Reformation date, were it not for the dramatic challenge of the concluding lines:

" As I would have if I were God,
And thou were Master Elginbrod."

The frequent allusion to "sleep," which is a common form, is worth some little investigation.

W. J. Locke quotes the following from a German churchyard, which is beautiful in its frank acknowledgment of human frailty: " I will awake, Oh Christ, when thou callest me, but let me sleep awhile—for I am very weary." [1]

This is quoted because it says honestly and in bold words what so many other inscriptions hesitatingly *suggest*, namely, that the dead are

[1] W. J. Locke, " The Morals of Marcus Ordeyne."

sleeping in a physical sense in their graves. We have noted that it was a very general superstition amongst various peoples, that the body confined to the ground remained there in a state of semi-consciousness, even suffering as the Jews believed, the actual pains of dissolution as a punishment for sins committed.

The ancient Greeks believed that in a material sense their dead were at rest. " Here sleeps so-and-so " they wrote over the grave. Have we not acquired from them something more of this superstition than is shown by our adoption of the word " cemetery." The Greek equivalent of this signified " to lull to sleep."

How do we behave in the presence of the dead? The sleep-like appearance of the body is undoubtedly the reason why we converse in hushed whispers, lest we should disturb the *sleeper* whilst one of the most popular hymns frequently sung in the church or at the grave-side expresses the same thought, " Leave we now thy servant *sleeping*." Of course it could be argued that whilst such terms are admitted and some reference to sleep is made on every other tombstone, the word is not intended to express actual sleep, but repose in a state of bliss which the Established Church, together with other Protestant bodies, believes the soul has attained, without the intermediary state of purgatory to which the Roman and Greek Churches subscribe.

That the letters R.I.P stand for something more material than a state of spiritual refreshment to the average mind, cannot, however, be honestly contradicted.

It is a popular belief that the erection of some sort of monument is a necessary finishing touch to the funeral ceremonies, and trading on this absurd

MEMORIALS, EPITAPHS, RINGS

conviction we shall find the marble mason's emporium exhibiting the horrors of his craft at the very gates of the cemeteries of any pretensions.

"Strike while the iron is hot," says an old adage, a truth which the Dismal Trader has learnt well enough to profit by, for well he knows that if a reasonable time were allowed for sentimental false values to adjust themselves, the greater part of his living would be gone.

What is true of the private funeral is not less true of the public funeral. Almost before the breath is out of the body, some well-meaning friend or relation starts a subscription list for the purpose of a " suitable " memorial, and according to the sum collected so a more or less expensive monument is erected. Subscriptions in such cases are largely made up of sums given for business or social reasons, and seldom represent, even at the time, any spontaneous offering. Not only is this sort of thing unjust to the living, but equally unjust to the memory of the dead, for after the wave of sentiment has passed the pretensions of the dead are judged not by the weight or costliness of the tomb which covers their remains, but rather by what they have done to further the cause of humanity.

The son of a self-made man erects a memorial at great cost at the death of his father, selecting for the purpose the finest position in the town where his wealth has been accumulated, honestly or otherwise.

By such means are we burdened with inartistic memorials erected to nobodies, which endure long after the reputation of those they represent has found its true level. Our churches and cathedrals suffer from exactly the same sort of thing, subscription tombs and monuments of forgotten politicians, painters whose pictures, once popular, now hardly fetch the price of their frames, poets whose work nobody reads.

To distinguish between the various forms of memorials, we must remember that some were erected over the place of sepulture, whilst others took the form either of a cenotaph or empty tomb, or merely a commemorative stone or tablet.

The tombstone took the place of the ancient obelisk or menhir (derived from the Celtic words signifying a "high stone"), the tomb itself was generally in the form of the Dolmen altar or table tomb.

A memorial stone or cross was at one time commonly placed where the coffin of a distinguished person had rested on its way to burial. At the foot of these crosses, all other coffins which passed that way, rested also.

The Elinor (Queen of Edward I) crosses are an instance of this. Twelve were erected, of which but three remain.

Charing Cross is a copy of the cross at Waltham. Incidentally, it is interesting to note that Charing Cross does not necessarily derive its name from the memorial, as is popularly supposed. The word Charing is said to be derived from the Saxon word, Cerran, which means a sharp turn or angle, and is thought to refer to the peculiar twist which the river takes at this point, which renders navigation very difficult to the larger crafts.[1]

We have inherited from past ages very few things which excite so great and general an interest as the monuments found in so many of our churches preserved from the time of the Crusaders.

It has been generally believed that from the crossing of the warrior's legs could be seen the number of wars in which the Crusader had taken

[1] Burns, "Journal of the London Society."

MEMORIAL BRASS OF A KNIGHT
WITH CROSSED LEGS.

CARD OF INVITATION TO A FUNERAL DATED
1779.

MEMORIALS, EPITAPHS, RINGS

part, or, as others supposed, it signified the taking of a vow to proceed to the Holy Land, and that the action often noted of the sword of the knight in the act of being sheathed represented the accomplishment of his purpose. Unfortunately, this interesting supposition does not always accord with historical facts; as Clinch points out, this view is not now generally held, and that the cross-legged attitude was merely a convenient and conventional manner of dealing with the limbs.[1]

The addition of a lion or a dog at the feet of the Crusader was a symbol of courage in the case of the lion and faithfulness in the case of the dog.

It is little wonder that the churches and cemeteries contain so many examples of neglected and decaying tombstones which it has ceased to be anybody's business or interest to repair, a matter which reminds us of that remarkable person Robert Peterson, from whom Sir Walter Scott took the character of "Old Mortality."

Peterson was born in Hawick, Scotland, and was brought up as a stone mason. He was a man of deeply religious convictions, and belonged to an austere sect known as the Cameronians. At an early date he deserted his wife and family and devoted the remaining forty years of his life to the erection and repair of the tombs of the Covenanters who had suffered persecution in the reign of Charles II. He wandered from churchyard to churchyard, his sole companion being an ancient shaggy white pony which lived on the rank grass growing round the neglected graves.

He died in the year 1801, a statue being erected to his memory which shows him engaged in his labour of love.

A society was founded in 1889 called The

---

[1] George Clinch, "English Costume."

Association for the Preservation of the Memorials of the Dead. This otherwise solitary instance of a mission in the service of the dead is in striking contrast to the damage and destruction of tombs of which we find so many instances throughout the pages of history.

In the latter years of the reign of Henry VIII the destruction of tombs was an obsession. Elizabeth, when she came into power, issued a special mandate against such vandalism, despite which, ruthless despoliation still continued. Tombs were hacked to pieces, and the marble of which they were composed was used for various secular purposes. Those especially suffered which bore the typical inscription of the old faith. It is said that Robert, Earl of Sussex, paved his larder and kitchen with the marble gravestones of his ancestors, to obtain which he did not hesitate to demolish the choir of Atlebrugh Church (Norfolk).

Perhaps nothing suffered more at the hands of the destroyers than the memorial brasses, which richly embellished the majority of the churches at that period.

No doubt this vandalism originated in a sort of religious frenzy, but it was certainly continued for the sake of profiting by the sale of the materials thus obtained. Brass, which always fetched a ready price, was easily removed, and the theft covered by melting down the metal into ingots or moulding it in the form of weights or other articles. In some instances memorial brasses were torn from the tombs for sheer mischief, and found their way more or less undamaged into lumber rooms and odd corners, from which they were later recovered and replaced in their original positions.

These simple and beautiful memorials followed the earlier forms of incised slate or stone. They

MEMORIALS, EPITAPHS, RINGS

came into vogue in Henry VIII's reign. Originally used as a coffin plate, they were frequently richly enamelled by the Flemish, who brought the custom to this country, but the art died out, later examples being of brass only. The best brasses are very fine in workmanship, the engraved lines being clear and simple. Gradually an attempt to obtain effects by shading with cross-hatched lines vulgarized the work, till it ceased to be of any artistic merit.

As in the case of the marble tombs, the brasses which bore the inscription "orate pro anima" were the first to suffer. It is not uncommon to find traces of still earlier workmanship on the reverse side of these memorials, which had been purchased as scrap brass from those who had stolen them, and later were worked up again for other purposes.

Occasionally memorial brasses are used to-day, but generally in commemoration of the clergy, whose robes or vestments lend themselves to a decorative and conventional treatment. It is an amusing comment on the ugliness of modern costume, which admits of no literal artistic representation, but our newly acquired sense of humour refused to submit to the substitution of the "toga," which was not long since a common expedient.

The coffin "furniture," dear to the undertaker's heart, is otherwise all that is left of the memorial brass. Anything more degraded in design and execution it would be impossible to describe. A glance through the catalogue of the wholesale firms who sell this rubbish to the trade will show a fearful collection of "new art" and other debased designs, if one may call them so, largely savouring of German origin. The cheaper variety were made before the war, by that enterprising nation, out of old tins and cans stamped under pressure and brass-plated.

The now abandoned custom of presenting

mourning jewellery in memory of the dead, was once a very general practice. Many of the old jewellers' trade cards show as an important part of the design a tomb on which an inscription was engraved, advertising all kinds of memorial rings and jewellery.

In the Middle Ages, and later, "mourning rings" were frequently mentioned in wills, a certain sum of money being set apart for the purchase and distribution of these mementoes to the relations and friends of the family.

Sometimes attendants and officials received their share also, as a curious extract dated 1719 reminds us. It is taken from the records of the Ironmongers' Company, and shows the Dismal Trade of the period in an unfavourable light.

"The master acquainted the Court that one John Turney, an undertaker for funerals, had lately buried one Mrs. Mason, from the Hall, but had refused the Master Warder and the Clerk each a ring, etc., according to his agreement, the persons invited being served with gloves, hatbands and rings."

Anne of Cleves left by will several mourning rings of various values for distribution at her death.

In Shakespeare's will (1616) sums of money were mentioned for the purchase of rings for several of his friends, three of which were for "My fellows" as he affectionately calls his brother actors, Hemynge, Burbage and Cundell. Izaak Walton in 1683 willed rings as "a friend's farewell," the cost of which he specified as 13s. 4d. each. For his wife and daughter he desired rings to be made and to be inscribed "Love my memory," whilst to the Bishop of Winchester he presented one on which

MOURNING JEWELLERY.
Brooches with Painted Memorial Miniatures and "Lockets," i.e. cases containing "locks" of human hair.

(*From jewellery kindly lent by Edwin Good, Esq.*)

MEMORIALS, EPITAPHS, RINGS

were engraved the words, "a mite for a million," I. W. obit.

In Pepys' Diary in the appendix appears a list of a number of persons to whom mortuary jewellery was to be presented at his death, which took place in 1703. Forty-six rings were to cost twenty shillings, sixty-two were to be of the value of fifteen shillings, and twenty of the value of ten shillings each.[1]

We may be certain that Evelyn, who so dearly loved to uphold the "funeral decencies," would not be behind in the matter of rings.

His child died in 1658, when he writes:

"I caused his body to be coffined in lead and deposited on the 30th at eight o'clock that night in the church at Deptford, accompanied with divers of my relations and neighbours, among whom I distributed rings, with the motto, 'Domincus abstutit.'"

For the burial of Charles I seven rings were made, containing a miniature of the King's head behind a death's head, and a motto, "Prepared be to follow me."

A sentimental attachment to locks of hair is of very old origin. The Greeks cut the first hair of a child, the beard of a youth, and the tresses of a maiden, these they offered to the gods. On the death of a parent the hair of the children, cut off as a token of grief, was placed with the body. Something of this practice was carried forward in the custom of preserving the hair of a deceased person in a special receptacle in memorial rings, brooches, lockets, etc.

The hair was woven or twisted in various ways,

[1] Wm. Jones, F.S.A., "Finger Ring Lore."

and formed quite a feature of the mortuary jewellery a generation since.

The use of black enamel in rings was much in vogue in England, white enamel being frequently substituted in the case of a child or young person. Some of the brooches of the eighteenth century are very fine in workmanship. They frequently contain as part of the design a miniature painted on ivory, representing an urn with a figure (sometimes a portrait of a bereaved husband or wife) weeping over a tombstone, with the usual accompaniment of willows and the like. Small seed pearls were very often introduced as an enrichment, and for the value of their symbol of tears.

Most of the brooches were so formed as to pivot on their frames, disclosing a miniature, or in later days, a daguerreotype of the deceased.

The habit of burying jewels with the dead has been largely responsible for many acts of sacrilege.

There have been many curious superstitions in relation to the wearing of rings.

The inhabitants of some of the Greek Islands believed that the soul could not leave the body as long as a ring remained on the finger. This rendered it necessary for those who watched over the dying to hastily remove the rings on the first symptoms that death had taken place, in order to allow the soul to escape from the body.[1]

Superstition still maintains that the turquoise is affected by the ill-health of a person wearing it, and that it remains dull and leaden in appearance after death, till worn by a person in good health, when it is said to regain the peculiar colour for which it is noted.

If these mortuary jewels were as a whole very ugly, what shall be said of the hideous lumps of

---

[1] E. C. Woodward, *The Englishwoman*, June, 1911.

MOURNING JEWELLERY.
Inlaid jet ear-rings, brooches, and gold and enamel rings.
(From jewellery kindly lent by Edwin Good, Esq.)

MEMORIALS, EPITAPHS, RINGS

crudely manufactured jet which it is still considered by some classes of society to be necessary to wear when "in mourning," or the even more preposterous "half-mourning" sets of ear-rings and the like, in which a little silver is introduced to lighten the effect. Whitby, which for centuries has been the seat of the jet industry, still carries on a trade on these ghoulish appendages, impervious alike to enlightenment or ridicule.

Even so sketchy a chapter on the subject of memorials must not be closed without mention of the still popular mourning card.

Here again, we find that in its original use, it was intended as a reminder of the departed, in order that the recipient might offer prayers for the repose of his soul.

In its present form the mourning card is a modest affair, printed in black and silver, and exhibiting all that elementary lack of taste which is so marked a feature of everything connected with our funeral customs. It contains, as a rule, in addition to the name and age of the deceased, some symbol of the Christian faith, sufficiently obscured by a wreath of lilies or ivy, in order to render it acceptable to all shades of religious opinion. A verse selected from some popular hymn expressing a pious aspiration, preferably in relation to "sleep," is added, but avoiding, of course, all the pitfalls, either definite or dogmatic.

In most family Bibles, earlier examples of the mourning card will be found. These are for the most part embossed in a white relief on a black background. The pierced or fretted variety was once very popular; these were most elaborate, and contained the usual symbols of grief—urns, weeping angels and willow trees.

Various degrees of black-bordered note-paper

and envelopes are still in use. Some few years ago, a revolutionary mind introduced an innovation which consisted of a black corner to the envelope in place of the sable border. Needless to say, this departure from orthodoxy had but a short life, and was soon overcome by the unwritten laws of funeral tradition.

The old-fashioned tradesman, on whose household death had laid a heavy hand, was wont to put up the shutters of his shop as a token of mourning. The consequent loss of business, in days of keener competition, suggested a modification, which took the form of a simple black-painted board in place of the shutters, a custom which is still to be met with.

EXTRACT FROM AN OLD LEDGER

An interesting record of the cost of various items supplied for a funeral in the year 1824.

Miss Harley
  To Geo. Stovell & Sons
   2 & 3 Lower Grosvenor Street

For the Interment of Miss Martha Harley at Brampton Bryan, Herefordshire – Died 25th January 1824.

£ s d	Item	£ s d
7.10 –	A Strong Coffin with white sattin lining and pillow	11 11 –
3.10 –	A Mattrass round sides head and foot of white sattin	9 10 –
. .	A Mattrass for the lid of same sattin	4 3 –
3.2 –	A White Sattin Sheet	3 2 .
– 12 –	8 Men in with Do.	1 4 –
– 7 –	Closing the same	9 –
18.18 –	A very strong outside Oak Case covered with superfine black cloth best silvered Nails & rich ornaments, silvered Plates and handles	22 10 –
2.15 –	An Engraved silvered plate of Inscription	3 13 6
– 15 –	Men in with the case	1 10 –
3.14 –	Use of Best Pall 11 days	6 – –
5.10 –	A Rich plume of best black Ostrich feathers	11 – –
3.6 –	Man to carry Do	9 – –
2.2 –	A Silk Scarf Hatband & Gloves Do.	3 3 –
– 11 –	2 Feather Pages & 2 Wand Do	1 10 –
1.1 –	2 Silk Hatbands & Gloves Do	1 16 –
24.4 –	2 Mutes on Horseback to Brampton Bryan	33 – –
2.4 –	2 Mutes off Stones	3 – –
8.8 –	4 Silk Hatbands & Gloves Do rich Silk Scarves	12 12 –
88.12 –	Card over £	138 13 6

		£ s d
88.12.—	Brought forward	138 13 6
2.—.—	4 Silk Dresses for Poles	9 — —
48.8.—	4 Horseman to Brampton Bryan ———	66 — —
4.8 —4	Do off Stones ———————	6 — —
	8 Silk Scarves for do 8 Silk Hatbands	
16.16.—	& 8 Pair Gloves —————	25 4 —
77.—.—	A Hearse and 6 Horses —————	86 12 6
	A Set of best black Velvets and a Set	
11.11.—	of Ostrich Feathers	22 — —
	2 Cloaks, 2 best Silk Hatbands & two Pair	
2.4 —	Gloves Coachman ——————	2 16 —
2.10 —	10 Pages with Truncheon —— — — —	7 17 6
5.10 —	10 Silk Hatbands & 10 Pair Gloves —————	7 10 —
110.—.—	2 Coaches and 4 Horses Each—— — ———	132 16 6
	2 Sets of best black Ostrich feathers	
9.—.—	Velvets ——————	16 — —
	2 Cloaks 2 best Silk Hatbands and 2 pair	
2.4.—	Gloves Coachman ..	2 16 —
2.—.—	8 Pages with Wands ——— ———	6 — —
4.8.—	8 Silk Hatbands & 8 pair of Gloves ——	7 4 —
	1 Best Crape Hatband & Gloves	
8.6	own Coachman...	— 14 —
2.4.—	2 Men on Horseback to Stones End....	3 — —
1.2.—	2 Crape Hatbands & Gloves Do ————	1 8 —
1.—.—	4 Pages with Wands —— ———	3 — —
2.4.—	4 Silk Hatbands & 4 Pair of Gloves	3 12 —
	1 Rich Silk Scarf & Hatband a rich	
6.6.—	& Silk Scarf and Hatband Nurseman	9 9 —
	A Rich Silk Scarf & Hatband & best	
	Gloves Sir H Halford	
9.9.—	A Do Do & Do Mr Jones ...	14 3 6
	A Do Do & Do Mr Higham	
409.4.6	Carr Over	£ 571 16 6

		£ s d
409.4.6	Brought forward	571 16 6
5.15.6	Own Attendance & Assistans	18 18 -
2.5.-	A Rich Silk Scarf do	2 5 -
18.-	2 Silk Hatbands & 2 Pair Gloves	1 16 -
4.2.-	Rooms on the Road & Coachman assisting	4 2 -
23.16.6	Turnpikes	23 16 6
125.-.-	Expences on the Road and back	174 3 -
3.17.-	7 New Hatbands the Mules & featherman the day of Interment	6 - -
11.-	2 Pair Servants Gloves silk	14 -
575.9.6		£ 803 11 =

INDEX

ALL HALLOWS EVE, 244, 245
All Saints, feast of, 234, 238, 244
All Souls, feast of, 234-6
Altars, origin of, 135
Ancestor worship, 101, 233, 251
Animals, slaughter of, 59, 60, 206, 235
Animism, 71
Ankow, 156
Anniversaries, 79, 84, 109, 235, 240, 242, 251
Ants, 13, 14
Arms, reversed, 204
Apples, 245, 246
—— Mass, 246
Associated ideas, 17
Averil, arvel, 104
Aya Marca, 234

BANSHEE, 21
Barbe, 91
Barrows, 131, 140
Baton, 128
Beds, 94
Bees, 14, 79
Belgium, 104, 108
Bellman, 84
Bell, mort, 82
——, passing, 82, 185
——, Rogation, 84
——, soul, 82, 83
Bells, 27, 53
Bidder, 84, 85
Bier, 35, 115, 116, 119
Black death, 183, 184
—— magic, 63, 71, 73
Body, burning, 208
——, disposal of, 222
——, disturbing, 173-5
—— snatching, 176-81
Bones, removal of, 137, 173, 174
Boots, reversed, 205
Breathing test, 23
Bridges, 123

Brittany, 64, 65, 94, 123, 154, 155, 162, 174, 175, 235
Bronze Age, 211
Brouardel, Dr., 23, 29, 220
Brunetti, 220
Bulgarian, 100
Bumping coffin, 124
Bunhill Fields, 259
Burial, cave, 43
——, chested, 42, 43
—— clubs, 96
——, congested, 146
—— costume, 39
——, cross-roads, 153
—— extravagance, 96, 97
——, face down, 151
——, garden, 159
—— grounds, 129, 137, 139-62, 218
——, infants', 37, 41, 151
——, kneeling, 239
——, naked, 37
——, night, 152
——, north, 149
——, responsibility for, 31, 32
——, secret, 143
—— shafts, 129
——, times for, 30
——, unconsecrated, 152
——, upright, 149, 161
—— versus cremation, 210
——, virgins', 169, 170
——, water level, 208

CANDLES, 117, 125
Cannibals, 47, 70, 99
Cat, phantom, 21
Catacombs, 134-8, 213
——, Paris, 137, 138
Catafalque, 118, 213
Catholic Church, regulations, 32, 33, 55
Cemeteries, Christian, 43, 139, 151, 247, 257
Cenotaph, 237

INDEX

Ceremonious anointing, 36
—— dress, 35, 36, 200
—— washing, 34, 213, 224
Certificates, 37
Chantry, 242
—— priest, 243
Charm, curative, 74
Charon, 51
Chevra Kadisha, 226
Chief, 15
Chinese, 36, 48, 51, 52, 211
—— child burial, 37, 41
—— coffin, 48
—— customs, 58, 73
—— plague, 182
Chrisom, 40
Christian practice, 30, 33, 34, 47, 95, 110, 134, 137, 140, 149, 150, 212, 223, 224, 240
—— sentiment, 51, 77, 164
Church, burial in, 254, 255
——, Greek, 109
—— guardianship, 166
—— neglect, 166
—— yards, 139-63
Cider, 18
Clipping festival, 165
Coaches, 121, 126
Cock, 151
Cockcrow, 236
Coffins, 42, 43, 44, 47, 48
——, furniture, 44, 267
——, preservation, 45, 46, 47
——, wood, 45
Coins, 51, 52
Common Prayer, 41, 42
Confirmation band, 40
Congo, 55
Consecration, 140, 184, 185
Coque-morts, 66, 67
Corn, 54, 109
Cornwall, 20, 75
Corpse, arresting, 122
——, ceremonious viewing, 104
—— derivation, 31
——, food, 101
——, lifting, 108
Corrosives, 46
Corsica, 68, 159, 169, 235
Crape, 92, 96
Cremation, 33, 209, 231, 214
——, scientific, 216-21
—— society, 222, 223
Crime, detection of, 46, 220
Cross-roads, burial, 153
Crusader, 264, 265

Curse, 164

DEAD, worship of, 66, 232, 233
——, kissing, 75
—— March, 205
Death hamper, 43
Decapitation, 23
Devon, 18
Defilement, 141
Dickens, Chas., 18, 148
Dii Manes, 235
Dirge, 119, 250
Dolmen, 130
Doole, 86-92
Douglas, 194
Dowager, 90
Drawing and quartering, 236
Dreams, 18
Dresden, 21
Drowning, 19, 238
Druids, 164
Drying body, 158

EARTH eating, 162
Earth in coffin, 162
Earth, thrown, 162
Egyptian, 53, 54, 58, 100, 101, 211, 234, 240
Embalming, 46, 74, 209-31
Epitaph, 173, 241, 242, 253-72
Excesses, 110
Execution, 25, 73, 206, 207

FACTION fights, 104
Feast, funeral, 33, 99-116
Fees, 122
——, interment, 139
Feralia, 235
Feudal, 160
Feuds, 103
Firing party, 205
Flag, 205
——, black, 207
——, half-mast, 206
Flowers, 86, 168-74, 210, 233
——, heather, 171
——, "immortelles," 172
Food offering, 99, 102, 172
Foul play, 103
France, 30, 41, 66, 93, 220, 247
Free Churches, 243
Funerals, civic, 196, 197, 199
——, conventions, 97
——, Mass, 114, 119

INDEX

Funerals, naval, 206, 238
——, processions, 99-128
——, public, 191-208
——, State, 88, 89

GERMAN, 30, 217, 220
Ghosts, 21, 77
——, raising, 62, 63
Gipsy customs, 42, 52
Gladiators, 214
Gloves, 106
——, white, 170
Good Friday, 19
Gorini furnace, 220
Gowns, black, 88
Gravedigger, 173
Grave goods 31, 49, 50, 55, 132, 175, 176
Grave, pagan, 131
Greece, 51, 211, 237, 244, 270
Gun-carriage, 205

HAIR, 269, 270
Hammer, 50, 52
Harrow, 117
Hatchment, 75, 118
Hearse, 116, 118, 203
——, light, 117
——, modern, 124, 125
——, motor, 125, 126
Heart beating, 23
—— burial, 151, 193, 194
—— forbidden, 194
——, stake though, 208
Heirs, 233
Helps, 36
Henry I, 41
Heriot, 80
Hohenzollern, 20
Horses, 125, 161
Hour-glass, 54
" House of Life," 161

INDIA, 56, 57, 58, 210, 234
—— fakir, 25
—— plague, 182-90
Infection, 29, 218
Innocents, Paris, 137
Insignia, 114
Ireland, 39, 52, 64, 77, 109, 124
Italy, 36, 145, 214, 220

JAPAN, 146, 234, 235
Jewellery, mourning, 176, 268-71
Jewish customs, 33, 34, 39, 46, 59, 61, 62, 66, 68, 91, 108, 134, 144, 161, 178, 224, 225, 226, 240, 241
Johnson, Ben, 161
Judea, 211
Jury, 28

KADAVAR UTILIZATION, 217
Kaddish, 240
Karlsruche, 20
Kattafin, 66
Keats, 215

LACERATION, 68
Lanhadron Park, 20
Last Post, 205
Leigh Hunt, 215
Lichgate, 144
Liripipe, 92
Looking-glass, 53
Louis XI, 93
Louisa of Saxony, 21
Lunatics, 143

MANDRAKE, 168, 169
Marini, 219
Martin, Saint, 34
Martyrs, 36, 142, 254
Mary, Queen of Scots, 93
Masks, 113, 213
Mazing the dead, 152
Memorial, 253-72
—— brasses, 40, 267
—— cards, 247, 271, 272
Mexico, 56
Military, 114, 127, 151, 201-6, 237
—— charger, 59, 80, 203, 206
Milk, 111
Mime, 66
Mirror, 19
Mohammedan, 239
Monks, 35, 47, 142
——, Capucine, 159
——, Trappist, 101
Montpensier, Mlle., 193
Mortalities, 182, 183, 184, 186, 188
Mort-cloth, 116
Mortuary, 27, 28, 114
—— chapel, 29
—— tax, 80-1
Mourning, 87-98
Murderer, 151
Mussulman, 210
Mutes, 61, 65, 66, 67
—— as waiters, 112

INDEX

NAILS, coffin, 39
Napoleon, 20, 201, 202
Nature, 11
Necrophorus mortuorum, 11
New Guinea, 72
Nomads, 211
No-man's-land, 186
Norway, 39, 109, 145, 159

OINTMENT, precious, 36, 113
" Old Mortality," 265
Oliver Cromwell, 177
Onions, 111
Orientation, 148, 150
Ossuary, 174

PACE, ceremonial, 125
Pagan, 237
Pall, 35, 115, 125
——, flag as, 205
Pancakes, 64, 235
Paper trade, 38
Parsees, 156, 157
Perfume, 36, 231
Persians, 157, 234
Peruvians, 234
Peterson, Robert, 265
Pillage, 178
Pinkings, 125
Plague, 182-90
——, Black, 182-6
——, Great, 188, 189, 190
—— pits, 189, 190
—— precautions, 215
Plays, 63, 144
Plumes, 128
Pompadour, Mlle., 138
Portugal, 30
Prayers, 103, 105, 109, 234, 240, 242
—— for dead, 250, 251, 255
Premature burial, 22, 23, 24, 25, 27
Preston, Robert, 260
Prickets, 117, 125
Processions, 48, 153
Prophet Elm, 20
Prunes, 108
Psychic investigation, 141, 226, 249, 250
Purgatory, 52, 239, 242, 243, 244, 262
Pyramids, 132, 133, 134
Pyre, 113, 212-5, 237

RAGGED REGIMENT, 113
Raven, 17

Registers, church, 38
Resurrection, 35, 39, 44
—— men, 178, 179, 180
Right of way, 122, 123
Roads, 120-3
Roman burial customs, 33, 41, 66, 78, 84, 112, 113, 123, 150, 173, 211
Romanoff, 21
Royalty, 20, 48, 74, 88, 93, 94, 127, 151, 176, 177, 178, 191-202, 208, 213, 214
Russian certificates, 54

SACRIFICE, 101, 235, 236
Sacrilege, 256, 266
Saddle cloth, 127
Sailors, 18, 206, 238
St. Chrysostom, 34
St. George, 236
St. Martin, 34
St. Odilo of Cluny, 244
St. John's Wood, 153
Salt, 53, 108
Sanctuary, 150, 154, 162
Sarcophagi, 135
Scarab beetle, 54, 55
Scotland, 18, 42, 62, 75, 82, 84, 85, 107, 116, 123, 201, 236
——, Assembly of, 143
Serbians, 236
Sermon, funeral, 107, 113, 192
Sexton beetle, 11
Shakespeare, 268
Shelley, 194, 214
Shrine, war, 248, 249
Shroud, 39, 42
——, woollen, 37
Shutters, black, 272
Siberian dogs, 157
Sin-eater, 69, 70
Skulls, 174
Skull boxes, 175
Slave burial, 136
Slave, slaughter of, 55, 56, 59
Sleeping, 256, 262
Solomon Islands, 100
Sorcerer, 72, 73
Soul bread, 104, 245
—— duality, 101
—— leaving body, 26
Souter, Charles, 179, 180, 181
Spain, 30
Spirits, 15
Spiritualist, 26
Starvation, 234

INDEX 283

State control, 139
State supervision, 28, 30
Stockings, 39
Stones, memorial, 254, 263, 265
Stuart, 94, 102, 146
Suicides, 150, 152
Sun worship, 158
Superstitions, 17
" Suttee," 56, 57, 58
Sweating sickness, 187, 188
Switzerland, 92

TABOO, 71
Tattooing, 204
Taxes, 80, 81
Thirst, 155, 156
Thompson, Sir Henry, 215
Toads, 26
Toll, 122
Tomb, access to, 173
" Tombe Issiore," 137
Torches, 76, 78, 115
Totemism, 71
Tower of Silence, 157
Toys, 53
Trade, 45
Tradition, 49
Travelling, 102
Trees, 163-90
——, ash, 164
——, box, 163
——, cypress, 163, 213
——, fir, 167
——, holly, 164
——, myrtle, 167
——, oak, 164-212
——, palm, 168
——, rosemary, 168
——, rowan, 164
——, sakaki, 168
——, willow, 163
——, worship of, 163, 164
——, yew, 163
Turkish, 59

Tyburn, 177

UNBAPTIZED CHILDREN, 143
Undertaker, 11, 30, 44, 75, 97, 98, 229, 231
Urns, cinerary, 227

VAULTS, decorated, 159
Verdi, 199
Viking, 158
Violet, 94, 95
Volley-firing, 205
Vowess, 90
Vultures, 156

WAGON, 119
Wagner, 159
Wailers, 66, 67
——, women, 113
Wakes, 61-81, 109
Wales, 21, 149, 247
Wands, 128
Warnings, death, 17
Waste, 45
Watching, 61
Watchman, 155
Water, 111
——, holy, 111
—— spirits, 20
Waxcot, 78, 80
Weeds, 86, 94
Weeper, 92
Wellington, 202, 203
" White Lady," 20
Widows, 58, 59, 76, 86, 89, 90, 91-4, 97
William the Conqueror, 191-3
Wills, 22
Witch-doctor, 14, 72
Witches, 21, 151
Woking, 221
Wreath, 171

ZUNA MOHAMMEDAN, 239

VINCENNES UNIVERSITY LIBRARY